Nineteenth-Century Major Lives and Letters

Series Editor: Marilyn Gaull

This series presents original biographical, critical, and scholarly studies of literary works and public figures in Great Britain, North America, and continental Europe during the nineteenth century. The volumes in *Nineteenth-Century Major Lives and Letters* evoke the energies, achievements, contributions, cultural traditions, and individuals who reflected and generated them during the Romantic and Victorian period. The topics: critical, textual, and historical scholarship, literary and book history, biography, cultural and comparative studies, critical theory, art, architecture, science, politics, religion, music, language, philosophy, aesthetics, law, publication, translation, domestic and public life, popular culture, and anything that influenced, impinges upon, expresses or contributes to an understanding of the authors, works, and events of the nineteenth century. The authors consist of political figures, artists, scientists, and cultural icons including William Blake, Thomas Hardy, Charles Darwin, William Wordsworth, William Butler Yeats, Samuel Taylor, and their contemporaries.

The series editor is Marilyn Gaull, PhD (Indiana University), FEA. She has taught at William and Mary, Temple University, New York University, and is Research Professor at the Editorial Institute at Boston University. She is the founder and editor of *The Wordsworth Circle* and the author of *English Romanticism: The Human Context*, and editions, essays, and reviews in journals. She lectures internationally on British Romanticism, folklore, and narrative theory, intellectual history, publishing procedures, and history of science.

PUBLISHED BY PALGRAVE:

Shelley's German Afterlives, by Susanne Schmid
Coleridge, the Bible, and Religion, by Jeffrey W. Barbeau
Romantic Literature, Race, and Colonial Encounter, by Peter J. Kitson
Byron, edited by Cheryl A. Wilson
Romantic Migrations, by Michael Wiley
The Long and Winding Road from Blake to the Beatles, by Matthew Schneider
British Periodicals and Romantic Identity, by Mark Schoenfield
Women Writers and Nineteenth-Century Medievalism, by Clare Broome Saunders
British Victorian Women's Periodicals, by Kathryn Ledbetter
Romantic Diasporas, by Toby R. Benis
Romantic Literary Families, by Scott Krawczyk
Victorian Christmas in Print, by Tara Moore
Culinary Aesthetics and Practices in Nineteenth-Century American Literature, Edited by Monika Elbert and Marie Drews
Reading Popular Culture in Victorian Print, by Alberto Gabriele
Romanticism and the Object, Edited by Larry H. Peer
Poetics en passant, by Anne Jamison
From Song to Print, by Terence Hoagwood
Gothic Romanticism, by Tom Duggett
Victorian Medicine and Social Reform, by Louise Penner
Populism, Gender, and Sympathy in the Romantic Novel, by James P. Carson
Byron and the Rhetoric of Italian Nationalism, by Arnold A. Schmidt
Poetry and Public Discourse in Nineteenth-Century America, by Shira Wolosky
The Discourses of Food in Nineteenth-Century British Fiction, by Annette Cozzi
Romanticism and Pleasure, Edited by Thomas H. Schmid and Michelle Faubert

Royal Romances, by Kristin Flieger Samuelian
Trauma, Transcendence, and Trust, by Thomas J. Brennan, S.J.
The Business of Literary Circles in Nineteenth-Century America, by David Dowling
Popular Medievalism in Romantic-Era Britain, by Clare A. Simmons
Beyond Romantic Ecocriticism, by Ashton Nichols
The Poetry of Mary Robinson, by Daniel Robinson

FORTHCOMING TITLES:

Romanticism and the City, by Larry H. Peer
Coleridge and the Daemonic Imagination, by Gregory Leadbetter
Romantic Dharma, by Mark Lussier
Regions of Sara Coleridge's Thought, by Peter Swaab

BEYOND ROMANTIC ECOCRITICISM

TOWARD URBANATURAL ROOSTING

Ashton Nichols

palgrave
macmillan

BEYOND ROMANTIC ECOCRITICISM
Copyright © Ashton Nichols, 2011.

All rights reserved.

First published in 2011 by
PALGRAVE MACMILLAN®
in the United States—a division of St. Martin's Press LLC,
175 Fifth Avenue, New York, NY 10010.

Where this book is distributed in the UK, Europe and the rest of the world,
this is by Palgrave Macmillan, a division of Macmillan Publishers Limited,
registered in England, company number 785998, of Houndmills,
Basingstoke, Hampshire RG21 6XS.

Palgrave Macmillan is the global academic imprint of the above companies
and has companies and representatives throughout the world.

Palgrave® and Macmillan® are registered trademarks in the United States,
the United Kingdom, Europe and other countries.

ISBN: 978–0–230–10267–5

Library of Congress Cataloging-in-Publication Data

Nichols, Ashton, 1953–
    Beyond Romantic Ecocriticism : Toward Urbanatural Roosting / by
Ashton Nichols.
        p. cm.—(Nineteenth-century major lives & letters)
        ISBN 978–0–230–10267–5
        1. English literature—19th century—History and criticism. 2. Nature in
literature. 3. Natural history in literature. 4. Human ecology in literature.
5. Philosophy of nature. 6. Urban ecology (Biology) 7. Ecocriticism. I. Title.

PR468.N3N53 2011
820.9'36—dc22   2010035165

A catalogue record of the book is available from the British Library.

Design by Newgen Imaging Systems (P) Ltd., Chennai, India.

First edition: March 2011

10 9 8 7 6 5 4 3 2 1

Printed in the United States of America.

To Lorenzo Kingsley Smiraglio and Grace Maria Smiraglio
first of a new generation

Previous Publications

The Poetics of Epiphany: Nineteenth-Century Origins of the Modern Literary Moment 1987

The Revolutionary "I": Wordsworth and the Politics of Self-Presentation 1998

Editor, *Romantic Natural Histories: William Wordsworth, Charles Darwin, and Others* 2004

CONTENTS

List of Illustrations   ix

A Scheme of Reference   xi

Prologue: Urbanatural Roosting   xiii

SPRING   Vernal Roosting: Romantic Ecocriticism

1 March: A New Urbanatural Year & The History of
   Natural History   3
2 April: Poetry and Science & Nature as Culture,
   Culture as Society   19
3 May: Species Science & Saving Cities, Saving Tigers   37

SUMMER   Estival Roosting: Ecocriticism

4 June: Vestiges of Time & Thoreau and Urbanature   55
5 July: Wild Animals Have No Souls &
   Ecomorphic Urbanature   69
6 August: The Loves of Plants and Animals &
   Romantic Poetry and the Pleasures of Nature   85

FALL   Autumnal Roosting: Urbanature

7 September: From Natural Pleasure to Natural Pain &
   A Perfect Bird, A Perfect Poem   105
8 October: Hawks I Have Watched &
   Urbanatural Roosting on Display   119
9 November: Science and Poetry &
   A Hard Rain's Gonna Fall   137

WINTER   Hibernal Roosting: Beyond Romantic
Ecocriticism

10 December: Zoos: Romantic Rhinos and
    Victorian Vipers   151

11   January: Displaying Human Beings &
       Romantic Urbanature   165
12   February: Death and Dying & Ecomorphic Ecocentrism   179

Epilogue   195
    Spring, Again
    March: Once More
    Life Returns Without Beginnings or Ends

Acknowledgments   209

Works Cited   213

Index   223

ILLUSTRATIONS

PROLOGUE

Parnassus as Urbanatural Roosting. This image of Mount
Parnassus in Greece—sacred to poets as the home of the
muses—reveals urbanature: sublime *natura*, the *urbs* of
Delphi, classical ruins, and Victorian buildings, all existing
in complete harmony. From *Gallery of English and
American Poets* (Philadelphia: E. H. Butler, 1870 [1858])   xii

SPRING

"Tyger Tyger, burning bright." Blake's tiger drawn from
Oliver Goldsmith's *Animated Nature.* Blake had
probably never seen a living tiger, but representations of
wild animals in volumes of natural history provided
images that helped clarify the place of humans in
the natural world. From *A History of the Earth and
Animated Nature* (New York: Thomas Kinnersley, 1825)   2

SUMMER

Dolphin on the beach. A creature in some ways as close
to humans as any in the animal kingdom, notable since
antiquity for its intelligence and its "playful and frolicsome
disposition." (John D. Godman, *American Natural History*,
Vol. III. Philadelphia: Carey, Lee, & Carey, 1828)   54

FALL

Unveiling the Secrets of Nature. The frontispiece to Erasmus
Darwin's *Temple of Nature.* The muse of poetry pulls aside
a curtain to reveal the many-breasted Artemis of Ephesus,
goddess of wild nature. Anthropologists now believe that
these were bull's testicles rather than breasts, signaling the

singular fertility of the goddess of wild nature. Drawn by
Henry Fuseli. (London: Joseph Johnson, 1803)   104

WINTER

The insect-eater, Dionea muscipula. The Great Chain of
Being is broken forever when a plant can kill and
consume insects. (*The Botanic Garden.* London:
Joseph Johnson, 1791)   150

EPILOGUE

The Fertilization of Egypt. The dog-headed god Anubis
assures that life will always return, even in a desert culture.
The deserts of Egypt are fertile because a god who is
half-man (culture) and half-dog (wild nature) has assured
that the floods of spring will bring water from the
monotheistic face of a Yahweh-like Urizen (or perhaps
The Ancient of Days) onto the flood-plain of the Nile.
Drawn by Henry Fuseli. Engraved by William Blake.
(*The Botanic Garden.* London: Joseph Johnson, 1791)   196

A Scheme of Reference

(primary sources abbreviated throughout the text)

Barr   Barr's Buffon. *Natural History*. Ed. J. S. Barr.
Blake   William Blake. *Complete Poetry and Prose*. Ed. David
            V. Erdman.
Botanic   Darwin, Erasmus. *The Botanic Garden*.
Buffon   Buffon. *System of Natural History*. Ed. R. Morison.
Coleridge   Coleridge. *Poetry and Prose*. Ed. Nicholas Halmi, Paul
            Magnuson, and Raimonda Modiano.
Darwin   Charles Darwin. Ed. Philip Appleman.
Keats   Keats. *Complete Poems*. Ed. Miriam Allott.
Letters   Keats. *Selected Letters*. Ed. Douglas Bush.
Prelude   Wordsworth. 1799, 1805, 1850. Ed. Jonathan
            Wordsworth, M. H. Abrams, and Stephen Gill.
Prose   Shelley. *Poetry and Prose*. Ed. Donald H. Reiman and
            Neil Fraistat.
RNH   *Romantic Natural Histories*. Ed. Ashton Nichols.
Shelley   Shelley. *Works*. Ed. Mary Shelley.
System   Buffon. *System of Natural History*. Ed. Morison.
Temple   Darwin, Erasmus. *The Temple of Nature*.
Tess   Thomas Hardy. *Tess of the D'Urbervilles*. Ed. Scott
            Elledge.
Thoreau   Thoreau. *A Week on the Concord and Merrimack
            Rivers, Walden, the Maine Woods, Cape Cod*.
Walden   Thoreau. *Walden and Other Writings*. Ed. William
            Rossi.
Wordsworth William Wordsworth. Ed. Stephen Gill. Oxford
            Authors.

J Hamilton after T Creswick

O thou Parnassus! whom I now survey,
Not in the frenzy of a dreamer's eye.
Not in the fabled landscape of a lay.
But soaring, snow-clad, through thy native sky,
In the wild pomp of mountain majesty!
What marvel that I thus essay to sing!

Parnassus as Urbanatural Roosting. This image of Mount Parnassus in Greece—sacred to poets as the home of the muses—reveals urbanature: sublime *natura*, the *urbs* of Delphi, classical ruins, and Victorian buildings, all existing in complete harmony. From *Gallery of English and American Poets* (Philadelphia: E. H. Butler, 1870 [1858]).

Prologue

Urbanatural Roosting

The time has come for a new idea and a new word to describe that idea. The new word is "urbanature." The idea this word describes suggests that nature and urban life are not as distinct as human beings have long supposed. *Urbanature* (rhymes with "furniture") suggests that all human and nonhuman lives, as well as all animate and inanimate objects around those lives, are linked in a complex web of interdependent interrelatedness. Let me explain.

Hawks are roosting on skyscrapers along Central Park East and Central Park West. Peregrine falcons are feeding on the Flatiron Building, and owls are nesting throughout Manhattan (Yolton). Meanwhile, thousands of environmentalists are boarding carbon-gulping airplanes, flying hundreds of thousands of miles—carrying tons of petrochemical Gore-Tex—to get "back to nature" in Montana and Mauritius. At the same time, the World Wide Web tells us that Henry David Thoreau said, "In wilderness is the preservation of the world." Over 600 websites say so. But Thoreau did not say, "In *wilderness* is the preservation of the world." He said, "In *Wildness* is the preservation of the world" ("Walking" 273, my italics). That difference—between "wildness" and "wilderness"—makes all the difference.

The interconnectedness demanded by *urbanature* insists that human beings are not *out of* nature when they stand in the streets of Manhattan any more than they are *in* nature when they stand above tree-line in Montana. When nature-lovers say that they long to *return* to nature, they are making what the philosophers call a category mistake. As Tyler Stalling has recently noted, "There is no 'real nature' to which to return. Rather, in the face of burgeoning technologies such as nanotechnology and genetic manipulation, the once defined border between nature and culture is obsolete" ("Lore of Humankind"). Urban culture and wild nature come to much the same thing: urbanature.

So far, only a handful of artists and designers have invoked the *portmanteau* word "urbanature" to describe this important link between city-style and wild-style. The designer and illustrator Shawna L. Handke invoked the term in 2008 as the name of an online shop ("Urban is our nature. Design is in our nature") she was opening "to create a world that shares life the way I see it. I get torn between the hustle and bustle of the urban world and the stillness that you can find in nature. Of course, if you look, you can find stillness anywhere you go" ("The Urbanature Way"). Urbanature is also the name of a group of landscape architects in New Zealand and Singapore who seek to exhibit the "interplay of nature in the urban city" (urbanature.org). A Seattle rock band has adopted the name Urbanature, and a German experimental electronic musician—Eoh Ganesh—calls himself UrbaNature. Most recently, Honda has announced "The UrbaNature Signature" in automobile design, an effort to combine sleek city-style with sustainable sensibility in its 2010 CR-V utility vehicle ("UrbaNature"). Until now, however, no one has offered this term as a way of pointing up the need for a less contested, more cooperative, relationship between urban-dwellers and wilderness advocates.

My coinage "urbanature" as a critical term has important connections to recent arguments about the need to rethink the idea of "nature" altogether. Enlightenment and post-Enlightenment ideas of "nature," like a number of other concepts, have been invoked in so many differing ways over centuries that they are now past due for a rigorous verbal and cultural critique. A number of such ideas—my own list would include at least "imagination," "identity," "self," and "consciousness"—are concepts that now seem worn down and enervated, often misunderstood and more often misapplied. A rigorous critique of "nature" is called for by a number of current scholars (William Cronon, Neil Evernden, and Dana Phillips, among others) and should also be of interest to all people who worry about their relationship to their nonhuman surroundings. This book will make use of numerous texts (Romantic poems, nineteenth-century nature essays, Victorian prose fictions, and contemporary ecocritical essays and books) as well as several methodological approaches (personal memoir, narrative scholarship, historical analysis, and ecocriticism) to argue for a rethinking of the idea of "nature" as it has been used since at least the mid-eighteenth century.

Crucial to *urbanature* is the idea that human beings are never cut off from wild nature by human culture. This is the central truth of all ecology. Nothing I can do can take me out of nature. There is nowhere for me to go. I am a natural being from the moment I am born (biologically) until the moment I die (organically). Instead of describing the nonhuman world anthropocentrically—in human terms—there are now good reasons to describe the whole world eco-centrically [eco-: *oikos*, house]. In addition, the wild places that environmentalists have set aside to preserve nature, have allowed those same environmentalists to ignore the people who may have been living on those places already—as well as urban-dwellers in general—to assume that urban spaces were somehow beyond their purview, somehow someone else's problem. As *Beyond Romantic Ecocriticism: Toward Urbanatural Roosting* will make clear, the nonhuman natural house I inhabit is the same place as my fully human, cultural home.

The time has come to apply the concept of urbanature widely, from the semi-wild edges of the Himalayas to the ecologically contiguous villages of the European Alps, from the Pacific islands of Polynesia to the Middle Atlantic hills of North America. Urbanature accurately describes wide suburban-sprawls filled with millions upon billions of flowers, trees, squirrels, and raptors, reaching from the Pacific edge of the Americas to the Ural edges of Europe, from Asian steppes to Andean fastnesses. This linking of urban spaces with natural places must also include wild and semi-wild creatures: animals in zoo cages and pets in high-rise condominiums, creatures on sidewalks, roofs, and skyscraper ledges from Bombay to Caracas, from Beijing to Brooklyn. Urbanature includes the biggest of all big pictures—every gust of solar wind and every swirl of every galaxy, every mountaineer climbing a mountain and every chemist making a new medicine, birds on buildings and fish in fishponds—as well as the smallest of all small pictures: rapidly evolving bacteria, pulsing microbes, and virulent viruses.

The globe is now completely mapped, filmed, and photographed, from those 1960s snapshots of the delicate blue-green planet seen from outer space down to Google Earth shots of the smallest streetscapes and streambeds. With my own computer mouse, and with MapQuest or Google Earth, I can move from Mauritius to Manhattan in a minute; I can spin from the Seychelles to Seattle in a second. I can zoom down onto every housetop. I can see almost every car in every parking lot. But this is not a problem. This is not a loss. In fact, my ability to scan the surface of the globe with my computer in seconds is part of what assures me that I am linked to every living creature, and every material object, that surrounds me. Children like those to whom this book is dedicated—growing up in their twenty-first century world—will never be able to conceive of the idea of *wilderness* in the same way that their parents and grandparents did, as a space so vast that the edges of it can hardly be conceived, as a mysterious wildness with which humans have almost nothing to do. The Romantic idea of wilderness may be gone, but it has been replaced by an idea of wild spaces that need to be saved, places that have already been saved—or still need to be saved—for human and, much less frequently, nonhuman reasons: the good of the biome, the lives of other species that live there. Modern society has reached a moment when many scientists and environmentalists, as well as a growing number of politicians and private citizens, understand that it all needs to be sustained: the nonhuman and human, the wild and tame, the rural and urban. The entire planet depends on a new willingness to see urban and nonurban spaces as equally worth saving.

Ecocritical awareness of the nonhuman world begins, in this sense, not with the environmental revolution of the 1960s and 1970s, but with a new definition of "Nature" first offered by Romantic writers in the late-eighteenth and early-nineteenth centuries. *Beyond Romantic Ecocriticism: Toward Urbanatural Roosting* examines a number of those writers and their ideas, and then charts a pervasive paradigm shift, a revolutionary turn away from a fallen version of "Nature" that was static and unchanging toward a Romantic "nature" characterized by dynamic links among all living things. This shift eventually leads toward a new emphasis on connections between nature and society. Current emphasis on evolutionary ecology arises not solely from a contemporary "Green" sense of the interdependence between organisms and their environments; it derives as well from Romantic and Victorian thinkers and their view of the interconnectedness of all living—and even nonliving—things. This book will thus link the zoological and botanical imagery of William Blake to the eco-awareness of William Wordsworth; it will connect the eco-sensitivity of John Keats with the eco-anxieties of Alfred, Lord Tennyson. By the twentieth century, the concept of Romantic natural history will allow for a critique of the eco-theology of Annie Dillard and a challenge to the eco-catastrophic thinking of Bill McKibben. Along the way, a number of contemporary ecocritics—Lawrence Buell, Jonathan Bate, and Timothy Morton, and numerous others—will reveal where the dominant current view of nature has come from, especially since that idea of "nature" is not now the same as the "Nature" described by Aristotle, Isaac Newton, or even Charles Darwin.

The "urbanatural year" chronicled in this book—from "Spring" to "Spring, Again"—links the ideas of Romantic natural historians and contemporary ecocritics to the pervasive current sense of an environmental crisis: Hurricane Katrina, the Gulf of Mexico oil-spill, climate change, species extinction, and an increasingly uncertain human future. A look at the legacy of Romantic natural history will move beyond the word "nature" as it has been employed since the Enlightenment—and beyond the nature versus culture split—toward the more inclusive idea of "urbanatural roosting." Finally, I will argue that Romantic ecocriticism should now give way to a more socially aware version of environmentalism, one less tightly linked to narrowly Western ideas about the self, the "Other," and the relationship between human beings and the natural world. Urbanatural roosting says that, if all humans are linked to each other and to their surroundings, then those same humans have clear obligations to each other and to the world they share.

How might human beings "roost" on the world? To roost is to make a temporary home (*oikos*) in the surrounding environment, the way hawks and ravens roost. Most birds roost in trees, while some roost just as successfully on the ground. Bobwhites roost in fields and in meadows, while screech owls find hollow cavities in tall trees. This is just one reason why meadows and tall trees need to be preserved, since even apparently "useless" natural sites, with no human purpose, are roosting-grounds for countless birds of many species. Even wild turkeys find thick roosting-branches high up in those trees. A bird initially roosts for its own benefit, and for the benefit of its species, but roosting also has consequences for other species and for the wider environment. Roosts have an impact on the trees in which they exist, on high ocean cliffs and other such nesting sites. They can generate massive quantities of guano, sometimes to the point of becoming commercially viable fertilizer harvesting spots. A bird gathers food where it roosts, and it may also find its mate there. Many birds build their nests where they roost, or they hide themselves and their young from natural enemies there. Roosts are crucial to the life cycle of most avian species (White, Dolbeer, and Bookhout). A roost, in this sense, is also beneficial to humans. Of course, the ideas of "benefit" and "harm" are completely human constructions, but the word "roost" at least describes a home, a home that affects, and is affected by, its inhabitants and their wider surroundings.

As humans, we roost no less than hawks, or eagles, or ravens. To roost is to know one place so well that you can create your home there, so well that you can use that local knowledge for your benefit and the benefit of those around you. Birds roost by using the natural resources around them, but they roost *without harming* those same resources—and those roosts—in the process. Human beings need to take a lesson from the birds; they need to start roosting more carefully on the earth. The phrase "urbanatural roosting" allows for a closer link between cities and the wilderness, between high rises and wild places. It also recognizes close ties between those who live within the city limits and those who live beyond the city limits: in the suburbs, the small towns, rural areas, even out in the middle of "nowhere." Roosting says that every "nowhere" is always a somewhere. Humans, like dolphins and dogs and mayflies, are natural beings. Instead of continuing to describe the nonhuman world anthropocentrically—in human terms—there are now important reasons to describe the entire world ecocentrically. This is part of the message about "nature" that poets like William Wordsworth, John Keats, and Percy Shelley began to offer to their culture. The scientist Charles Darwin understood these same links, as did the poet and novelist Thomas Hardy. The literary works analyzed in the following pages will provide an index to the emergence of a broadly ecological awareness in Western culture. At the same time, the scientific works examined here will offer a revealing look at links among aesthetics, emotions, and the natural world over the past two centuries.

Many of the great "nature" poems of the Romantic era were actually written in the suburbs, in the back gardens of great cities, or in the midst of the largest urban space on the planet at the time: London. To be "natural" originally meant, not to be nonhuman—as it now often seems to mean—but, "to be born": *natura*, "birth," and also "essence," as in "the *nature* of the problem." *Beyond Romantic Ecocriticism* will return the term to these original meanings: "nature" is about things that are born and about the essence of things, not a dubious philosophical essence, but simply the heart of the matter, the center of the issue (i.e., "what is the *nature* of the problem here?"). The human-made object is no less natural because human beings have shaped it, no less "born" or "essential" because it has been fashioned by human hands. The bird makes a nest, and that nest is just as natural as the bird herself. Human hands make a house, and that house is no less natural than the materials that fashioned it, or the human hands that shaped it.

So where does my concept of urbanatural roosting begin? It begins with a bit of Romantic natural history, with William Blake claiming that "A Robin Red breast in a Cage / Puts all Heaven in a Rage" (*Blake*, "Auguries of Innocence" 5–6). Around the same

time, William Wordsworth read Erasmus Darwin's natural philosophy and used his psychological theories in lyric poems. Meanwhile,
this earlier Darwin (Charles's grandfather) wrote book-length poems
of botanical observations in heroic couplets, while his good friend
Joseph Priestley penned theological essays at the same time he was
discovering oxygen. The poet Percy Shelley experimented with chemical and electrical equipment in his rooms at Oxford—he almost blew
them up!—and Mary Shelley was talking about the Italian electrical scientist Luigi Galvani on the night she initially conceived Victor
Frankenstein's monster. Samuel Taylor Coleridge sought poetically
and philosophically for the "one Life, within us and abroad" ("The
Eolian Harp," 26) that would unify the apparently disparate elements
of creation:

> And what if all of animated nature
> Be but organic Harps diversly fram'd,
> That tremble into thought, as o'er them sweeps,
> Plastic and vast, one intellectual Breeze (36–39)

Galvanic nerve responses, luminous plankton, sensitive plants
(*Mimosa*), poison trees (*Bohun upas*), intelligence in animals and
sexuality in plants: ideas and images like these fostered poetic reflec-
tion and scientific lyricism throughout the century before Charles
Darwin's *On the Origin of Species* (1859). This link between science
and poetry in the eighteenth and nineteenth centuries is a crucial
aspect of the origin of current ideas about environmental sustainability. These ideas continue to suggest close links among various parts
of the natural world but also close connections among the natural,
social, and urban worlds in which these versions of nature are, more
than ever, being described.

All of these nineteenth-century nature writers—and their
"*Major Lives and Letters*" as this current Palgrave Macmillan series
suggests—along with their successors down to the present day, reveal
ways that human beings are part of a vast urbanatural web of organic
interrelatedness. From William Blake to Lawrence Buell, from Alfred,
Lord Tennyson to Terry Tempest Williams, poets and prose writers
have come to understand that humans share one finite globe with
all other living things: not one world called "nature" and another
called "culture." This is why the "lives and letters" of these writers
link directly to my assertion that humanity's material and nonhuman "house"—once called "nature"—is the same place as its fully
human and cultural home. Scientists now know that I share genetic

information with chimpanzees and crustaceans. They have mapped the human genome down to the precise gene for breast-cancer, or the specific genes that make my brain a human brain and not a chimpanzee brain. They are on the verge of transplanting animal organs regularly from nonhuman species into human beings. Surgeons can already insert human genes directly into other species and vice versa. Each living being is genetically related to every other species in countless ways: humans to gorillas, whales to dogs, fish to foxgloves, fungi to bacteria, and all of these to each other. The family of "man" has become the family of all living things.

By the time a fully developed ecocriticism emerged in the twenty-first century, some ecologists and social critics had already begun describing the "death of environmentalism" or even a "post-environmental world" (Nordhaus and Shellenberger 2004). One ecocritic and environmental activist described the "end of nature" (McKibben 1989) and six years later his "hope" for some ongoing and successful version of urbanature (*Hope, Human and Wild* 1995), while another has posited the end of the very idea of nature (Morton, *Ecology without Nature* 2007). In *The Abstract Wild*, Jack Turner says, "I do not believe that modern convenience is incompatible with the preservation of the wild because I have a good deal of both in my life"; although Turner loves his "Ford 4x4 truck [...] Powerbook [...] Zeiss binoculars [...] and E-mail," he is nevertheless able to call for "a culture that deeply loves the wild earth" (xvii). A sense of honest balance and proportion like Turner's will be required by urbanaturalists in the coming decades. Michael Bennett, in "Urban Nature: Teaching *Tinker Creek* by the East River," notes the tendency of traditional—I would say "Romantic"—ecocriticism to "romanticize natural environments without realizing their connection to larger socioeconomic forces" (54). Bennett argues for "an ecocriticism which blends a traditional focus on 'wild' nature with the diverse ecology of urban environments" (56). Bennett anticipates my emphasis on urbanature in many ways. Such post-Romantic and urbanatural versions of ecocriticism echo Andrew Ross's criticism of the "powerful sway of neoromanticism over the ecology movement," on a Romantic version of ecocriticism that has too often ignored, for example, "the environmental racism practiced upon targeted populations of color" (9). As early as 1981, the urban-planner Kevin Lynch called for accepting "that the city is as natural as the farm and as susceptible of conservation and improvement"; once ecocritics and planners do so, he noted, "we work free of those false dichotomies of city and country, artificial and natural, man versus other living things" (Stein 475). Nature-lovers from Ralph Waldo Emerson to modern deep ecologists have too often embraced the wild at the expense of the tame; they have emphasized the nonhuman at the expense of the human.

My emphasis on *urbanature* and *roosting* emerges out of my own contention that gentrification, postindustrial waste, environmental racism, and other forms of urban degradation can come about when land-use urban planners or environmentalists say that wild nature takes precedence over urban wastelands: "well, vast tracts of wild forests and wilderness areas have been saved; what difference does it make what happens to a few under-resourced, devastated sections of this postindustrial city?" This assumption is especially easy to make when those same planners or environmentalists are describing vast sections of once-great cities that upper middle-class "nature-lovers" will never visit. In this regard, my argument echoes David Orr's emphasis on the "new urbanism," a movement that seeks to bring numerous urban life-activities physically closer together: "housing, employment, shopping, culture, public spaces, recreation, and health care" (*Design* 52) instead of having them sprawled out over vast sections of the landscape. Orr has also called for an educational system based on "global ecological enlightenment," one that will allow students to see how closely their human lives are linked to the nonhuman world, how "all education is environmental education" (*Earth* 12). In *The Nature of Cities: Ecocriticism and Urban Environments*, Michael Bennett—author of the quotation on environmental racism in the previous paragraph—and David W. Teague link an uncertain ecological future to several urbanatural solutions: (1) the preservation of urban gardens on once "wasted" ground (think Detroit, Pittsburgh, or Akron); (2) ecofeminisms that emphasize nurture in urban planning; (3) nature writing in the city and the suburbs; and, (4) the term "park" as a word that reaches from Frederick Law Olmsted's "Central Park" to F. V. Hayden's and Ulysses S. Grant's "Yellowstone," from the earliest urban parks of Europe to the carefully planned Kaza Park, a twenty-first century game-reserve in southern Africa that will be roughly the size of Italy. A final example of applied urbanature comes from Terrell Dixon. In his collection *City Wilds: Essays and Stories About Urban Nature*, Dixon reveals ways that "the wild—once we choose to recognize it—inhabits the city as well as the country" (xiii). As is so often the case, the truth is simply a matter of people opening their eyes and seeing what has been right there in front of them all along.

One element of Romanticism has contributed to the problem that urbanature seeks to resolve. This idea underpins a version of environmentalism that has held powerful sway for more than two centuries. In this view, nature is somehow opposed to urbanity, the wild is what the city gets rid of, human culture is the enemy of nature. Adam and Eve were the only threat to a once pristine (nonhuman) Garden of Eden. According to this narrative, human beings tore down their garden; they messed in their nest. Wordsworth's poem "Nutting" chronicles this myth in detail: "Then up I rose, / And dragged to earth both branch and bough, with crash / And merciless ravage" (41–43); the result of this violence is that the elements of nature give up "[t]heir quiet being" (46), while the ravenous intruder learns that "there is a Spirit in the woods" (54). Yet, that harmonious Garden of Eden, Wordsworth's "one dear nook / Unvisited" (14–15), never existed in the first place. Nothing more than careful roosting is required to clean up that messed-up nest for good. This earlier Romantic version of environmentalism—the one that saw human beings as the problem—revealed serious limitations whenever it was applied to a world in which "nature" and "culture" merged into a unified vision. Humanity now inhabits a unified organic and inorganic biosphere, one that all of its members need to learn to care for and share. At the same time, the immediate needs of social and ecological—that is, human—justice reach well beyond Romantic ecocriticism. Twenty-first century humans should live closer to the ways that animals live, that is, in harmony with their surroundings. From a Darwinian perspective, human beings are genetically related to every other creature on this shared planet. The human species now needs to roost with its fellow species, no longer to have dominion, no longer to dominate. If I take any lesson from my fellow creatures, I should learn that the planet is here not for my ruling but for my roosting.

One final example of urbanatural roosting will conclude my prologue. Where would we be without *penicillium*, that invisible fungus-spore that flew through Alexander Fleming's window in his London laboratory—in 1928—and led to penicillin, a drug that has saved millions of lives? Was Fleming functioning in wild nature or in urban culture when he came upon that fungus? He was operating in both. A purely natural object (the airborne *penicillium*) had landed on a purely cultural production (a Petri dish smeared with agar) and the result was penicillin, a natural product of human culture that has changed life on this planet forever. Behind Fleming's discovery of the *penicillium*-mold were almost two centuries of debate (c. 1750–1930) about medicines possessing aspects of nature that could change human existence: the microscopic world, germ theory, the immune system, and vaccination. Ahead of Fleming's production of penicillin stretched another century of debate about the results of these discoveries. Who should have access to such biological lifesavers? Which societies would control the natural knowledge that might save lives or might lead to the loss of millions of other lives? Would the power of such knowledge reside only with the developed world, only for the benefit of the cultures that had created such advances? Or might there be a means of moving from a monocultural view of nature to a multicultural one, from a world of self-isolating societies to a world of unified and unifying cultures? As the discovery of penicillin suggests, urban culture and wild nature once again come to much the same thing: urbanature, a new model for roosting on the planet that each of us shares with other human beings and also with the rest of animate nature.

SPRING

—VERNAL ROOSTING—

ROMANTIC ECOCRITICISM

"Tyger Tyger, burning bright." Blake's tiger drawn from Oliver Goldsmith's *Animated Nature.* Blake had probably never seen a living tiger, but representations of wild animals in volumes of natural history provided images that helped clarify the place of humans in the natural world. From *A History of the Earth and Animated Nature* (New York: Thomas Kinnersley, 1825).

MARCH

The world is the fairest of creations.

—*Plato,* Timaeus

I have come to a rustic stone cabin that my family has always called "The Roost" to begin a process that I will call "roosting." Roosting describes a new way of living more self-consciously on the earth. This book will be a "meteorological journal of the mind" (see Henry David Thoreau and Annie Dillard), but one drawn from this world, the world in which—as William Wordsworth says—"We find our happiness, or not at all!" (*Prelude* 11.144 [1850]). A decade later, Thoreau said, "in Wildness is the preservation of the world" ("Walking" 273). Wordsworth and Thoreau linked our life as humans to the nonhuman world around us, and they both echoed the Franco-German *philosophe* Baron D'Holbach, who had said, in 1834, "Man always deceives himself when he abandons experience to follow imaginary systems. He is the work of nature.—He exists in nature.—He is submitted to her laws" (1: 9). I propose to accept the claims of Wordsworth, Thoreau, and D'Holbach as starting-points for the urbanatural year I will chronicle in this book.

The wildness of which Thoreau speaks can be found as easily on Beacon Street in downtown Boston as it can on the rural shoreline of Walden Pond. Thoreau's wildness is also available in Manhattan or Montana. Thoreau says so in the rarely cited sentences that immediately follow the famous "Wildness" quote: "Every tree sends its fibres forth in search of the Wild. The cities import it at any price" ("Walking" 273). So wildness is not only about wild places; it is also about cities and about a state of mind. Thoreau's "Wildness" can be found in the minds of all those who have read and understood his message. Likewise, Wordsworth's "world / Of all of us" (*Prelude* 11.142–43), is as likely to be found in the center of Paris or London as it is in the rugged rock piles and tarns of the Lake District or the Alps. With this in mind, my goal is to move, not only back (to nature) but also forward (toward urbanature), forward into the experience of living in a world where nature and culture are no longer seen as distinct. This new world is one where the natural and the urban mingle—just as they do so easily on any map these days—just as they do now in my computer screen on Google Earth or MapQuest. Now that human beings have begun to accept the idea that they need to live more sustainably on the earth if they are going to survive as a species, it is essential to describe just how such sustainable living might take place. To do that, it is important to go back to a time when humanity and nature were seen as unified for the first time. Where am I heading during my "natural" year? First, back to Romantic ecocriticism; then forward, toward urbanatural roosting.

A NEW URBANATURAL YEAR

The ancients began their new year during the month that is still called March (named for Mars, the god of war) because that was the time when life began again every year, once a year, as it had forever. In Finland, this month is still called *maaliskuu*—which means "month of earth"—because this is the time when the bare soil shows itself again each year from beneath a deep cloak of winter's snow. The long months of cold have seemed interminable. The frost has seemed forever. Then the sun reappears, the snow melts, and the icy soil begins to grow warmer again. The new life of spring begins to sprout: crocuses push up through the scattered morning rime, green buds poke out at the end of the branch tips, scurrying feet leave tiny scratches in the cold, still icy groundcover. All at once life begins again, and the whole world seems suddenly fresh and new. Throughout Scandinavia, young people and old alike step outside on the first really warm day and turn their bodies eastward to face the sun. They turn their faces and their palms toward the light and the warmth. Even today, with central heating running throughout the winter, whole villages of northern people turn out to perform this simple ritual every spring. The sun has come back and, with the sun, life itself has come back.

This same seasonal cycle begins again every year all over the planet—except near the North and South Poles and in the tropics, where four seasons tend to be reduced to two: wet and dry—at different times for sure, but always right on schedule. This year, I find myself on top of the Blue Ridge Mountains, near the Virginia-West Virginia border, on the precise day that the new natural year begins. It feels like New Year's Day. Like an earlier forest wordsmith, I have come to these woods because I wish to live deliberately, but I also wish to live quietly and peacefully, away from the ringing of cell phones and doorbells, away from the clanging of town bells and sirens, and away from intruding thoughts of taxes and rapid transportation. I won't stay as long as I might like to during each of my mountain sojourns—I still have a human life to lead—but I will return to the Roost whenever I can carve out the necessary days or weeks, a natural life artificially distinct from my urban life. I will be here for as many days as I can manage this year, at least some days during every month, from now until next March: one natural year to think about urbanatural roosting.

This book will set down the story of my "roosting" year. I will not pretend—as so many nature writers have done before me—that the rest of the world does not continue to exist beyond me, that urban life does not continue busily, and noisily, during each of my sojourns away from the city. Cabs are still racing down Broadway in Manhattan as I write these words. Jumbo jets are landing at Dulles airport, and sirens are whining throughout cities around the world. In fact, a central thesis of my upcoming year is that the world of nature and the world of human beings are not as separate as many of our best nature writers have long imagined them to be. Hence "urbanature" and hence "roosting." Nature does not end where the wild woods stop and the hard pavement begins. Nature does not cease because a human being has appeared on the scene.

Thoreau, remember, often walked into Concord for dinner with his mother or an evening conversation with Emerson. Indeed, Thoreau was arrested and sent to jail in the middle of the two "wild" years he spent at Walden. The Concord town center was only a mile-and-a-half from the shore of the pond. Thoreau's successors—Aldo Leopold, Edward Abbey, Annie Dillard, and Terry Tempest Williams, to name just a few of my own *genii loci*—have all admitted that their lives away from urban life are only a part of the nature-writing story. In a similar spirit, I want to spend some extended time at my own non-human Walden—the Roost—and some equally valuable time during this year in the urban world of men and women. Indeed, I will report back from several cities in America and in Europe while I am roosting. As Dillard once said, I want—like the bear—to go "over the mountain" to see "what I [can] see" (11). But unlike Annie's bear, I want to go to town, too; I want some urban life linked closely to my natural, roosting year.

"I have a great deal of company in my house; especially in the morning, when nobody calls," Thoreau says in the chapter of *Walden* called "Solitude" (95). That is how I feel this morning, alone in my 25-by-50-foot cabin, "alone" in a small room full of inhabitants: camel crickets, spiders, a lone wasp buzzing against the window pane, a tiny ring-neck snake no longer than my thumb wriggling toward the porch door. There was a wolf spider in the outhouse this morning; he was a full three inches from leg tip to leg tip. With his legs extended he covered my palm—if I dared pick him up—and I did dare to pick him up, not because I am brave but because I know that wolf spiders don't bite, nor do they have any desire to hurt humans. For the same reason, I have always encouraged my daughters to pick up spiders and snakes, not to scare my children but to help them to grow up free from the fear of reptiles, bugs, and mice. Many children grow up these days full of fear of the natural world around them, especially the wild world of bats and snakes and snails. Such fear poses a serious danger.

These unfortunate children are taught to fear nature by their nature-fearing parents. As Richard Louv says in his masterful *Last Child in the Woods: Saving Our Children from Nature-Deficit Disorder*, "Our society is teaching young people to avoid direct experience in nature [...] Children and adults are even beginning to see nature as our natural enemy" (2, 130). My children actually have very little to fear from the animal world, except perhaps their fellow human creature's ignorance. My children should mostly fear human animals, and the ways those animals often treat one another and the rest of the nonhuman world. My family and I do not generally fear spiders and snakes and wasps; these creatures are like us. As Darwin says, they want to find food and find a mate and then go off to eat their meals and rear their offspring in peace. Here is how John Keats expressed this important connection across the species boundary: "I go among the Feilds [*sic*] and catch a glimpse of a stoat or a fieldmouse peeping out of the withered grass—the creature hath a purpose and its eyes are bright with it—I go amongst the buildings of a city and I see a Man hurrying along—to what? The Creature hath a purpose and his eyes are bright with it" (*Letters* 285). Anyone who has seen the bright eyes of a deer mouse, as I did this morning, knows this vivid facial mouse-expression that Keats describes: it "hath a purpose and its eyes are bright with it." In the same letter, written in March 1819, Keats reveals a central truth of all Darwinian thinking, four decades before Darwin: "The Hawk wants a Mate, so does the Man—look at them both they set about it and procure on[e] in the same manner—They want both a nest and they both set about one in the same manner—they get their food in the same manner" (285). Mates and food: those details begin and end the story of natural selection.

"You only need sit still long enough in some attractive spot in the woods that all its inhabitants may exhibit themselves to you by turns" (155), Thoreau wrote in his chapter called "Brute Neighbors." I took his advice this morning and sat stock-still on a rock near the top of the mountain ridge for almost an hour. Dappled light shifted and fluttered against tree bark and lichen-encrusted rocks. A single spring moth flapped and then landed, folding its wings into perfect triangles of dusky brown and gray, holding them horizontally like a patterned carpet of pale color that suddenly flashed bright yellow at its base. A chipmunk appeared from a distant pile of leaves, running straight toward me until he realized my startling human presence. Then he bolted, full tilt, almost bouncing off of sticks, logs, and rocks, until he finally looked back over what passed for his chipmunk shoulder and then disappeared down a hole at the base of a towering oak tree. He was only one of several creatures that, as Thoreau promised, exhibited themselves to me, "by turns": another butterfly, then a small flock of warblers, and finally a centipede, swirling in a sinuous s-curve from side to side, finally disappearing down a narrow crevice in the rocks at my feet.

Back in the cabin, even the wasps are waking up now. Somehow they have survived the cold winter between the Roost's thick wooden shutters and its thin glass windows, somnolent for months at temperatures that have reached into single digits. How can their tiny insect bodies not freeze when the night's cold drops close to zero degrees Fahrenheit? Their thin exoskeletons must be able to keep enough liquid—is it bug-blood?—unfrozen in their veins—do they even have veins?—so that when these first warm days arrive, the wasps wake up sluggishly and walk along the rocky ledges of the windowsills, still unable to balance, still unable to fly. Soon they fall off the windowsills and crash to the ground, unhurt because their body weight is so slight. Finally, some of them become airborne and fly off to nearby tree branches that still look as dead as December; or they land on the edge of the windowsill, unfolding their wings and turning their tiny heads—all eyes and antennae—toward the sun, facing the warmth, just like me. I still wonder, how did they survive such winter temperatures? These are cold-blooded creatures; they have no internal means of keeping warm. What allowed those few drops of cold-blooded fluid not to freeze solid in their tiny wasp bodies? I have no idea.

Early warblers skitter close-by through low shrubs and tree-tops. Shuddering vultures carve great winged circles across a cloud-streaked, pale morning sky. A yellow-shafted flicker *clack-clacks* through a brambly bush in the distance, in search of early spring insects. Even today, on this day after the last day of winter, I spot three fully developed butterflies—all mourning cloaks—in the space of a single morning hour. How can they all have emerged so early in the season? When did they pupate and mature? Where did they manage to hide from the winter frosts? What force kept them from freezing, like those unfrozen wasps, during these recent icy nights? Wordsworth was equally impressed by creatures as simple as these butterflies, as was John Keats, as was John Clare.

As to my own argument, I will invoke not only these poets, but also scientists, to support my claims. Each twelve-month chapter in my "meteorological journal" works to explain how poets and scientists think alike, even though they also think differently. For starters, both poets and scientists need powerful metaphors. In fact, every writer—poet or scientist—relies on metaphoric analogies to make any new idea, and some old ideas, comprehensible. This point may seem obvious, but it is crucial to my argument. All human creators, from poets or physicists, rely on metaphors to make the unknown—what William Blake called the "once, only imagin'd" ("Marriage of Heaven and Hell" Plate 8)—into the well-known and newly understood. In that fact resides another important truth about the limits of the idea of "nature." Writers and critics have made and remade the idea of "nature" so many times since the Enlightenment that it is now a concept that is worn down; in some ways it has outlived its usefulness. Nature no longer lingers in the dark, wild forest; it is now found from the Himalayas to Houston, from the Maldives to Manhattan.

A low light is shining across the gray-green water of the Shenandoah River at the foot of the mountain. A smoky half moon and a few dusky stars are visible through barred clouds in the west. The sky holds its final trace of last night's darkness. The hillside has grown suddenly still. The woods surrounding me are stunningly silent. It is rare these days to sit outside anywhere in the world and hear nothing but the sound of one's own breathing. Out beyond these woods lie the rolling fields of Loudoun County, spreading away toward Leesburg and the nation's capital in the distance. Even here, in this thick forest, so close to the sprawling megalopolis that reaches from Richmond to Boston—past Washington, Baltimore, Philadelphia, New York, New

Haven, and Providence—even here, the woods fall so silent for some rare moments, in certain spaces and some liminal (border) traces, that I can only hear the sound of my pulse in my ears. I can hear it right now.

This book begins by exploring the way the mind makes metaphors from the nonhuman ("natural") world as often as it does from the human ("urban") world. In a similar way, the symbolic world still inhabited by our culture began only within the last three centuries, when the analogies of emerging ("Enlightenment") science began to be drawn from the same sources as the analogies of ancient ("primitive") poetry. "Pain penetrates me drop by drop," Sappho said in the seventh-century BC. "My love is like a red, red rose," Robert Burns added in the eighteenth-century AD. "The sun is like the still point at the center of a spinning wheel." Who said that, or something very much like that? Nicolaus Copernicus. Copernicus arrived in the fifteenth-century AD and said, approximately, "you see the sun, the sun *seems* to be moving, but it is not. In relation to our world it is standing still, just as the wagon wheel's center stays still while the wagon wheel is spinning." The scientist always needs a metaphor, just as the poet does, to make any new idea comprehensible. The sun is like...My love is like...The solar system is like...An atom is like...and so on, on and on.

Such metaphors from science and from poetry will become one of my organizing principles, taking on the material spirit of each season in sequence, month by month, from a section called "Spring" to a section called "Spring, Again." The spirit of this place—The Roost—will become the spirit of this book. What does "spirit" mean, after all, but "breath"? "Inspiration" comes from "to breathe into," from the Latin, *in-spirare*. There is no magic here, just the living breath, call it the life force if you will, the *élan vital*, organic life breathing in and out, at least as long as each organic life lasts. To understand these links between science and poetry, I need to go back at least as far as Romantic natural history: "Romantic" from Romantic poetry, "natural history" from those early scientists who made long lists of animals and plants with scientific names and consistent morphological characteristics. Romantic natural historians produced a *picture* of a world beyond social and civic concerns and called it the natural world. "Romantic" nature was not the earlier nature that had been given to human beings in *Genesis* by an all-powerful deity; rather, it was a humanistic nature that human authors acknowledged having shaped out of the contents of their own minds. Romantic nature was not a world over which humans had entire "dominion," but rather a world that humans were meant to care about and share with others.

Poets and scientists, from the mid-eighteenth century onward, helped to shape a version of nature that was linked directly to human feelings: Romantic emotions and values. This new Enlightenment nature was not only for human beings to control and constrain but also for them to understand and value, in part because it was so closely linked to their entire world. *Beyond Romantic Ecocriticism: Toward Urbanatural Roosting* will begin by looking back to a time when poetry (in fact all art) and natural philosophy (in fact all science) were more closely linked than they often seem today. Such an analysis will reveal where the current sense of "nature" has come from; today, it is clear that poets think more like scientists than many poets often realize, and scientists think more like poets than many scientists are willing to admit.

Terrell F. Dixon, in the introduction to his anthology *City Wilds*, says that his own goal is to "help us learn to see and cherish nature in the urban places where most of us now live" (xviii). I concur with Dixon, but I would add an even more radical proposal; nature is not *in* urban spaces any more than nature is *in* Yellowstone or the Tetons. Those places *are* natural as much as Manhattan and Beijing are natural, or—to put it more clearly—this now is a postnatural world and a postenvironmental world. The term "nature" served a crucial political and literary function from the time it was invoked by Locke and Rousseau to describe the source of humanity's inalienable rights and the inviolable laws that controlled the material world. The term "environment" has been invoked more recently by environmentalists to make a precise argument for the need to clean up the streams, and the lakes, and the rivers of Europe and North America and to clean up the air of Los Angeles and Mexico City. But nature is now no longer distinct from something mysteriously "non-natural," nor is the environment limited to nonhuman spaces that need a thorough cleanup. Skyscrapers and suburban sprawl are surely parts of the broader natural environment, but nature also exists in every fenced backyard and along every interstate highway's dingy median.

Dixon traces the important historical sources of America's cultural separation of the natural and the urban. American settlers, he argues, were particularly inclined to see the city and the wilderness in oppositional terms. Having come from Europe with a desire to leave behind cities that had been inhabited and developed for hundreds—sometimes thousands—of years, these pioneers favored the wide-open spaces of the American frontier. These were the same settlers who helped to create an apparent separation between the natural and the urban out of their need to leave the cities behind to carve out new lives from the hitherto unoccupied wilderness (with little—if any—recognition of the long-standing human cultures of the indigenous inhabitants: the Cherokee and Cheyenne, the Navaho and Sioux, the Iroquois and Algonquin). Dixon also notes that Emerson and Thoreau, as the most influential of America's early nature writers, "inherited a distaste for the city from European Romanticism" (xii). Dixon is right in the broadest sense about the way the Romantic writers of Europe and America disdained the city. Like Thoreau's two years at Walden Pond, Wordsworth preferred the Lake District to London. Shelley stood in awe at the foot of Mont Blanc, and Keats sought out the nonhuman spaces of a stubble farm-field in autumn. But this is a point that can be easily overstated. Keats's nightingale was singing in a suburban back garden, Shelley's skylark is a bird of the small cities and the town lands, and one of Wordsworth's greatest poems reveals that "nature" can be found in the heart of the world's largest city.

An Urbanatural Poem

One of the greatest nature poems in English, by one of the greatest nature poets in the language, is a poem set in the center of the largest city in the world:

> Earth has not any thing to shew more fair:
> Dull would he be of soul who could pass by
> A sight so touching in its majesty:
> This City now doth like a garment wear
> The beauty of the morning; silent, bare,
> Ships, towers, domes, theatres, and temples lie
> Open unto the fields, and to the sky;
> All bright and glittering in the smokeless air.
> Never did sun more beautifully steep
> In his first splendor valley, rock, or hill;
> Ne'er saw I, never felt, a calm so deep!
> The river glideth at his own sweet will:
> Dear God! the very houses seem asleep;
> And all that mighty heart is lying still! (*Wordsworth* 285)

A city of one million people (the approximate population of London in September 1802, when the experience described in this lyric occurred) is the setting for a sonnet that makes several remarkable claims. I have left the poem without its title on purpose. The "heart" that is lying still here is clearly the heart of the city, but it might also be called the being, the essence—the *urbanatural* energy (human and nonhuman)—that is about to be released when this city wakes. Wordsworth catches that dawn-moment when the day is all anticipation, when only the slightest of fulfillments are barely imagined. The word "fair," the first direct attribution made by Wordsworth in this poem, comes from an Old English word meaning "beautiful," but the word also means equitable or balanced, as in a "fair deal" or a "fair plan" (*OED*).

What is balanced so perfectly here are the details of urban buildings and spaces with the natural earth and sky. The beauty being described is at once "silent" and "bare," bare as in lacking a cover, open to plain view, but also as in "bare" bones, the "bare" necessities, that is to say, all that is needed. Nothing more is required; the scene is complete. The scene also offers numerous imposing human creations—"Ships, towers, domes, theatres, and temples"—that "lie / Open," like the pages of a book to the nonhuman, and therefore "natural," world of fields and sky. "Fields" is the perfect transitional word here, suggesting as it does a piece of land that is nonhuman in its origins—there are fields in the world that no human hand has ever touched—but also fields as in farm fields, pieces of land that have been carved out, set aside, shaped, and tended by human agency.

What is perhaps most powerful here is precisely the lack of human agency expressed in this scene. Human beings are all literally out of this world—they are all asleep or indoors, except for the speaker ("Ne'er saw *I*"; italics added)—so that this sight reminds the poet of a remembered nonhuman equivalent: another scene, an imagined rural scene, composed of "valley, rock, or hill." Because Wordsworth is the speaker, the English Lake District must come to mind, but at the same time—so the "nature" poet says—an imagined scene of nature without urbanity, would not (or could not) be any more beautiful. This purely imagined natural sight—the one of "valley, rock, or hill"—can lay claim neither to more beauty nor to greater calm than the largest city on the planet. No purely natural landscape could offer a sight of more splendor than this morning view of vast London from the bridge over the mighty Thames at Westminster. This recognition is the key to the poem's power, especially as part of Wordsworth's "natural" *oeuvre*.

The mighty river Thames glides without any need for humans or human agency: "The river glideth at his own sweet will." There is not any personification or any anthropomorphism here, however, because the river glides without any force helping it, except perhaps gravity.

The river's potential energy is turned to kinetic energy by the slope of the riverbed and by the sea-level out beyond Gravesend that keeps it flowing in an easterly direction, except when the tide rises. The river's "sweet will" echoes the earlier dull "soul who" might miss such a scene. This scene too has a "soul," but it is a soul only in the sense of energy, only in the sense of a potential for action, just like the action of a slow-moving river. There is nothing magical here. As is so often the case in Wordsworth's writing, an almost godlike power is nothing more than a combination of the physicist's matter and energy: water and light, houses and gravity.

Wordsworth, at this pantheistic stage in his own life (before the middle-aged, Anglican Tory settled in), is perhaps even worried that such a soul is the only soul that humans might have, not some mystical, quasi-spooky (ghost-in-the-machine) soul, but merely a potential for action, a soul that can express the very movement and activity that is so lacking in the "calm" of this scene from an urban bridge. This masterful sonnet is written in praise of potential: the potential of a river to flow, the potential of these houses and their occupants to wake up (they seem "asleep"), and the potential of an urbanatural city to come bustling to life in the moments after the poem ends. Even the "smokeless air" is a reminder that the morning's fires have not yet been lit. Dorothy Wordsworth captured the urbanatural power of this precise light in her own *Journal*, where she wrote of this identical morning scene, "The sun shone so brightly with such a pure light that there was even something like the purity of one of nature's own grand spectacles" (Wordsworth, *Oxford Authors* 710n). She and her brother have shared a similar urbanatural moment. Soon there will be tens of thousands of wreaths of smoke curling up from London's Blakean chimneys (and a few "Satanic mills" perhaps?), clouding out the "bright and glittering" air, smudging up the fair clarity of a sky through which all of London's human creations now lie "open to" the wide expanse of field and sky that rolls out in the distance toward Keats's Hampstead.

The energy of this city is obviously embodied in the countless people who are living within these silent houses, but this heart that is still—not yet pumping with the full measure of its daytime vigor—represents at once the literal beating hearts of all those sleeping people and also the "heart" of London itself, the combined energies of the life force: fields full of plants and animals, the wide river swarming with fish, the sun's energy expressed in all of that bright "glittering," this clear combination of human and natural energies. The sun's energy, expressed as light, is what literally creates "splendor"—the word means "brightness" or visual "brilliance"—and so the "Dear God!" invoked at the end of the poem *is* the pagan version of God that so worried Coleridge in Wordsworth's "The world is too much with us" ("Great God! I'd rather be / A pagan suckled in a creed outworn" [9–10]). "It's God; I see God" any pagan-pantheist might say when a "divine" (natural) force is revealed in forest, sea, or sky. For Wordsworth, in "Composed Upon Westminster Bridge," such a naturalized, non-Judeo-Christian, deity is revealed within the urbanatural scene itself. A purely *material* god is made manifest in the unification of human and nonhuman, the domes and fields, the temples and sky. The sight and the feeling are both part of a revelation of something new ("Ne'er saw I, never felt,"), but the divinity revealed here is no supernatural force beyond the material world of our knowing; rather, this is a god in and of this world—the same world, as this poet said elsewhere, in which humans find their happiness, or not at all.

THE HISTORY OF NATURAL HISTORY

In the twenty-first century, it is hard to appreciate the power of the intellectual bomb that Charles Darwin dropped on the world when he first proposed the concept of mutable species in *On the Origin of Species*. So great was Darwin's own anxiety about the revolutionary power of his idea that he wrote to J. D. Hooker in January 1844, claiming that he felt like a violent criminal: "I am almost convinced (quite contrary to opinion [*sic*] I started with) that species are not (it is like confessing a murder) immutable" (*Letters* 81). But the bomb that Darwin detonated was actually a long time coming. Many naturalists before Darwin had anticipated the idea of mutable species. In fact, the idea stretches all the way back to the pre-Socratic Greeks. In addition, many books of "natural philosophy"—the early word for "science"—going back to the herbals and bestiaries of the Middle Ages, argued for an organic and dynamic view of life that described species as much more closely related to one another than traditional scientific or religious views had allowed. Such writings reveal how late eighteenth-century and early nineteenth-century science connects to a much wider Romantic sensibility. Romantic natural history comes, by 1796, to link all of "animated nature" with what the poet Samuel Taylor Coleridge called "the one Life, within us and abroad" ("The Eolian Harp" 26). This idea of an organic unity linking all living things directly challenged a dominant view of nature that went all the way back to Genesis.

The Genesis picture saw species as separate creations. It described all life as irrevocably arranged along a strictly hierarchical Great Chain of Being. Here is one version of that so-called chain:

GOD
ANGELS
BLESSED SPIRITS
GHOSTS
HUMAN BEINGS
MAMMALS
BIRDS
REPTILES
AMPHIBIANS
FISH
INSECTS
PLANTS
MICROSCOPIC CREATURES
INANIMATE OBJECTS

What were the implications of this hierarchy? According to any literal reading of Genesis, God had to make dinosaurs and trilobites; otherwise, where could they have originated? On this same view, God also had to make the AIDS virus and cancer cells, or where could they have come from: not from nothing? When Issac Newton said that matter could not be created or destroyed, a major problem appeared. If matter has always existed, there is no need for a beginning. Likewise, if the Great Chain of Being is unbreakable, then where do the Venus flytrap and the sundew plant fit, lowly botanic forms that catch and eat insects, creatures that are apparently higher on the chain than they belong? If a plant can capture and consume "higher" creatures, then the chain is less stable than it had seemed. Once plants like the Venus flytrap and the sundew arrived in Europe from the swamps of the American South, two lowly organisms stepped out of the Great Chain of Being and into a world of more confused being, no longer a chain, but now a web of complex organic interrelatedness or—as Charles Darwin would soon announce—a tree of life whose branches would eventually reveal the connectedness, and also the precise relations, between and among all living things.

This new idea of nature, which broke the Great Chain of Being, derived from Copernicus, Galileo, and Newton by way of Rousseau, Goethe, and Coleridge, among many others. Romantic nature replaced separate creation—six days, every species utterly separable and distinct—with a dynamic and organic model, a much less stratified and indivisible version of the order of the nonhuman world. Between 1750 and 1859, a new narrative came to challenge the earlier story of divine order. Romantic natural history—not only in scientific works but also in poetry, prose, personal narratives, and the visual arts—emphasized not *separate* but rather *connected* creation, a unified tree or web of life and living things. This Romantic view saw humans, animals, plants, single cells, and all other living organisms linked together in ways that would have been unimaginable to many earlier thinkers, that remain unimaginable to fundamentalist creationists in the twenty-first century. Humans were themselves gradually incorporated into the emerging narrative of dynamic change. The Great Chain of the Genesis account was not a rigid chain but was actually more like Darwin's "tangled bank," a jumble of complex living things, all connected in complex—or perhaps ultimately simple—ways:

> It is interesting to contemplate an entangled bank, clothed with many plants of many kinds, with birds singing on the bushes, with various insects flitting about, and with worms crawling through the damp earth, and to reflect that these elaborately constructed forms, so different from each other, and dependent upon each other in so complex a manner, have all been produced by laws acting around us. These laws, taken in the largest sense, being Growth with Reproduction; Inheritance which is almost implied by reproduction; Variability from the indirect and direct action of the conditions of life, and from use and disuse; a Ratio of Increase so high as to lead to a Struggle for Life, and as a consequence to Natural Selection, entailing Divergence of Character and the Extinction of less-improved forms. Thus, from the war of nature, from famine and death, the most exalted object which we are capable of conceiving, namely, the production of the higher animals, directly follows. There is grandeur in this view of life, with its several powers, having been originally breathed into a few forms or into one; and that, whilst this planet has gone cycling on according to the fixed law of gravity, from so simple a beginning endless forms most beautiful and most wonderful have been, and are being, evolved. (*Darwin* 174)

Every human is an animal. Every animal, and every plant, is related to every human.

This new natural history led straight down the path to the present day. Even though the radical split between C. P. Snow's "two cultures"—of science and art—has been a twentieth-century phenomenon, what I call Romantic natural history is an essential precursor to current ideas about "ecology" defined as "the branch of biology that deals with the relationships between living organisms and their environment," deriving etymologically from the study of the "house, dwelling": *oikos* [*OED*]. Ecology, in this sense, might be described as Romantic natural history infused with, and altered by, the scientific discoveries of the past century-and-a-half. Beyond Romantic natural history, however, lie a cluster of closely related concepts: not just ecology but also ecocentrism, not only anthropomorphism but also ecomorphism, so-called second nature (nature altered by humans) and also the idea of urbanature: *urbs* ("city" or "metropolis") and *natura* ("nature" or "essence") combined.

So what does all of this have to do with roosting, with my urbanatural year on the Blue Ridge? By roosting, I hope to link the rhythms of the nonhuman seasons to those writers and thinkers who have helped to alter one view of nature over the past two centuries. These poets and scientists have turned environmentalists away from one view, in which humans dominated the planet, toward a new view of a sustained, and sustainable, ecology. I will not remain on the Blue Ridge every day during the coming year, because I want some of my observations to come directly from the urban side of urbanature. I will report from Manhattan and Rome, from Philadelphia and Florence. I want my links to the city to remain alive and well. I want to embrace the seamless continuum that stretches from a single microbe on the tip of my finger to the entire contents of the Museum of Natural History in New York, from the smallest salamander and screech owl to the tallest steamship and skyscraper. When modern urban nature lovers try to escape the "confines" of the city for the wide-open spaces of the "natural world," they are chasing a chimera. I hope to reveal that chimera for what it is, an illusion created by a misreading of certain elements of nineteenth-century—Romantic—thinking about nature, the self, and especially urban society.

Yellowstone National Park, to choose just one American example, is a naturalistic theme park that relocated thousands of indigenous people (members of the Shoshone, Blackfoot, Bannock, and Crow tribes) to start using this land as a self-described "wilderness" for the benefit of mostly upper-middle-class, mostly white, nature lovers. At the same time, the US government approved the slaughter of tens of thousands of wild animals (elk, antelope, moose, and bighorn sheep) in order to feed government workers so that this "wilderness" park could be created (Neuzil and Kovarik). Likewise, the "Grand Teton National Park" (appropriately described by the Park Service in one phrase along with the "John D. Rockefeller, Jr. Memorial Parkway"),

Yosemite ("one of the first wilderness parks in the United States"), and many other wild, Western places, were all fashioned by land-use planners out of whole cloth, carefully crafted by well-meaning federal employees to satisfy the wilderness needs of the times, not primarily to reflect the "natural history," or the human history, of any of these spaces. A 2005 US Park Service map indicates twenty-six separate tribes—"tribe" is a European word, not theirs—all currently identified with land set aside for "reservations." These indigenous groups of people are historically or culturally "associated" (i.e., the Park Service's polite term) with the land now called "Yellowstone." Wilderness, indeed. To move toward such current realities, however, it is necessary to go back. To get a clear understanding of urbanature, I need to move from Romantic natural history to Romantic ecocriticism and beyond.

*   *   *

The precise moment of this year's spring came at 7:33 a.m. today, not long after sunrise, to the small stone cabin where I was slowly waking up on top of the Blue Ridge. The sun rose halfway along its daily march from a northern spot on the ridgeline of the winter solstice to a southern spot further down the same ridge, where the same sun will rise again on the morning of this year's summer solstice and again at this morning's same vernal spot next spring. I will be here then as well. At almost the same moment that the sun rose this morning, a line of low barometric pressure pushed across the wide valley, moving rapidly toward the Potomac River, the coastal plain, and finally out to the wide Chesapeake Bay beyond. A brief rain shower fell softly and stopped. The sky cleared and became a patchy world-roof of pale whites and blues. The only sound that announced the coming of spring was a single mourning dove *coo-cooing* and *cack-cackling* over the boulder-line below the screen porch on which I was still waking up. This green spring dawn is the morning that I should call the real New Year's Day.

2

APRIL

Realize thy Simple Self; Embrace thy Original Nature.

—*Tao Te Ching, 19*

So I convince myself—might it actually be true?—that I can hear the sap rising when I stand close to the towering oak tree by the front door of the cabin. I press my ear to the rough bark to be sure. Do I hear it, or is that just the blood pumping in my ears? The green treetops all around me are literally exploding along the hillsides now, across the river bottom and up the edges of the valley, reaching all the way to the mountain ridge-tops beyond. The trees on the crest of the Roost's low mountain—from 1,000 to 1,200 feet in altitude—are still caught in the cold of winter, but one five-pointed flower (a blue periwinkle, my field guide says) has unfolded its petals on the forest floor. A large mat of thick moss shoots spiky pistil-stalks above soft and spongy moss-tops. The light carpet of gentle greens—this moss-bed, a few lichens, and the earliest of the spring grasses—spreads out across the ground into the distance, like a rolling carpet of motley.

Butter-yellow forsythias burst their bud-tops all around me. Another periwinkle pushes its pointy leaves upward. The leaves unwrap and unfold, each plant revealing a startling purple-blue flower within. Drab—almost gray—ivy grows greener along the walls of the cabin and around the rocks that form the Roost's pathways and rustic yard. Near the ridge line behind the cabin, a huge pileated woodpecker works hard against the bark of a spreading oak tree. The huge bird *ham-hammers* until he can latch his massive beak under a slab of lichen-covered bark. Then he pops the rough slab off the tree, sending it crashing to the forest floor. When this hardworking

woodpecker finds a wriggling, fat white grub in the oak tree, he bur-
ies his thick beak deep into the softer inner wood and pops the moist
blob of squirming insect life into his mouth. Then he shakes his wide
woodpecker-head rapidly up and down—up and down again—as he
swallows.

Unfolding red maple blossoms unfurl to become more blossoms
and shimmering leaves. Each quaking-aspen bud opens as a cluster
of heart-shaped green leaves, quivering and quavering in the sun.
White dogwood blossoms unfold to spread out as glorious leaf-flow-
ers (dogwood flowers are actually modified leaves). Countless shades
of green—the green of untold flowers and twigs and shoots and
leaves—will soon fill the whole forest: first slowly (day-by-day) and
then faster (days turning into weeks), but always silently and steadily,
always without the aid of any human being. The plant world performs
its magic so slowly and soundlessly that human beings barely notice,
unless they take the time to watch carefully. Watch these buds and
shoots every day, and the scene changes: imperceptibly at first, then
noticeably, and finally with the evidence of a total transformation. Sit
very still, observe one flower or vine-tip long enough, and it is possible to literally watch it unfold. I can almost sense these individual
cells swelling and dividing.

For the first time in the early months of my "natural" year, the
bug world is also waking up in earnest. A few gnats skitter across
my face and hit my hands in the sunlit clearing. A thin, silvery moth
crawls up the rock wall of the cabin. A larger moth flutters near the
porch lamp, where he had alighted and rested last night. More wasps
are waking up as well, still stumbling along the window ledges and
eaves. Some of them crawl slowly and then halt, as though they are
still too cold to move or have forgotten how to fly. One white-faced
hornet buzzes by the side of the house, rising and falling, testing his
thin, still-warming wings. A small white butterfly dances among dead
brown leaves and pale green shoots on the hillside behind me, darting
from forsythia blossom to forsythia blossom, taking advantage of the
first bright gush of nectar before the full flowering of spring. Soon,
bigger butterflies will emerge to challenge this small white-sulfur for
supremacy on the hillside.

As I cock my head to one side, I can suddenly hear the spring
migration of countless April birds. Flapping and gliding masses come
through trees and shrubs, along rocky ledges all around me, sometimes like a distant breeze, sometimes like a full-blown flutter of
feathery leaves on the wing. First come small clouds of multicolored,
skittery warblers, then a tight bundle of rusty, thudding robins. All at

once, there are literally dozens of songs and calls echoing in the curve of the hillside, filling the air around me with the only sounds amid an otherwise silent world around me. There is nothing remarkable here beyond these diurnal and seasonal matters of fact, just the ordinary miracle of morning.

A white-throated sparrow calls from far off in the distance. The dozen notes of his special song are as sweet as the clang of the most delicate wind chime: plaintive and clear, high pitched with an unmistakable meter, like a well-known and often-remembered poem: *I-I Pea-bod-y, Pea-bod-y, Pea-bod-y, I.* To the north, in this hemisphere, the ornithologists say *O-O Can-a-da, Can-a-da, Can-a-da-a.* Always and everywhere the conspicuous towhee can also be heard: a slurry, slurping *che-wink, che-wink,* followed by an unmistakable, clattery *drink-your-tea, drink-your-tea-he-he.* Suddenly, a melodious wood thrush breaks through—the nightingale of the eastern American forests—louder than all the rest, sweet and liquid: singing *here-I-am, here-I-am.* This song is as sweet and melodious as any sound offered in any forest in the world. Meanwhile, the cardinals have stayed around all winter. They have no need to migrate. They manage to find resilient winter seeds, or small shrubs and tree buds, right through all of the short, cold days of winter. The swirling birds around me are now so thick in the low bushes and trees that their wing-beats sound like wind. In fact, their wings are among the loudest sound I hear in the greening woods of morning. All afternoon I find fallen feathers scattered in the forest around me.

POETRY AND SCIENCE

When Mary Shelley sought to explain Victor Frankenstein's reason for creating his monster, she wrote that a "new species" would bless its human creator for existence. What did Mary think the word "species" meant in 1816? By this time, throughout Europe and North America, poets and natural historians were hinting at the biological connectedness of all living things, even without the precise scientific details that would allow them to explain such links. When Coleridge refers to "the one Life, within us and abroad, / Which meets all Motion, and becomes its soul, / A Light in Sound, a sound-like power in Light" ("The Eolian Harp" 26–28), he is imagining a naturalized version of a divine force, but he is clearly not describing any version of the Judeo-Christian God. Erasmus Darwin might have called Coleridge's "one Life" a "vegetative" energy, an *élan vital*, which pervades all living things ("all objects of all thought, / And rolls through all things" as Wordsworth would add in "Tintern Abbey" [1798, 102–3]). In "The Eolian Harp," Coleridge describes "all of animated nature" as "organic Harps diversely fram'd" and refers to the animating principle as "Plastic and vast" (36, 37, 39). The phrase "animated nature" was widely used by natural historians to distinguish those aspects of creation that were responsible for their own motion (*anima* deriving from the word that means "breath" or "wind") from inanimate objects, those without *anima* (*spirit*-less equals *breath*-less). To lack a spirit meant to lack a breath. There was nothing magical here, nothing immaterial. The phrase "animated nature" also hinted at a vital principle that distinguished living from nonliving things.

These authors, poets, and early scientists, consistently claim that human beings are contiguous with the natural world rather than distinct from it. They collapse the distinction between nature and culture at the same time that they point out similarities between and among all living things. Even a brief survey of well-known Romantic writings reveals how frequently the claims of early-modern science were connected to ideas and images drawn from these poets. When, for example, Percy Shelley says, in 1816, that "Nought may endure but Mutability" ("Mutability" 16), he is arguing, much as a scientist might, that change is the only constant in the physical universe. Shelley's statement concludes another poem about the Eolian harp or lyre—a wind-vibrated musical instrument—that gives "various response to each varying blast" of the breeze (6). Such a claim is a poetic restatement of a scientific principle that stretches from the flux of Heraclitus to Heisenberg's Uncertainty Principle. In the material world, change is the only thing that remains ever the same: change of seasons, change of form, change of characteristics, and change of state: $E=mC^2$ was Einstein's version of this same truth.

Shelley, for example, believes in a unifying principle that can link the force (energy) of the wind to the materiality (matter) of the objects that the wind affects. In his poem "The Cloud," he describes how each sky-born cloud is an example of natural renewal, an image that affirms the permanence of transience. In the process, the poet—for the first time in any work of literature—offers the precise details of what scientists call the hydrologic cycle, in verse. "The Cloud" accurately describes how each sky-borne collection of H_2O molecule takes shape out of vapor drawn from the ocean waters (by the heat of the sun) and then replenishes those same waters when it falls back to the earth and sea: "I pass through the pores, of the ocean and shores; / I change, but I cannot die" (75–76). With each of these cycles of watery renewal, the cloud notes its ability to laugh at its own "cenotaph" (81), its own tomb. Shelley takes his readers beyond any personal or egocentric longing for eternal life; instead, he grants "immortality" of cyclical, natural process. This is nature's only promise of eternal life, but for Shelley it is a sufficient one:

> All things that we love and cherish,
> Like ourselves must fade and perish;
> Such is our rude mortal lot—
> Love itself would, did they not. ("Death" 1–4)

Likewise, in each hydrological cycle, the cloud repeats a process of making and unmaking that represents, not only a version of immortality, but also the world's only form of permanence: "Like a child from the womb, like a ghost from the tomb, / I arise and unbuild it again" (83–84).

Shelley's cloud image, and its cycle of building and rebuilding, can be linked directly to current science's idea of the hereditary germplasm, that aspect of genetic material that survives the death of each individual and continues from life to life. Like the water in any cloud, each creature's genetic imprint—its DNA—is a direct copy of the hereditary cells of its parents and of countless individuals stretching back through time. Most of my own direct ancestors are centuries and millennia dead, but their DNA, their hereditary imprint, survives in me: in my eye color, my baldness, my height, even in the details of my personality. In this sense, I contain material strains (or replicated versions) of the actual germplasm that was contained in the bodies of my predecessors. Everything in me—except for mutations that I may have added—I owe to them. This germplasm stretches far back beyond humans and hominids to every creature, of every kind, that gave rise to the species I became, and even to me. The biological permanence I possess *is* the coiled DNA (arising from my parents into me and from me into my offspring) that I have already passed on to my children at the moment of their conception and—potentially—to their children and their children's children as well. Shelley, confronted with the precise details of twenty-first century genetics would probably ask, "What more immortality might I need than this?" His answer, in "The Cloud" and elsewhere in his work, is resounding and persuasive: "none."

Shelley's "Sensitive Plant" presents another example of the science of natural history invoked for poetic purposes. The sensitive plant (*Mimosa pudica*), as Erasmus Darwin had noted in his *Botanic Garden* (1791), posed a continuing scientific mystery because its visible movements seemed so much like those of an animal. Sensitive plants possessed rudimentary forms of sensation; they responded to touch and folded up their leaves (some observers said they "slept") at night. The earlier Darwin had said, "Naturalists have not explained the immediate cause of the collapsing of the sensitive plant; the leaves meet and close in the night during the sleep of the plant [...] in the same manner as when they are affected by external violence" (*Botanic* 2: 40). A plant that can be said to "sleep," even metaphorically, easily provides Shelley with a botanical example of more widely organic, and even human, characteristics. Earl Wasserman points out that "the sensitive plant was one of the most frequent examples of those ambiguous border-forms sharing both vegetable and animal characteristics" (157). Such forms broke down the integrity of the "Great Chain of Being" by suggesting that "fitness" was a matter of practical success, not of objective or ideological standards. Venus fly-traps—brought to Europe first from the swamps of the southeastern United States—could capture, kill, and digest whole insects. Erasmus Darwin's "Loves of the Plants" linked the sex lives of flowers directly to the sex lives of humans. Some plants are polygamous, while others are adulterous. Some flowers are seductive, and others are chaste. Such links between organic forms reach all the way to humans.

Shelley's "Power"—like Coleridge's "a sound-like power in Light" and Wordsworth's "motion and a spirit, that impels / All thinking things, all objects of all thought, / And rolls through all things" ("Tintern Abbey" 101–3)—is in front of me all the time: in rocks, in trees, in everything I see. This is why Romantic writers were so often described as pantheistic; they located their versions of divinity in the world of nonhuman nature, or they imagined capital-"N"-Nature possessing all of the "spirituality" that any human might need. Shelley is, however, not like the twenty-first-century nature lover who says that she gets in touch with her spiritual side during long walks in the springtime woods. Shelley clearly distinguishes "Power" from the effects of power in such a way that the two can never be confused with one another. For him, it is only the effects of "power" that are ever fully evident in the human realm: "Power *in likeness* of the Arve comes down" ("Mont Blanc" 16; italics added). Such Romantic natural power is sometimes seen as synonymous with the life force, the *élan vital*, what Dylan Thomas later calls "The Force that Through the Green Fuse Drives the Flower" (a Romantically ecocritical poem if there ever was one). Authors and readers claim to—or get to—experience this Romantic "spiritual" power through the five senses, but Romantic authors and Romantic readers both claim to be receptive to the presence of this power—some more than others—even if that possibility requires a "sixth" sense. This is the same force, of course, that can be sensed by each Romantic's *sensorium* (the sum of all five physical senses) through the vehicle of clouds, mimosa plants, skylarks, and nightingales.

Other borders—between the living and the nonliving, the organic and the inorganic, plants and animals—are comparable to the barrier that separates Shelley's unseen "Power" from its visible effects in nature. The *Cyclopedia* compiled by Ephraim Chambers in 1728 described the sensitive plant as "an herb sufficiently known to the world for its remarkable property of receding from the touch, and giving signs, as it were, of animal life"; similarly, the natural historian Soames Jenyns compared the sensitive plant to a "shell-fish," noting that the "lowest" animal and the "highest" plant are both distinguished by sensitivity— this bivalve opens "to receive the water which surrounds it," just as the sensitive mimosa is observed "shrinking from the finger" that touches it (Wasserman 157n). All sensitive plants embody a general anxiety about hybrids (half-and-half organisms) that plagued early naturalists. If everything had been separately created and then uniquely placed in its proper spot along the Great Chain of Being—by divine fiat—how might an organism look like a plant but behave like an animal? In the process of exploring such curious cases, early naturalists found apparent species boundaries to be much less absolute than had been previously imagined. A plant (the mimosa) might move like an animal. An animal (the sea anemone) could behave much like a plant. Which was which, who was what? It would take Charles Darwin, and then Gregor Mendel, to resolve this particular border dispute.

Shelley's "Ode to the West Wind" includes another of the most powerful Romantic depictions of sympathetic interactions across an apparent natural boundary. In one of his typical border-crossing images, Shelley claims that the wind that influences plants on the land can have a comparable effect on plants in the sea. Shelley imagines undersea plants responding to the terrestrial change of seasons brought about by the West Wind:

> The sea-blooms and the oozy woods which wear
> The sapless foliage of the ocean, know
> Thy [the wind's] voice, and suddenly grow grey with fear,
> And tremble and despoil themselves: O hear! (*Shelley* 3.39–42)

Shelley's science is not accurate here, but his impulse is proto-ecological, as he indicates in his own footnote: "The phenomenon alluded to [...] is well known to naturalists. The vegetation at the bottom of the sea, of rivers, and of lakes, sympathises with that of the land in the change of seasons, and is consequently influenced by the winds which announce it" (*R NH* 311). Plants in the sea enter into a natural cycle that includes plants on land. In addition, terrestrial plants have literal sympathy for aquatic ones. What happens on land influences what happens beneath the waves. Scientists have now proven how right Shelley was, even though he may have been wrong in his specifics; what happens on land has a direct impact on what happens under the sea: natural climate and human pollution both produce versions of Shelley's sympathetic interactions between various parts of the ecosystem. Even the modern term "ecosystem" suggests just the sorts of connectedness that Shelley and other Romantic writers intuited, and sought to describe, in the nonhuman world.

Ideas about the relationship between the natural world and human culture have been part of English literary criticism since its beginnings in the eighteenth century. Coleridge, another of those Romantic poets and critics who consistently and carefully scrutinizes literary representations of the natural world, praises Prince Hamlet's focus on the smallest physical detail in his naturalistic surroundings, noting that "attention to minute sounds,—naturally associated with the recollection of minute objects [...] gives a philosophic pertinency [...] and [...] really is, the language of nature" (*Shakespeare* 347–48). In a related way, Shelley's prose essay "On Love" notes that

> Hence in solitude, or in that deserted state when we are surrounded by human beings, and yet they sympathise not with us, we love the flowers, the grass and the waters and the sky. In the motion of the very leaves of spring in the blue air there is then found a secret correspondence with our heart. There is eloquence in the tongueless wind and a melody in the flowing of brooks and the rustling of the reeds beside them which by their inconceivable relation to something within the soul awaken the spirits to a dance of breathless rapture, and bring tears of mysterious tenderness to the eyes like the enthusiasm of patriotic success or the voice of one beloved singing to you alone. Sterne says that if he were in a desert [*sic*] he would love some cypress. (*Poetry and Prose* 504)

Ever since this Romantic idea of a direct (if "secret") organic correspondence between human emotions and the objects of the natural world, imaginative writers in English have sought to explore and explain the connection between humans and nature for literary effect. Some of the greatest passages in English poetry and imaginative prose—since 1820—have emerged out of this belief in Shelley's "secret correspondence" between the brooks, the weeds, the wind, and the human "heart."

My point is not that Shelley anticipates the precise details of subsequent thinking—much of his science is simply wrong—but only that his awareness of natural history allows him to imagine nature as an interdependent realm (depending on the relationship between and among it parts) while also seeing wild nature and human culture as interdependent systems, eventually leading to the idea of urbanature. Of course, this notion of an interdependence between human mental activity and organic nature also drives the imaginative impulse in poems like Shelley's "Ode to the West Wind," Keats's "Ode to a Nightingale," and Coleridge's "Frost at Midnight." In each of these poems, the human speaker longs to possess, or link to, a nonhuman energy that he identifies with the wind, the bird, or the frost. The force that causes the wind to blow, in Shelley's poem, is credited with planting "winged seeds" in the ground, bringing them to life in the spring, driving "loose clouds" across the sky, dropping "rain and lightning," even causing waves to roll the entire length of the ocean along the "Atlantic's level powers." One unified power causes all of these natural effects, but this power is nothing more than a series of physical processes contained in nature, what John Locke and others had called "natural law." Shelley, as the speaker of his poem, addresses the wind self-consciously and says, in effect, "I feel a sense of connection to the power within these natural processes linked to the West Wind. Now let me be even more fully identified with that power" ("Oh! lift me as a wave, a leaf, a cloud!" 53). Let me feel its force directly and grow more forceful in the process, "Be thou, spirit fierce, / My spirit! Be thou me, impetuous one!" (61–62). In all such Romantic poems, the speaker longs to identify with, or to be identified with, a nonhuman object or force that possesses a power the poet lacks: be it wind, bird, or frost. Numerous other Romantic poems rely on similar versions of natural forces: waterfalls, sunsets, and skylarks, even glow-worms.

Biology, the science that would eventually explain the physical facts behind such Romantic "nature" poems, came into being early in the nineteenth century—the term originated around 1800 (*OED*)—and helped to show how the 1859 world of Darwin's *On the Origin of Species* differed so greatly from the 1735 world of Linnaeus's *Systema Natura*. Biology did not determine destiny in the nineteenth century—as it seems to do so often in our own cultural moment—but Romantic natural history helps us see how the "Nature" of Issac

Newton and Linnaeus becomes, via Wordsworth and Shelley, the "nature" of Stephen Hawking and Stephen Jay Gould. If species are mutable, as Darwin and Mendel prove them to be, then all species are connected in ways that no static view of creation could allow. As we now know, through DNA testing, every species is genetically linked to every other species, alive or dead, extant or extinct. In addition, the barrier that once appeared to separate species from one another has now been replaced by a dynamic system that produces new species out of older ones, evolution via natural selection. The mimosa is related to all of the motile animals it mimics. The biochemical processes that cause its leaves to open and close are directly related to the nervous impulses of the animals it seems to imitate. The nightingale (we now know) does sing for a biological reason, and that reason is related to the very issues that are lurking in Keats's human mind: the search for a mate, the need to declare the range over which he has control, and the necessity to reproduce before "a few, sad, last gray hairs" (25) disappear. Hairs for the human, like feathers for the bird, announce the end of those shared expectations of lifespan and species reproduction.

One implication of genetic inheritance is that there is, in one sense, no such thing as a species at all; or rather, many species are regularly transforming themselves into new forms, new species and subspecies, new aspects of biological creation. If every species emerged out of earlier species, then it is precisely the liminal border states—subspecies, varieties, subpopulations, transitional forms—that reveal points of contact between one species and another: domestic dog and wild wolf, coyote and coy-dog cross, competitive chimpanzee and cooperative bonobo, primitive Neanderthal and sophisticated Cro-Magnon. Mary Shelley did not know precisely what a "species" was when she published the term in the first edition of *Frankenstein* in 1818, but neither did the Comte de Buffon, Erasmus Darwin, or Charles Darwin. The word "species" is a generalized word we use to describe populations that share genetic material and are unable to breed with other species. But the crossing of the complex borders between species and among species is precisely the point at which new species emerge. Romantic anxiety about species was not merely the result of uncertainty about the origins of organic nature. Such anxiety was part of a much wider cultural movement away from an atomized view of discrete natural types toward the current model of nature as an organic whole, what scientists now call an ecological system.

Romantic writers were not always good scientists, nor did all of their literary images derive from accurate scientific information. But sensitive plants, western winds, and the idea of new species chart a pervasive paradigm shift, away from a "Nature" that was static and unchanging toward a "nature" characterized by dynamic links among all living things. Such a view is much closer to the contemporary claim that nature is not here for human beings, but that human beings are—in one sense at least—here for nature, as part of its continuing processes. It now does make sense for me to say that I am here *for* nature; I am part of the vast web of genetic links and animate inter-relatedness that Shelley, Keats, and Coleridge (among others) clearly intuited in their writings. Twenty-first-century cultural emphasis on ecology links directly to many of these earlier Romantic thinkers. In the century before Charles Darwin, scientists and writers saw human beings as organisms with important connections to their surround-ings. These same connections, as science has come to understand, have profound implications for life on the planet that human beings share with the rest of the living world.

Nature as Culture, Culture as Society

At this point I need to offer a version of nature that can help us break down the conceptual separation between two worlds: nature and culture, the natural and the civilized, the natural and the human. I am not the first to make such an effort. Wendell Berry, in his essay "Preserving Wildness" (1985) says, "The argument over the proper relation of humanity to nature is becoming, as the sixties used to say, polarized....At one extreme are those who sound as if they are entirely in favor of nature...At the other extreme are the nature con-querors, who have no patience with an old-fashioned outdoor farm, let alone a wilderness" (137). A decade later, William Cronon made the crucial observation that "wilderness is not quite what it seems. Far from being the one place on earth that stands apart from humanity, it is quite profoundly a human creation" (69). By this time, Cronon was one of a number of historians, environmentalists, and land-use planners who agreed that the idea of "wilderness is itself no small part of the problem" (70) in humanity's relationship to the nonhu-man world. More recently, Timothy Morton has said that, for Shelley, "nature and culture were coterminous," since Shelley argued that "Man in his wildest state is a social being" (*Companion* 185). Morton then develops this idea of Shelley's as a central aspect of his own argu-ment in *Ecology Without Nature*; for Morton, the cultural creation called "wilderness" expresses "fingers wagging, strongly or weakly, at modern society. To the extent that wilderness spaces and the laws that created them persist, we are still living, literally, within the Romantic period" (*Without Nature* 114). The modern idea of "wilderness" was largely a Romantic invention, no longer just the ancient idea of a terrifying place where the wild things are, but now a place where the urban is absent, a combination of ancient pastoral and Renaissance rural. Contemporary humans are still caught in the grip of this idea, insofar as they cannot see that the wild and the tame, the natural and the urban, are often overlapping and always closely linked.

Scott Hess has helped to bridge this gap by calling for a new emphasis on "everyday nature," a concept that exists in opposition to a "nature" that has "been defined by the mainstream environmental movement and a variety of post-Romantic aesthetic traditions as existing apart from the social and economic structures of everyday life" (91). Hess's "everyday nature" has important parallels to my "urbanature." It exists in cities, in towns, in parks, and in cars, anywhere that humans acknowledge their connection to the nonhuman world. Of course, the idea of sustainability also indicates this necessary link between organisms—human organisms included—and their environments, as "everyday nature" suggests. So "urbanature" and "roosting" provide ideas that clarify the current idea of sustainability. In addition, the idea of urbanatural roosting may help backpacking environmentalists find common ground with condominium-dwelling urbanites, and vice versa.

"Urbanature" takes in, not just Thoreau's "Wildness [that] is the preservation of the world," but also the self-consciousness that is, according to Annie Dillard, "the curse of the city and all that sophistication implies" (81). The wild is traditionally identified with innocence, the civilized with experience. Urbanature, as I invoke the term, comes close to Blake's idea of "organized innocence"; that is, a natural, childlike, "wild" innocence *after* experience has had its way with my "natural" self. Urbanature can return me to a state of innocence, even after experience has altered the person that I was before my own fall into self-consciousness. Dillard says that self-consciousness is the novelist's world, unselfconsciousness the poet's. Nature is raw, while the urban is cooked. For my argument, it is all nature, wherever it is located, whatever its surroundings: the Sierra Nevadas, the silicon chip, the Humboldt squid in the ocean depths, my trash can full of organic and inorganic garbage. That much is easy. What is harder is to talk about this sense of nonhuman nature as continuous with human nature. To that end, each of my monthly chapters will work toward a new way of thinking: *ecocentrically*. Instead of describing the nonhuman world anthropocentrically—in human terms—there are now good reasons to describe the nonhuman world as the human home [eco-: *oikos*, house]. My material, animal, wild, and nonhuman house (once called "nature") is the same place as my emotion-rich, socialized, familial, and fully human home. Ecology—the study of this natural house that is also my social home—is the science that allows each of us to appreciate the richness of our widest (not just "wildest") surroundings. In fact, I need a number of new words—and new meanings for older words—to help move toward this view: not only "roosting," but also "ecocentric" and "ecomorphic," as well as "ecotecture" (see *New York Times Magazine*, May 20, 2007), "ec(o) home," "ambience," "wilding," and—of course—"urbanature."

The earliest nature writing in America emphasized the openness and limitlessness, the sublime emptiness, of a vast continent. But even the social act of publication—a publisher, an editor, type, press, paper, ink, binding, marketing, and distribution—gave the lie to the idea that this new nation was somehow more natural than it was urban. No writing in Europe had quite the American outlook or context, however, since Europe—like much of Africa and Asia—had been occupied by advanced human civilizations for thousands of years when authors began writing about the nonhuman, natural world as a subject in its own right. When Gilbert White, for example, in *The Natural History of Selborne* (1789), first wrote about his home village in the county of Hampshire in England, he was describing a plot of land that had been continuously occupied by human beings since at least the Bronze Age (c. 2,000 BCE). Likewise, the celebrated Chinese nature poet Wang Wei (701–61), although he lived in the eighth century ACE, describes images of natural landscapes that had been inhabited for countless human generations when he began to write.

In America, by contrast, even eighteenth- and early nineteenth-century authors described their surroundings as though these writers were the first humans ever to cast their eyes on these wild landscapes. Such a perspective is offered—or assumed—even when these authors knew perfectly well that American Indians had already lived on these lands for millennia. American nature writers are often masters of the ability to turn their faces away from the facts of human habitation when those facts do not suit the agenda of the author. Morton notes that a "white male nature writer in the wilderness may be 'going native' to some extent, but he is also usefully distancing this wilderness, even from himself, even in his own act of narration" (*Without Nature* 126). Thoreau was no rustic living in wild nature. He was a Harvard-educated scholar living a short walk from the town center

of Concord, Massachusetts. America is typically presented by early
nature writers as a virginal, pure and untouched, wilderness. It would
have been a different story if indigenous Indians had established a literary culture during their millennium in North America before white
Western Europeans first landed on their shores (492–1492 ACE).

Even more significant than the question of how long humans
have occupied a particular piece of land, a fundamental philosophical difference also separates the literary impulse toward nature and
nature writing, as in the example of American and Asian—specifically
Chinese—contexts. As James J. Y. Liu notes, in his landmark study
The Art of Chinese Poetry:

> Nature to these Chinese poets is not a physical manifestation of its
> Creator, as it is to Wordsworth, but something that is what it is by vir-
> tue of itself. The Chinese term for "Nature" is *tzu-jan*, or "Self-thus,"
> and the Chinese mind seems content to accept Nature as a fact, with-
> out searching for a *primum mobile* [first-cause or first-mover]. This
> concept of Nature somewhat resembles Thomas Hardy's "Immanent
> Will," but without its rather sombre and gloomy associations. (49)

Here, in the Chinese setting, is a world of nature and nature-plus-
culture that could not be more different than that of Hobbes, or even
Rousseau. From Liu's trenchant observation it flows that Chinese
nature "is neither benignant nor hostile" to mankind; hence, Asian
"man" is not conceived of as "for ever struggling against Nature but
forming part of it. [...] Man is advised to submerge his being in the
infinite flux of things and allow his own life and death to become
part of the eternal cycle of birth, growth, decline, death, and re-birth
that goes on in Nature" (49). This passage by Liu also accurately
describes American—and generally Western—responses to the need
to "struggle against" the natural world, at least up until the nineteenth century. By the 1850s, writers like Emerson and Thoreau—
both of whom were powerfully influenced by their reading of Eastern
texts: the *Bhagavad-Gita*, the *Upanishads*, the *Vedas*—were starting
to argue for "Eastern" beliefs about continuity between human and
nonhuman worlds. By the twentieth century, a great deal of American
nature-writing comes to be pervaded by a philosophical view much
closer to the Eastern one described by Liu, a non-monotheistic perspective that argues for submerging the cultural fiction of the "self"
into the "infinite flux of things." Gary Snyder, to choose one contemporary example, is no less at home amid the nature-plus-culture
of Lao-Tse and Basho than he is among the naturalistic images of
Walt Whitman, Herman Melville, and D. H. Lawrence.

Early American nature writers often assumed, even when they knew it was not true, that the world they were describing had been untouched by human hands. This ability to ignore the indigenous inhabitants of the continent—there were at least several million Indians in North America by the year 1700—was aided by the fact that, as primarily nomadic cultures, American Indians left very few material remains behind. (The Anasazi cliff dwellers of the southwestern deserts—Arizona, New Mexico, Utah, and Colorado—and several mound-building tribes throughout the country are notable exceptions.) What seemed to be the empty palate of American natural riches became a powerful symbol for the new nation and its possibilities. Early descriptions of this vast continental land mass and its features emphasized just these aspects of North America's nonhuman resources. Writers ranging from Christopher Columbus, in the log of his earliest voyage (1492), to Meriwether Lewis and William Clark in the journals of their expeditionary trek across the Louisiana Territory (1803), described the New World as largely empty in terms of human settlements, and undeniably endless in terms of the abundance of its plants, animals, minerals, and landscapes. This "absence" of humans was just another index of the possibilities this "new" nation held for exploitation, colonization (of the few "nonresistant" peoples who were found here), and further exploration of the continent.

Nature writing in the United States, as in Britain and elsewhere, often represents a complex combination of natural and human history. Such complexity is evident in writers during the early years of the colonies and, later, the young republic that was the United States. Hector St. John de Crèvecoeur and Alexis de Tocqueville, both best known for early works on the development of America, link American politics and culture directly to their crucial connections to the natural world. Crèvecoeur titled his major volume *Letters from an American Farmer* (1782), signaling the extent to which an agrarian and agriculturalist vision was at the heart of the American idea of the frontier and the pastoral dream of the new United States. Likewise, in *Democracy in America* (1835–1840), Tocqueville writes, "the Americans themselves [...] are insensible to the wonders of inanimate Nature, and they may be said not to perceive the mighty forests which surround them till they fall beneath the hatchet. Their eyes are fixed upon another sight: the American people views its own march across these wilds—drying swamps, turning the course of rivers, peopling solitudes, and subduing nature" (559). Tocqueville stresses the point that, from its earliest European settlements, America was characterized by a group of people who set out to enact the biblical injunction to subdue the earth. The Hebrew God—Jaweh—had told Adam and Eve that they (and their descendants) would have "dominion" over the beasts of the fields, the birds of the air, the fish of the sea, and the wild landscapes that contained all of these creatures. Humanity's role, according to this Judeo-Christian injunction, was to subdue and control nature, not to preserve or sustain it. This view, of course, had powerful consequences for interactions between Americans and the lands that would become the United States, as well as interactions with the indigenous people. In the first place, as Tocqueville notes, Americans do not know what they have until it is gone; they only lamented the loss of wild lands when those lands had already fallen "beneath the hatchet."

So what does this history have to do with the idea of "roosting"? How might I "roost" on the world? To roost is to sit and observe, the way a hawk or a crow sits and observes, in order to figure out what is going on in a particular place, to experience the surroundings more carefully, and to come to know a precise piece of environment more clearly. A bird's roost has a direct impact on the tree in which it exists, on the cliff or other nest-site, and on its wider environment. Roosting, as I invoke the term, involves a wide range of verbs: perching, surveying, resting, feeding, hunting, nesting, and mating, at the very least. It can occur in rural isolation. Such isolation, however, is not the solution for most humans, since living in rural isolation requires airplanes and automobiles to get there, gasoline and gasoline-powered machines (to maintain each personal piece of property), and lots of wire or wireless technology (to keep rural people connected to the wider culture around them). Roosting can occur in small towns (perhaps the ideal urbanatural solution), or in suburban sprawl (clearly the current reality for vast swathes of human culture, with all of its attendant asphalt, colorless chain-stores, plus glaring street lamps and garish signage without end). Of course, roosting can also take place in the world's massive urban spaces, modern civilization's greatest—at least in impact, size, and cultural progress—but also most problematic, contribution to world civilization, planetary culture, and recent ecoculture.

Urban ecology is a reality that has become increasingly necessary as more and more humans occupy less and less land area. Only in recent years have humans become a predominantly urban species. The United Nations recently reported that the "world's mega-cities are merging to form vast 'mega-regions' which may stretch hundreds of kilometres across countries and be home to more than 100 million people" [each]; this same "trend helped the world pass a tipping point in the last year [2009–10], with more than half the world's people now living in cities" (Vidal). But such concentrations of humanity produce more than one option for a shared urbanatural future. Imagine urban, suburban, small town, and rural places in which the water and the air are clean, in which the food is fresh, local, and preservative free, in which the energy is used but also used wisely—reused and not wasted—in which human spaces are built with an eye to nonhuman needs and built to blend the inner world (of human consciousness) with the outer world (of nonhuman nature): minds and weather, emotions and plants, health and animals, vegetables and computers. Imagine human spaces in which plants are pervasive and always generously included: buildings full of trees, and plants, and vines, and useful gardens everywhere. Imagine buildings oriented always toward the sun and the wind and the natural forces that will help to improve human and other organic life within those porous walls. Imagine human culture always benefiting from animal nature, whatever the setting: birds and plant-fertilizing bees, cats and protective dogs, but also raccoons and squirrels, hedgehogs and coyotes, pond fish and frog-legs, all integrated with other species into mutually beneficial spaces and places. Detroit is about to turn "large swaths of this now-blighted, rusted-out city back into the fields and farmlands that existed before the automobile....Roughly a quarter of the 139-square-mile city could go from urban to semirural" (Runk). Detroit is the same postindustrial and urbanatural city that now boasts a three-acre Earth Works Garden, one of hundreds of "community gardens" and "thousands more food gardens that are not part of any network," scenes of an "apple orchard, horses, ducks, long rows of cauliflower and broccoli" in a city center that is "still beautiful, both in its stately decay and in its growing natural abundance" (Solnit 72–73). Urbanature calls for this Detroit option in many postindustrial cities, as well as the wider possibility that architects and ecoplanners of all kinds will develop urbanatural solutions to a whole range of design problems.

What humans need now is a new paradigm, a paradigm that will leave them no longer feeling separate from the world around them. Instead, they will come to see themselves as roosting in a natural world that they helped to make. No longer will human beings coop themselves up in airtight spaces, shut up with oil-heat all winter and air-conditioning all summer. No longer will they move from one climate-controlled enclosure to another. Instead, they will live in environments in which the natural and the urban interpenetrate: sun flooding though vast glass-walls designed to manage solar radiation, roof surfaces designed to collect water and let light in and air out, the barriers that once separated people from their surroundings (windows, walls, doors, and roofs) now conceived as permeable membranes designed to take advantage of sun and wind and weather in ways that will make the indoors seem more like the outdoors and vice versa. Twenty-first-century people need to see themselves both *in* and *of* the integrated world they inhabit. The urban and natural environments need to be seen as continuous, not divided. I cannot get "back to nature"; I am always already there. I cannot escape from nature into culture, since nature follows me wherever I go, and vice versa. I am not living in the country or the city. I am urbanaturally roosting.

*   *   *

I just heard the fluty wood-thrush sing again. I stepped out of the screen door of the Roost to breathe the bright April air, just as freshly as I breathe it inside the cabin (the door onto the screen porch is wide open on the other side of the cabin). I touched a rock on the outside cabin wall and held my hand there for only an instant. Although it is not yet noon, the rock is warm to my touch. I was not exaggerating earlier. I can feel the warm spring rising.

3

MAY

Man alone contains within himself as many species as exist on earth.

—Boehme

May birds are out in their forest-filling droves now: late warblers—Blackburnian, Kentucky, black-throated blue, Parula, black-and-white, myrtle, cerulean—plus vireos, black-capped chickadees, tufted titmice, towhees, flickers, phoebes, blue jays, robins, flycatchers, kingbirds, mockingbirds, mourning doves, and wrens, among many others. Fiddlehead-tops on lavish fern-fronds are unfolding. The tightly curled leaves on every tree branch above the ferns are unrolling. Wild columbines stand straight upright in the woods amid the full flowering of their ornate orchid-style blossoms, red and purple, blue and creamy white. When I turn over each flower's floret, I find insects sucking on every one: little aphids and bigger gnats, countless tiny winged things, all clinging to stamens and pistils, slurping nectar, nibbling pollen, soaking up the sticky sex-stuff of late spring.

By the middle of this bird-drenched morning, I have seen a pileated woodpecker at closer range than ever before in my life. I just paced off the distance to the midsize sapling on which he has been ham-hammering, precisely twenty-four feet from the Roost's front door. This male was as big as this largest of North American woodpeckers ever gets in these woods, a full foot-and-a-half from red-tipped crest to black-tipped tail. He returned twice after my clumsy stalking sent him flapping warily back into the deep woods. He *peck-pecked* the ground, as well as the tree's sides, waddling in an ungainly fashion over small rocks and crunching leaf piles. Then he sat on a thick fallen log, looking from side to side between taps, first at me, then back into the deep woods. When I go and pull several flakes of bark from the tree and stump on which he has been so earnestly engaged, I find several fat, shiny glistening grubs full of spring dampness in the bark of this great tree, still wet, still wriggling.

SPECIES SCIENCE

As she worked on the draft of her remarkable first novel, Mary Shelley penned a famous sentence that offered natural history as the explanation for Victor Frankenstein's desire to create a new *kind* of living being: "A new species would bless me as its creator and source; many happy and excellent natures would owe their being to me" (Robinson 1: 85). The line appears in the 1818 edition of the novel and is unchanged in the revised 1831 version. Charles Robinson's facsimile edition of the manuscript reveals that "species" was Mary Shelley's third word choice after considering "creation" and "existence" (1: 85). A great deal of scholarship has emphasized Mary Shelley's life experiences and state of mind during the famous Frankenstein summer of 1816. Additional criticism of the novel has analyzed specific scientific advances of the era. In Italy, both Luigi Galvani and Alessandro Volta were experimenting with electrical impulses and muscular contractions during the 1790s. Life science was in the air (even without the word "biology"), and the eighteen-year-old Mary Shelley had a shadowy concept of "species" in her mind in 1816, a concept that related clearly to a wider Romantic natural history.

J. S. Barr's English edition of the Comte de Buffon's magisterial *Natural History* echoes the traditional view of species as it was understood in 1792: species are "ancient" and "permanent," "always the same," organized in a divine, and rigid, hierarchy: "Of these units the human species is to be placed in the first rank; all the others, from the elephant to the mite, from the cedar to the hyssop, belong to the second and third orders" (*Barr* 10: 343). Buffon's effort to argue for the fixity of species is complicated by one question that he has particular difficulty in answering: "What purposes then are served by this immense train of generations, this profusion of germs, many thousands of which are abortive for the one that is brought into life?" (10: 347). Buffon wants to argue for "fixed" and "constant" species, but he is forced to acknowledge that nature often produces "failures," "abortions," and "monsters." These failed examples of supposedly stable "types" pose continuing problems for Buffon's definition of species. In fact, Buffon anticipates Darwin—and famous lines by Alfred, Lord Tennyson—when he notes that "individuals are of no estimation in the universe; it is species alone that are existences in Nature" (10: 342): "So careful of the type she seems, / So careless of the single life" (*RNH, In Memoriam* 54.43–44). Individuals die in untold numbers so that each species can be preserved and can evolve. Even species, however, are soon understood to be temporary creations; a species is just as likely as an individual to die out—to become extinct—if conditions change so that the species can no longer survive. Take away food and individuals will die in untold numbers, up to and including the death of the species. Take away the ability to mate, and the species will become extinct.

The solution to the problem of difference in Buffon's account is not variation of stable species (hybridization), but the production of "varieties": "the figure of each species is an impression, in which the principal characters are so strongly engraven as never to be effaced; but the accessory parts and shades are so greatly varied that no two individuals have a perfect resemblance to each other; and in all species there are a number of varieties" (10: 353). So species are fixed but varieties within species are not. The test case for Buffon is our own. The human species, he says, is "fixed and constant," and yet "in all species there are a number of varieties. The human species, which has such superior pretensions, varies from white to black, from small to great, &c. The Laplander, the Patagonian, the Hottentot, the European, the American, and the Negro, though the offspring of the same parents, have by no means the resemblance of brothers" (10: 353). Buffon needs a way not only to explain variation but also to argue for the stability of types. As a solution he offers a theory of "varieties"—actually an attempt to explain human races—which undermines the boundary between species.

Erasmus Darwin, grandfather of Charles, takes Buffon's troubling question and turns it into a new way of thinking about natural order and biological unity. The earlier Darwin is the natural historian most directly responsible for many of the ideas that made their way into a wide range of Romantic literature. He was referred to in the introduction to Mary Shelley's 1831 *Frankenstein* (*RNH* 287), praised by Coleridge as having "a greater range of knowledge than any man in Europe" (Barber 210), and made use of by Wordsworth in his poem "Goody Blake and Harry Gill" (*Wordsworth* 688). Erasmus Darwin's capacious and synthetic mind worked consistently to question the notion of immutable species. He not only personified and humanized the sexual life of plants—some plants are "polygamous," others engage in "clandestine" sexual "rites"—he also anticipated the outlines of his grandson's theory of evolution. In his *Phytologia* (1800), Erasmus Darwin described the "muscles, nerves and brain of vegetables" (132), concluding that plants have sensations and volition, "though in a much inferior degree even than the cold blooded animals" (133). In *The Temple of Nature* (1803), he describes the *Lycoperdon* tuber, a plant that "never rises above the earth, is propagated without seeds by its roots only, and seems to require no light. Perhaps many other fungi are generated without seed by their roots only, and without light, and approach on the last account to animal nature" (48–49). Such shared lives of plants and animals can, relatively easily, be linked to human life.

Darwin also argues, in *Zoonomia* (1794), that nature is full of complex forms of variation and metamorphosis within the lives of single creatures as well as species. He cites caterpillars changing into butterflies, tadpoles into frogs, the "feminine boy" into the "bearded man," and the "infant girl" into the "lactescent woman" as examples of dynamic and mysterious changes in individuals (1: 500). So humans undergo forms of metamorphosis that are parallel to those seen in animals: ecomorphism; humans are more like animals than animals are like humans. He also marvels at "great changes introduced into various animals by artificial or accidental cultivation, as in horses" (1: 500). This line of thinking allows him to conclude that "all animals have a similar origin, viz. from a single living filament" and that "it is not impossible but the great variety of species of animals, which now tenant the earth, may have had their origin from the mixture of a few natural orders" (1: 498–99). "A single living filament" or "a few natural orders"? In either case, all life on earth traces back to, and is thus related to, primordial ancestors from whom all subsequent generations and species have descended.

Darwin's choice of the word "filament" to describe the original piece of matter that came to life is suggestive, because it so closely approximates science's current descriptions of the double-helix of DNA, the twisted and self-replicating ladder-like structure that seems to have arisen from complex combinations of carbon and organic compounds and formed the necessary building block for all subsequent living things. Darwin cites David Hume's claim that "the world itself might have been generated, rather than created" with the resulting conclusion that all living organisms derive, not only from earlier organisms, but ultimately from inorganic compounds (2: 247): from inorganic to organic, then from conscious to self-conscious. Darwin offers another powerful image that will dominate the thinking of the next two centuries when, in a note to *The Temple of Nature*, he imagines life originating from the ancient seas as part of his claim that "all vegetables and animals now existing were originally derived from the smallest microscopic ones, formed by spontaneous vitality" (Add. Notes VIII 38). This speculation leads to perhaps the most often-quoted lines from *The Temple of Nature*:

> Organic Life beneath the shoreless waves
> Was born and nurs'd in Ocean's pearly caves;
> First forms minute, unseen by spheric glass,
> Move on the mud, or pierce the watery mass;
> These, as successive generations bloom,
> New powers acquire, and larger limbs assume;
> Whence countless groups of vegetation spring,
> And breathing realms of fin, and feet, and wing. (295–302)

Here is Charles Darwin's own theory in embryo, but already complete. Erasmus Darwin even argues that sexual reproduction is far superior to asexual reproduction because it introduces hybrid variation and mutability into individuals, hybridity that can then be passed on—and altered—in subsequent generations. The only piece of the puzzle missing in the earlier Darwin's account of evolution is the idea of natural selection, the idea that nature herself does the selecting that determines which characteristics survive and prosper and which are eliminated through competition, death, and extinction. That piece of the equation would have to wait over half a century until Charles Darwin said, quite simply, "any being, if it vary however slightly in any manner profitable to itself, under the complex and sometimes varying conditions of life, will have a better chance of surviving, and thus be *naturally selected*" (*Darwin* 97; Darwin's emphasis). If organic matter has only one source, then all life on earth is technically the extended history of a single organism. Of course, it is also possible that life itself, just as details within each species, can have originated more than once, under more than one specific set of circumstances.

The science of biology was soon to be revealed as at least as complex as the science of geology. From the time of Christopher Columbus to Captain Cook, global exploration introduced to the Western world new species of plants and animals, and even "new" groups of human beings, all of which had emerged over periods of time that could barely be imagined. Real dragons (the komodo: *Varanus komodoensis*), actual sea monsters (giant squid: *Architeuthis dux*), and literal cannibals (e.g., in New Zealand and New Guinea) were all parts of the stories brought back by European expeditions to the four corners of the earth. Many of these "creatures" (human as well as nonhuman) were discovered and transported to Europe and America for exhibition. The Prussian polymath Alexander von Humboldt was the personalized embodiment of such explorations. His ascent of Mount Chimborazo in Ecuador took him to the highest altitude ever reached by a human up until that time. Von Humboldt received life-threatening shocks of organic, animal voltage while wrestling with electric eels from the Orinoco River in the Amazon basin. He collected bird guano (for manure), and his description of its properties made it into one of Europe's most important fertilizers. He argued that Africa and South America were originally part of the same landmass, long before the theory of plate tectonics, and he virtually invented the subsequent science of meteorology (Sachs).

Many such explorations to the world's continents, and to far-flung oceanic islands, introduced Europeans to plants and animals—not to mention human beings—with remarkable shapes and habits. Snakes that could swallow goats whole, spiders as large as a human hand, people who filed their teeth to sharp points: these tales revealed the world of "nature" to be at once wider and wilder than anyone had yet imagined. Discoveries were catalogued and then presented in exquisite books of illustrated natural history, or captured and then displayed in early zoos and cabinets of curiosities, private precursors to public museums. There were, of course, wide variations among all of this flora and fauna, but there were also stunning similarities, even among plants and animals that were continents away and oceans apart. It is clear that Europeans standing in front of these animal and plant displays—in Naples, Florence, London, Dublin, Paris, Berlin, and elsewhere—noticed patterns and similarities that connected fish with reptiles, reptiles with birds, and birds with mammals. Some describable force, acting on organisms, had to explain these similarities as well as the differences among living things. Why did so many creatures have tails? Why were those tails so similar? Why were so many creatures bilaterally symmetrical? Why did no creature have three arms, or five legs? Why did all creatures with eyes also have big brains (relative to body size)? Reflections on this variety and these likenesses led directly toward Charles Darwin's final understanding of these relationships.

In addition to all of this life, neither amateur naturalists nor dedicated scientists could ignore the vast amount of fossil evidence that flooded into view by the mid-nineteenth century. Geological hammers were uncovering an earth that had been, and still was, constantly changing. Scientists like Richard Owen were describing reptiles as big as dragons that had lived on earth for millions of years, millions of years ago: Owen called them *dino-saurs* ("terribly-great lizards"). Some natural theologians were so upset by this picture of the past that they argued that God had hidden all of these fossils deep in the earth to test the commitment of the faithful. Other fundamentalists claimed that *Tyrannosaurus rex* and *Stegosaurus* were the remnants of giant antediluvian creatures that did not make it onto Noah's small ark. Then, around 1811, a preadolescent girl, walking on a cliff-side English beach, uncovered ancient bones of gigantic dimensions. Mary Anning had literally been struck by lightning—her nurse had died—when she was barely one-year-old. Now she struck figurative lightning into the scientific world by finding the first virtually complete skeleton of an ichthyosaur, a gigantic "fish-lizard" that had roamed the Mesozoic seas for tens of millions of years, millions of years ago. Her brother had found the skull of this same creature a year earlier. Mary Anning's actual dinosaur still hangs on the wall of the Natural History Museum in London. I gazed long at it during my last visit there. The confusion created by such a discovery was not just religious, however. The way people thought about their own world was changing. That sturdy mountain over there that had once seemed to be such an image of permanence? It will not last forever. That mighty river yonder that has flowed here for all time? Not so. As Charles Lyell had shown with geologic evidence, that river was not flowing in this valley five million years ago, and it might not be here a million years from now. If poets and scientists wanted images of permanence, they would have to look somewhere else, not to the mutable natural world.

These same certainties about change and wonder applied to the animal kingdom. Until the mid-nineteenth century, the gorilla was the Loch Ness monster or the *yeti* of its time, a mythical creature existing only in the local legends of several central-African tribes. Then in 1847, an American medical missionary—appropriately named Thomas Savage—described a creature he named *Troglodytes gorilla*. "Troglodytes" means caveman; "gorilla" was the name of a "tribe of hairy women" encountered by Hanno, the famous Carthaginian explorer of the fifth century BCE. But Savage had apparently seen only a few skeletons. The first gorilla hunter and collector was Paul du Chaillu, a larger-than-life Frenchman who killed and collected specimens until he was himself almost killed in several dramatic encounters with the local human population. Du Chaillu was also the first person to confirm the existence of the group of people who came to be known as "pygmies." So this once-mythic gorilla-animal really existed, as did human beings of a type so alien that it was hard to see them as human. It is easy to imagine the level of challenge to conventional thinking posed by sudden discoveries of this wide range of physical similarities and organic differences in places as far flung as central Africa, southeast Asia, and the wilds of an island like Madagascar.

Physical similarities between apes and humans were as unsettling as they were hard to explain. The orangutan was called *Homo sylvestris*—"man of the woods"—well into the nineteenth century. As early as 1800, visitors to La Specola (The Observatory) museum in Florence had been able to gaze upon a perfectly preserved chimpanzee in a glass case. He is still there today. From up close, his hands look just like human hands, his tongue looks like a human tongue, and his eyes—though made of glass—gaze out at viewers with a strange sense of recognition. This is most likely the same great ape that Byron saw when he visited this museum in the early years of the nineteenth century. By the late eighteenth century, public zoos had begun exhibiting living specimens of these exotic creatures (I will discuss the details of these museums and zoos later in my urbanatural year). For now, let me just say that no human—whether fundamentalist or atheist—can look upon a living (or even a stuffed) great ape without an unnerving, or perhaps exciting, sense of recognition, a sense that continues from Byron's day down to the present. Such a creature must be humanity's kin; there is no other possible explanation: he has toenails and finger prints, the skeletal remnants of a tail (just like all people do), and a brain that is often—relative to his body size—larger than the human brain. Researchers who have worked closely with Tarzan's cheetah or Koko the gorilla report that great apes are creatures with a full claim on self-consciousness and an ape-sense of personal identity. In the eighteenth and nineteenth centuries, theorists from the grandfather Erasmus Darwin to the grandson Charles Darwin hinted at evolutionary explanations that linked human beings directly to monkeys and apes by way of common ancestors. Maybe my ancestors did swing through the trees? Perhaps those people who are still born with a visible tail—this fact is true—possess this extra appendage (really just an external coccyx) because of humanity's close connection to these creatures? Human beings have been "roosting" on earth for a long, long time; that much is certain.

SAVING CITIES, SAVING TIGERS

This morning's scene outside my door recalls Thoreau's willful essay "Walking": "I wish to speak a word for Nature, for absolute freedom and wildness, as contrasted with a freedom and culture merely civil,—to regard man as an inhabitant, or a part and parcel of Nature, rather than a member of society" (260). We need precisely such a model of "wildness," the sentiment that Thoreau echoed often throughout his writings. The word he emphasized was not "wilderness." He never said, "In *wilderness* is the preservation of the world" (italics added), as those more than six hundred mistaken web pages currently claim that he did. His quotation was "in *Wildness* is the preservation of the world" (273; italics added). Thoreau's "wildness" is not only, or even primarily, about wild places. His "wildness" is about a state of mind. Thoreau says, again and again, that people need to "wild" their personal retreats (often located in the wilderness), but they also need to "wild" their minds. Each of us needs to *wild* not just our external places but also our internal spaces. Thoreau advocates "wildness" as a verb, as in, "I hope that I will be able to *wild* my mind during this ecocentric year of roosting." There may be wildness in all wilderness places, but wilderness is never a prerequisite for wildness. This lesson is even more important for the technocentric twenty-first century than it was for Thoreau's industrializing nineteenth century. The wildness I need is in London and in the Laurel Canyon. I can feel Thoreau's wildness in the noise of Manhattan just as I feel it in the silence of Montana.

Do not get me wrong. I include myself in this critique of modern life, and, at the same time that I am calling for wild minds, I am also calling loudly for the preservation of wild places. Every person needs to help preserve wilderness spaces—just as I need to "preserve" the Roost—with a clear sense of the distinction between human activity and those nonhuman activities that can only be thought of as "wild." Just as important as my set-aside spaces, however, is the wider wild-sense that I want to call "roosting." As much as humans need hands-off, wheels-off wilderness, they also need hybrid places and mixed-use spaces, human landscapes that are ecocentrically reimagined and redefined, nonhuman spaces mixed with human places that will produce sunsets for the city masses and computers for the wilderness dwellers. This is why the time has come to recognize that human beings are always *in* nature and that nature pervades *every* last human space. A new sense of internal and external balance can emerge out of recent rhetorical uses of the prefix "eco"—ecocentric, ecomorphic, ecotecture—and also my feeling for my widest ec(o)h(o) me (eco-, echo, home, me): a unified dwelling place that includes not only human habitation (the valley below me filled with the towns of Charles Town, Harpers Ferry, Martinsburg, and all the human places in between: drive-in theaters, fast-food restaurants, convenience stores, gas stations, churches, motels, and houses), but also the non-human habitation all around me (the wild ridge above me, the river and its uninhabitable flood-plain, steep unlivable mountainsides, the sky above, the underground below).

The recognition of these two sorts of spaces is already occurring on the part of many architects, urban planners, and urban (or rural) designers who are seeing their task as one of integration. These planners seek to bring the wild, nonhuman world into the buildings and parks and roadways of the social world, and they also strive to take human beings into wild places of every size and kind, but only with concern for a world that existed long before any members of the species *Homo sapiens* arrived. A school of urban planning has already emerged around this idea. In "Urban Nature and Human Design: Renewing the Great Tradition," Anne Whiston Spirn claims that

> Nature pervades the city, forging bonds between the city and the air, earth, water, and life within and around it. Urban nature consists of air, the materials suspended within it, and the light and heat transmitted through it. It is the landforms upon which the city rests and the minerals embedded in the earth beneath it; the water in rivers and reservoirs, pipes and soil; and the organisms that live within the urban habitat. But urban nature is more than a collection of individual features like wind, hills, rivers, and trees. It is the consequence of a complex interaction between the multiple purpose and activities of human beings and the natural processes that govern the movement of air, the erosion of the earth, the hydrologic cycle, and the birth and death of living organisms.
>
> The city is part of nature. Recognition of that basic fact has powerful implications for how the city is designed, built, and maintained, and for the health, safety, and welfare of every resident. For the past century, however, consideration of nature has been viewed as pertinent mainly to the design of parks and new suburbs... Unfortunately, especially in this century, planners and designers have mostly neglected and rarely exploited natural forces within cities....A few cities, however, have exploited nature ingeniously to shape an urban habitat that is safe, healthy, economical to build and maintain, beautiful, and memorable. Although such cities are not common today, they are part of an abiding tradition in city design. (Stein 475–77)

I quote Spirn at length because her argument is the planner's version of my ecocritical and literary argument. She first wrote these words in 1985, and yet, twenty-five years later, urban designers are still struggling to take Spirn's words seriously, to move beyond the long-standing "belief that the city is apart from, and even antithetical to, nature" (476). The hope now is that city planners and developers will continue to learn from examples such as those Spirn cites—Woodlands, Texas; Stuttgart, Germany; and Denver, Colorado—urban locations that have made use of natural facts and forces (geology, the hydrologic cycle, weather patterns) as part of their planning processes and ongoing development.

As David Orr has recently said, "Designing with nature...disciplines human intentions with the growing knowledge of how the world works as a physical system. The goal is not total mastery but harmony that causes no ugliness, human or ecological, somewhere else or at some later time" (*Design* 4). Such environmental design implies that humans are always among natural processes which they did not create, yet which they often can control—for good or for ill—and just as often not control. The good part of this equation is easy: fresh water and clean air, ocean sunsets, autumn hillsides, nesting swallows, and fields full of wild flowers. But the "ill" side of nature is no less natural: harsh climate, violent weather, dangerous animals, poisonous plants, disease-causing organisms, and toxic chemicals. Illnesses, allergies, accidents, and injuries: all are fully natural, all are part of the story; so, is nature good for human beings, or bad? This is the question, and distinction, that each person needs to move beyond. My "urbanature," like Orr's "designing with nature," is about "remaking the human presence in the world in a way that honors life and protects human dignity. Ecological design is a large concept that joins science and the practical arts with ethics, politics, and economics" (4).

This is another reason that the prescriptive and integrative aspects of urbanature are essential. If I assume that my life in the urban world of humans separates me from the wonder of wild nature, then I am unprepared for crime, the swine flu, AIDS, or a massive hurricane, like Katrina, that can destroy a major city in a matter of hours. If I imagine that my weekend escape (my "Roost")—which enables me to leave the "bad" city in favor of the "good" wilderness—keeps me free from the negative aspects of urban life, then I am that much more likely to ignore the city or at least let it fend for itself. Let the city become the place where dirt, chaos, and human misery collect; I always have the pristine wilderness of my "second" home, my rural retreat, my illusory escape *back* to a wild nature that I never really left in the first place. AIDS—like the bubonic plague of an earlier era—came into my own city perfectly naturally, according to the CDC in order to thin-out the gene pool of a particular species in the way pandemics have always done. Katrina rolled ashore in New Orleans, bringing with it essential warm air and water that were desperately needed by the dried-out sections of the East Coast of North America in late summer, just as hurricanes have been doing since long before New Orleans, before the French and the Spanish, before the Indians, eons before any human inhabitants at all.

The implications of such a view in terms of social class are too unsettling to require much explanation. The rich and the well-to-do seek to escape from the "unnatural" city for the relative safety and imagined security of their "natural" lakeside retreats. Meanwhile, the poor and the underprivileged are left with only urban spaces, waste-lands of postindustrial ugliness, cut off from the forces and the sub-stances that might sustain them: pure air, clean water, fresh food, and pleasant surroundings: the quiet, the safe, and the naturally healthy. The "Fresh-Air Fund" is a perfect example of this contradiction. Every summer, since 1877, this well-meaning charity has collected money to take urban young people to the pristine "wilds" of rural nature-camps and host-family homes outside the city. The young people get a pleasant break from the challenges of their impoverished lives in the city. The donors get their guilt assuaged; they are freeing these victims of poverty for a glimpse of the way the other-half lives (*Fresh Air*). I do not mean to suggest that this is not a well-intentioned and beneficial experience for these urban young people. But imagine, instead, that these Fresh-Air Fund donors went to spend a long week-end with these young people in the South Bronx or Spanish Harlem, showing them how to make vegetable gardens in their backyards or neighborhood waste-grounds, teaching them how to build and estab-lish bird-feeders, nesting boxes, and frog ponds. Then at least New York's children would have learned that they live in a space worth saving, not just a place that needs leaving.

All of the "positive" natural substances (air, water, soil) and quali-ties (fresh, clean, pleasing) have come to be associated with a version of nature that has been separated from urban blight. The "cutting off," however, is always done by humans; it is not the result of any natural differences. Human beings created the images of Romantic nature just as they created the images of the blighted city. Humans forget, however, that the devastated slashes of vast volcanic wasteland on Mount St. Helens were created by a natural eruption, not by any human action. Nature is only "good" when it provides the things that humans like: sparkling water, pastoral landscapes, food-supplying plants, and harmless animals. Once I consider wolves, mud-choked rivers after a storm, poisonous plants, or the barren wastelands of the desert, however, nature is no longer a world I would choose to inhabit, any more than I would choose the slums of South Central Los Angeles. The conclusion is obvious. It is necessary now for humanity to save it all (the whole world) and make it all into something valuable—urban and natural, civilized and wild—to recognize the interconnectedness of every place and every aspect of human and nonhuman life.

Let me offer one final example of the way ideas of disconnectedness—and connectedness—trace back to an earlier moment in natural history. The imaginative separation between the natural and the human is starkly evident in a poem like William Blake's "Tyger." Blake's tiger is an animal that embodies the sort of destructive wildness that humans do not want to associate with themselves or with benign nature. Blake's capacious imagination could make space for gentle lambs but also for voracious tigers. Each human being—according to Blake—contains a lamb-force and a tiger-force. Romantic writers often posit a unifying force that transcends such separation, a force that moves beyond good and evil toward a Thoreauvian version of amoral wildness. Blake's lyric insists that this single force exists within both the tiger and the lamb: "Did he who made the Lamb make thee?" (20). The rhetorical question contains its own answer. Of course the same force that made the tiger made the lamb. How else could the two have come into being? Blake describes his tiger possessing a fascinating beauty: "Tyger, tyger, burning bright" (1), just as beautiful as any lamb with its, "clothing of delight, / Softest clothing wooly bright" (5–6). This wild cat is beautiful because of, not in spite of, the power of its destructive energy. The same is true of wild nature itself.

Oliver Goldsmith's *Animated Nature* (1774) was published two decades before Blake's poem and presents a naturalist's version of a tiger very similar to the poet's. After describing the astounding physical beauties of the creature, Goldsmith says, "Unhappily, however, this animal's disposition, is as mischievous as its form is admirable, as if Providence was willing to show the small value of beauty, by bestowing it on the most noxious of quadrupeds" (2: 135). The small value of beauty, indeed. Imagine a tiger crouching low in thick bushes. She pounces suddenly onto the back of an unsuspecting gazelle as the innocent creature steps into a clearing. The tiger's claws slash at the throat of her vulnerable prey. The gazelle falls to the ground, and the predator guts her tigerish maw, burying long, blood-soaked fangs into the flesh of the soft, blood-warm gazelle's underbelly. The tiger rips and tears, bites and chews, slashing at the fur and the flesh of the still-living, still-breathing creature. This tiger, however, is in no way evil. She is simply being a tiger. After she eats her fill, she will take food home to her beautiful tiger cubs. Blake knows that human beings want to *read* nature in their own image, just as they often want to imagine God only in their own image. Humans want to see themselves in nature and nature in themselves. Nature itself, however, can never—in any sense—be evil. Only humans are evil, only they can judge their own actions as moral or immoral. No AIDS virus is evil; no cancer cell is wicked. The moralistic values of nature and of human nature are all in the mind, and only the human mind.

By the time that Blake imagines his animal "burning bright, / In the forests of the night" (1794), the wider European imagination was fully saturated with descriptions of this mysterious and apparently bloodthirsty creature. George Louis Leclerc, Comte de Buffon, for example, completely anthropomorphizes the tiger, which he calls "the scourge of every country he inhabits" (*System* 132). Buffon's tiger has "no characteristics but those of the basest and most insatiable cruelty. Instead of instinct he has nothing but an uniform rage, a blind fury; so blind indeed, so undistinguishing, that he frequently devours his own progeny, and, if she offers to defend them, he tears in pieces the dam herself" (132–33). Buffon even attributes the tiger's ferocity to a strangely anthropomorphic class-structure within the animal kingdom. The tiger is more vicious than the lion because of his second-class social status within the cat family: "The first class [the lion] is less tyrannical than the inferior classes, which, denied so full an assertion of authority, abuse the power with which they are entrusted" (132). Buffon implies that if such class-envy is true of animals, perhaps we should also fear all human beings who find themselves members of inferior social classes. So anthropomorphism applied to the world of tigers can even be used to support a blatant form of class-based bias and implied racism among humans.

By the time Thomas Bewick published his *History of Quadrupeds* in 1790, he was already drawing on such well-established textual versions of tigers. Like Goldsmith, he had certainly never seen a tiger in the wild. Like Blake, if he had seen a tiger at all it was only the emaciated old male that was kept in the king's menagerie at the Tower of London, but that was unlikely, since the royal zoo was not yet open to the public. Like virtually all Romantic natural historians, Bewick's knowledge of "nature" has as much to do with what he has read and seen in books as with any experiences he has had of wild nature. The same was true with the great Romantic nature poets; their "nature" was derived from books as much as it was from lived experience.

Most of what Keats knew about nightingales had come from field guides and volumes of natural history, like those written by Bewick or Buffon. Like poets and natural historians, Bewick draws on earlier works of natural history to claim that the tiger is "the most rapacious and destructive of all carnivorous animals" and "is even said to prefer human flesh to that of any other animal" (171). Like Buffon, Bewick connects this creature with precise geographic locations, once again linking the animal to the human societies near which it is found: "The Tiger is peculiar to Asia; and is found as far north as China and Chinese Tartary: It inhabits Mount Ararat, and Hyrcania of old, famous for its wild beasts. The greatest numbers are met with in India" (171). Bewick also emphasizes tigers' generally hostile interactions with humans, regardless of circumstance. The animal "does not seem sensible to the attention of its keeper; and would equally tear the hand that feeds, with that by which it is chastised" (172). Only the most vicious of creatures, human or animal, would bite the hand that feeds. Once again, the colonial implications are clear: beware of viciousness, human or animal, from those parts of the world that produce such traits.

Next, comes a curious anecdote in which a colonial party subdues one of these rapacious felines in a surprising, and quite Kiplingesque, way: "Some ladies and gentlemen being on a party of pleasure, under a shade of trees, on the banks of a river in Bengal, were suddenly surprised at seeing a Tiger ready to make its fatal spring: one of the ladies, with amazing presence of mind, laid hold of an umbrella, and unfurling it directly in the animal's face, it instantly retired" (172). A second party was less lucky: "A Tiger darted among them whilst they were at dinner, seized on a gentleman, and carried him off in sight of his disconsolate companions" (172). The fearful side of traditional views of nature is nowhere more evident than in descriptions of wild animals killing and eating humans. Few images are more horrific to the mind than the idea of a tiger, or a python, or a shark, literally ingesting the body of another human being. But even a man-eater, like this one described in such detail by Bewick, is not evil. Man-eating is what some tigers do; it can be completely natural. Our modern version of such a tiger, the man-eating great-white shark in the movie *Jaws*, is fearful for just the same reason: the true violence of nature is startling, terrifying, and always random: first a young woman, that careless swimmer, then the seasoned sea-captain who sets out shark-hunting just one too many times. Herman Melville's killer white-whale Moby Dick was based on the 1820 ramming of the whale-ship Essex in the South Pacific in by an enraged sperm whale (Philbrick). Such violence never makes sense except in relation to the "rules" of nature. Carnivorous animals are violent when they eat; they are likewise violent when they protect their mates or their young. Nature only *seems* evil when it threatens humans or human order. The only thing humans have to fear from nature is our fear of nature itself.

Blake's poem "Auguries of Innocence" reminds his readers that whenever they upset the balances of nature, they do so at their own peril: "The wanton Boy that kills the Fly / Shall feel the Spiders enmity" (33–34). Blake's proto-ecology is one reason that preservation of the human world also resides in Thoreau's idea of wildness. Only the wildness in each of us can reconnect us to our wild surroundings and, in turn, preserve the air, the water, the resources, and the nutrition that the world will need to sustain creatures from the simplest one-celled animals to humanity's own complex societies in the future. To save *Homo sapiens*, humanity will need to save the whole world, all of it: from spiders to tigers to humans, from wild lands to suburbs to cities.

SUMMER

—ESTIVAL ROOSTING—

ECOCRITICISM

Dolphin

Dolphin on the beach. A creature in some ways as close to humans as any in the animal kingdom, notable since antiquity for its intelligence and its "playful and frolicsome disposition." (John D. Godman, *American Natural History*, Vol. III. Philadelphia: Carey, Lee, & Carey, 1828).

4

JUNE

He who is in harmony with Nature hits the mark without effort
and apprehends the truth without thinking.

—Confucius

It rained all night. This morning the forest is alternately dripping
and swelling with moisture and dampness. The drops run down the
cups of leaves and blossoms, then along the smallest branches to larger
branches, from these branches toward the trunk, and finally down
the deep grooves of the trunk to the wide arching roots at ground
level. Once at ground level the water follows the roots, spreading out
into an area almost as big as the mass of the tree above ground. For
many trees, the total amount of root-matter equals the amount of
tree that is visible above ground. Stand back from a tree and imagine
as much tree as is visible above ground growing down into the earth,
a sort of mirror-tree reaching deep into the dark earth and humus
and rock, anchoring the massive trunk and branches, sucking up the
moisture and minerals needed for life. The entire tree acts as a funnel,
directing the water that falls onto it down the tree's body to the spot
where the water is most needed, down deep into the mirror-tree of
mighty roots underground.

A salamander stands sentinel on the stoop in front of the cabin
this morning, his head cocked to one side, his eyes staring. His tail
is gone, now just a flat red stump, probably snapped off during some
recent battle with an enemy. Unlike a scaly snake, this amphibian salamander really is slimy to the touch. He has to be slimy, since he has to
stay wet. He is almost an aquatic creature. In fact, he can be aquatic
whenever he wants, although forest salamanders like this one can also

live their entire lives without ever submerging their bodies completely in water. They manage to gather moisture from damp spaces under logs, hollow holes between roots and earth, or soggy spots of leafy mulch that never quite dry out. This astonishing salamander in front of me—like all of his amphibious brothers and sisters—has brought aquatic life out of the ponds and streams and has figured out a way to live a liquid life on land.

The wounded tip of his blunt tail has almost healed. Hungry predators often bite off a salamander's tail, or the salamander can whip his own tail and snap it off; then, the tail wriggles with life for a few valuable seconds to draw the attacker's attention away from the rest of the living body of the creature. Salamanders are among the most complex creatures that can regenerate an entire limb, like many simpler animals. Scientists still do not completely understand the precise process by which a salamander's leg "knows" how to regenerate a hand and fingers if it is severed at the wrist, and an entire leg if it is detached next to the body. Recent research in this area, however, is very promising: "By tracking individual cells in genetically modified salamanders, researchers have found an unexpected explanation for their seemingly magical ability to regrow lost limbs. Rather than having their cellular clocks fully reset and reverting to an embryonic state, cells in the salamanders' stumps became slightly less mature versions of the cells they'd been before. The findings could inspire research into human tissue regeneration" (Keim).

Like all amphibians, this creature is among the last aquatic landanimals on earth. In the Darwinian sense, he is a perfect missing link, a completely transitional type, poised halfway—in genetic terms—between water animals and land animals. The reason scientists could not identify missing links in Darwin's time was because they did not realize that they were looking at them all the time. Every amphibian is a missing link between creatures of the ocean and creatures of the shore, a living embodiment of every creature that crawled out of the sea to live on land but still had to have some fishy-way to keep his bodily moisture around him. I pick him up off the drying stoop and drop him into the damp leaf-mold beside the cabin.

There is a female five-lined skink on the path. She is a reptile, not a wet-skinned amphibian, but a dry-skinned, sharp-clawed tiny dinosaur. Many of the earliest dinosaurs were not the towering thunderlizards of childhood terror; they were about the size of house cats. So here, on a sunny Roost morning, in a matter of minutes, I have observed the transition from slimy-skinned, amphibious salamander to scaly-skinned, shiny lizard. This finger-sized lizard has plated scales just like those on the largest land creatures that ever lived. These skink-scales also adapted marvelously over countless millennia from dinosaur scales into feathers like those on every bird I now see flying in the sky above me. Every bird feather, from the smallest hummingbird's covert to the most massive eagle's primary wing-feather, is nothing more than the elongated and unfolded scale plate of a dinosaur adapted into this new use. If anyone doubts that all the birds are descended from reptiles, they only need to get up close to any chicken or parakeet and notice the leathery-scaled skin around the beak, the eyes, and the claws. Then notice the claws themselves, hooked and razor sharp, just waiting like a lizard's claws to grab onto some prey or hold tightly onto a perch.

VESTIGES OF TIME

This morning I read about Robert Chambers, the anonymous Victorian author of *Vestiges of the Natural History of Creation*, the book that out-Darwined Darwin a decade-and-a-half before *On the Origin of Species* (1859). Chambers's *Vestiges* set Victorian London on edge in 1844 with grand claims about churning masses of stardust that swirled together to form planets and stars, with detailed descriptions of the way life popped up *ex nihilo* out of blobs of literal nothing (Secord). This life then started to change and kept on changing until, by way of characteristics passed from one generation to the next, it led to Robert Chambers, and to me. Chambers knew a great deal about chance mutations first hand—and first foot—as it were. He was born with six fingers on each hand and six toes on each foot. Intelligent design? Chambers did not think so. When these added vestigial digits were amputated on the doctor's advice, the surgery resulted in a great deal of pain, and mildly mutilated hands and feet that never healed properly. Six toes were not part of any plan; they were just a genetic accident that led to unnecessary pain and suffering. As Darwin would soon reveal, natural selection makes as many mistakes as it does successes.

Vestiges of Creation was a sensation from the day it was published, but the book was so controversial that Chambers did not allow himself to be revealed as its author, nor was the book's authorship known for forty years, until a decade after Chambers's death. In America, the book was read assiduously by Abraham Lincoln, then an unknown Illinois attorney who had been born a quarter of a century earlier on precisely the same day—February 12, 1809—as a young English naturalist named Charles Darwin. Meanwhile, Queen

Victoria listened attentively to her consort Prince Albert read *Vestiges of Creation* out loud to her daily, along with regular readings from the poet Alfred, Lord Tennyson. This was, of course, the monarch who would announce, following the death of this same beloved Prince Albert, when he was only forty-two, that "Next to the Bible, *In Memoriam* is my comfort" (Sinfield 1). *In Memoriam*, Tennyson's evolution-anticipating masterpiece, was directly influenced by Chambers's *Vestiges*. Tennyson's poem, so beloved by the Queen after her own beloved's death, is the source of the famous description of nature as ever-violent, always "red in tooth and claw." The violence of nature, especially in the form of accident and illness, was reported in the lives of virtually all of the great literary and historical figures in the eighteenth and nineteenth centuries. Tennyson's own best friend—his classmate, the poet, Arthur Henry Hallam—fell victim to a massive, completely "natural," brain hemorrhage at the age of twenty-two. Darwin lost his beloved Annie when she was just ten years old. Wordsworth lost a son at six and a daughter before she turned four (see his lyric "Surprised by Joy"). Not "red in tooth and claw"; rather, dead of diphtheria and TB.

The impact of these frequent early deaths on the lives of their famous survivors is hard to overstate. Wordsworth and Keats had lost both of their parents before they were fifteen. Mary Shelley's first child died in her arms eleven days after a premature birth. Percy and Mary lost two more children in the years 1818 and 1819, while both of these young parents were still in their twenties. Byron lost his father at three, his mother at twenty-three, and his daughter Allegra died before her sixth birthday. Coleridge's father died before his son was ten. The consequence of such early deaths of parents, children, extended relatives, and friends has never—to my knowledge—been fully investigated. All of this death played an undeniable role in the psychic lives of most people in the eighteenth and nineteenth centuries. When Darwin announced that death was the engine of evolution, that it took a great many dead individuals to support the few breeding adults who survived in each generation of a species, this was not news to many Romantic and Victorian authors: "So careful of the type she seems, / So careless of the single life" ... "'So careful of the type?' but no...[Nature cares] for nothing, all shall go" (*In Memoriam* 54.43–44, 55.57, 60). The idea that not only individuals, but also entire species, were the price that had to be paid to evolution for the possibility of beneficial changes in nature, prepared the way for a great deal of twentieth-century hopelessness, existential angst, and nihilism.

Perhaps the most shocking aspect of Chambers's thesis in *Vestiges of Creation* was its thoroughgoing materialism: the idea that there was a purely physical means by which everything on earth, indeed everything in the universe, came to be. Creation did not need a proximate cause. The world did not need a willful creator, nor did it require an intentional deity. All that was required, according to Chambers, was the inorganic matter that made up the planets and stars, followed by complex combinations of inorganic compounds and energy into organic molecules, then simple animalcules into creatures small and finally larger: first slug-slime and all of those invisible living things, next creepy-crawlies, then fishes and amphibians, reptiles and birds, mammals and man, all made up of stardust, all wriggling not upward but only outward toward more spaces (Darwin would call them "niches") and more places within these natural spaces. In the view set forth in *Vestiges*, there was never any "progress" in nature, no movement toward a goal, just steady change and constant newness. This idea that nature might just be changing—not changing for any purpose or toward any goal—was as threatening as the idea that human beings were merely another species waiting for extinction, little more than the latest arrival in a long list of new forms that would come and go like the dinosaurs and the dodo bird.

Chambers did not claim his role as author of this work because he knew, as Darwin would know fifteen years later, the sort of repercussions that this line of reasoning was going to create. Nineteenth-century England was not ready to learn that the Archbishop of Canterbury and Queen Victoria had ultimately emerged from the primordial ooze of some antediluvian swamp. Thoroughgoing materialism of this sort had gotten the French *philosophes* into all sorts of trouble and had led to Romantic versions of atheism that are still with us in the twenty-first century (Priestman). Chambers, however, knew that he had gotten the basic facts right, even if he had gotten some of the precise facts wrong. That is the way science works; little bits of "right" knowledge emerge in the midst of incomplete knowledge, wrong knowledge, and just plain guesses. But Chambers, like Copernicus three centuries before him, and like Lucretius two millennia before both of them, had laid out a fairly accurate template for "the way things are." He created a full-blown Victorian sensation by saying that creation was an ongoing process, not a single moment of divine *fiat*. Creation did not take seven days or seven billion years; it had not ended yet, nor would it ever.

Creation, as Chambers and Darwin after him understood, is not an event but a process, the endless unfolding of the laws of matter and energy, the comings and goings of bits and pieces of matter from a stable table of elements, with the less-stable influences of heat and light and sparks of various forms of energy acting upon them. There is no need for any supernatural agency to make any part of the universe happen. As Stephen Hawking and others have pointed out, once the final laws of nature have been resolved into one single principle (already reduced to four: the strong force, the weak force, electromagnetism, and gravity), into the so-called unified field—Hawking says that the unifying force will be a lot like gravity—then science will know pretty much exactly how it all works. Here is how he put it to Gregory Benford in 2002:

> "I suggested we might find a complete unified theory by the end of the century." Stephen made the transponder laugh dryly. "OK, I was wrong. At that time, the best candidate seemed to be N=8 supergravity. Now it appears that this theory may be an approximation to a more fundamental theory, of superstrings. I was a bit optimistic to hope that we would have solved the problem by the end of the century. But I still think there's a 50–50 chance that we will find a complete unified theory in the next 20 years." (Benford)

Until that time—just like Lucretius, Galileo, Newton, Darwin, Einstein, and Hawking—scientists and nonscientists will have to be satisfied with bits of accurate knowledge amid the continuing confusion of the rest of what they think they know.

One of the central issues for Chambers, as for Darwin, was time, time and the problem posed by too much of it. What science now calls geologic time—and adolescents learn about in high school—was almost unimaginable even to well-educated thinkers in the late eighteenth and early nineteenth centuries. As the actress Fanny Kemble said, upon putting down a copy of *Vestiges of the Natural History of Creation*, "its conclusions are utterly revolting to me,—nevertheless they may be true" (Secord 270). What revolted so many Victorians about these ideas was not merely the sense that every human being might be descended from ape-like ancestors, but that the vastness of evolutionary time made all human beings seem much less significant than ever. If humanity traced it origins to 4,004 BCE—as the Irish Bishop Ussher had calculated in 1650—then humans might feel comfortable in a tidy and coherent family of man that seemed imaginable and comprehensible. If, however, my ancestors reach back millions and billions of years, and if they include gorillas and viruses, slugs and bacteria, then I clearly am a different sort of creature than the descendant of Adam and Eve. The problem was not just how much time had been required for the changes that Chambers, and later Darwin, were describing, but rather how insignificant human life—and all of human civilization—seemed in the face of the timeline required for these incremental biological changes to occur. Assyria, Babylon, Egypt, Greece, Rome, London, probably New York, and perhaps even Los Angeles: every one of these great civilizations gone in a relative heartbeat of geological time; every human culture's own brief moment on the stage nothing but a blip on the radar of scientific—not historic—time.

To understand the problem posed by time for these Victorians, it helps to consider time in reverse, from this current instant as far back as the human mind can imagine. On this warm June afternoon in the eastern United States, just below the Roost, in the Shenandoah River, numerous mayflies and winged-insects are being born and emerging into the sunlight. Some few of them will mate and will then die in the time it takes me to write these few paragraphs. Likewise, there are countless tiny creatures in the air around me now that will live for two or three days and will die by the time this weekend begins. A week, two weeks, a month: all of these time-frames encompass the life spans of countless insects, and many other small creatures above, alongside, and beneath my own human life: flying insects, hair-thin worms, tiny spiders, and pin-head sized arthropods.

Keep moving back. A year ago today was the birthday of many creatures that will die before the sun sets this evening. A worker-bee, several mice in the outhouse and cupboards, most bugs, an opossum: all of these creatures have life expectancies close to twelve months. The ants in their complex communal ant-nests live only an average of six months. Worker bees in their remarkable hives survive for roughly one year. A bat can live twenty-four years, a crocodile almost fifty. Today, the average human being in the developed world can expect to live roughly eighty years. Of course, if I am a male in many West African nations, my life expectancy is still more like forty years. If I combine the current life expectancy worldwide with the estimated lifespan of hunter-gatherers, the average life expectancy of all human beings who have lived for the past ten thousand years, would fall somewhere between thirty and forty years of age, especially given all those early *Homo sapiens* who were felled by unplanned accidents, unknown diseases, and saber-toothed tigers ("Age database").

Now, leave the human scale behind in this backward march through time. The longest-lived organism on planet earth is the bristlecone pine, a gnarled, wind-blown tree that inhabits altitudes where the air grows thin above tree-line in Colorado, New Mexico, and eastern California. The bristlecone can survive five thousand years if conditions of light and water are right. They live so long partly because of the density of their resin-filled wood. These stunted pines of the windswept southwestern hillsides live more than twice as long as the oldest giant sequoia ("Ancient Bristlecone"). There are bristlecone pines alive today that were shoots and saplings when Tutankhamen and Christ walked the earth, when Cleopatra ruled Egypt and King Priam reigned in Troy.

But all living things are babies, mere infants, in the sweep of the time during which significant natural change occurs. One million years ago? The first Ice Age was freezing the planet then, while the first fossil hominid that has a direct claim to human lineage, *Homo habilis*, was walking upright. Go back an additional three million years to reach the earliest hominids that can be identified as genetic kinfolk of twenty-first century humans. But not even this time-frame gets close to the geological clock, to real rock-time. No monkeys had appeared until thirty-nine million years ago, no horse (*Eohippus*) ever trotted, or cantered, or galloped until fifty-five million years before the human era. It was sixty-five million years ago, or thereabouts, that a meteor or comet hit the planet humans call home, probably in the vicinity of the Cancun Peninsula in Mexico, wiping out countless living things and innumerable kinds of living things, ending an entire era—the one called the Mesozoic—in the process.

That meteoric extraterrestrial bomb was probably no bigger than a small city—say three miles across—but it had a greater impact on life on this planet than the combined effects of tens of millions of earlier years ("What Killed the Dinosaurs?"). What about those dinosaurs that were all but wiped out by this extra-planetary disaster? Was this planetary collision a disaster to them? Probably not. The dinosaurs run backward again from about seventy million years ago (*Tyrannosaurus rex* and Jurassic Park's velociraptor), through Stegosaurus and Allosaurus (about 150 million years ago), all the way to the first dinosaurs of all: 228 million years in the temporal distance of clock time. Those earliest dinosaurs were about the size of a housecat. Along the way, flowering plants showed up a mere 115 million years from this morning, the first bird (*Archeopteryx*) flapped in around 155 million years ago, and the first mammal—tiny shrews with wriggling faces like mine (two fleshy ears, two eyes, one nose with two nostrils, one mouth full of teeth; maybe my cousin)—221 million short years ago, short that is compared to this long Age of Reptiles.

Now it is possible to talk about real extinction, once again in a way that would have seemed unthinkable and unspeakable to most

Victorians. At the end of the Paleozoic Era on earth, about 245 million years ago, more than 95 percent of all life vanished. That statistic is correct: 95 out of every 100 creatures and kinds of creatures—gone. Science does not know why this greatest of all of the great extinction events (there have been at least five) happened, but the fossil record does not lie about destruction on this scale. All of those individual animals and plants—and all of those types of animals and plants—were here, and then they were all gone. All of them. Gone (Stanley and Yang).

My backward time clock is finally reaching significant geologic time. The coal I burn in my coal-grate at home was laid down in the swamps of Kentucky about 320 million years ago. In the blink-of-a-cosmic-eye (50 million years before that) species like the shark in "Jaws" were appearing in the world's oceans for the first time, swimming fast and far, looking for meat to eat. One hundred million years before these sharks, the first land plants had sprouted out of their water-borne seeds, and a mere 200 million years before that there were watery jellyfish pulsing along the sandy shorelines of the entire globe. Out beyond and beneath all of those jellies were many more solid bottom-dwelling ocean worms, crawling and wriggling, looking for love, well, at least looking for a mate. Three hundred million years ago, every living creature that could not divide asexually was looking for sex with a mate. Now that is a genesis story.

I do not want to scare myself or my readers, but I will take all of the time span I have covered so far—670 million years back—and more than double it; double it with a mere snap of the fingers. Now, I have arrived at the origins of multicellular organisms, but that is only 1,500,000,000 years ago, and I am still only half-way—back and back once more—to bacteria. No wonder those Victorians got scared. I know I am, and I am still not close to the time that many geologists care most about, the time that matters, the time when the third planet from the sun really got going. Roll back, roll back, and back again from bacteria and my timeline reaches the origins of life on earth. When? That is still a good question, according to most of the scientists who study this question: "Some of the oldest rocks on Earth, found in Greenland, hold important clues to life's beginnings. The problem is, experts disagree both about how to interpret the clues and about how old the rocks really are" (Tenenbaum). Probably some number rounded off to 3,900,000,000 million years ago, that is roughly 46,800,000,000 months, that is 1,404,000,000,000 days from today: that is one *trillion* four hundred and four billion days. Days? The age of the earth itself? By this point, what the *tick-tock* difference does it matter at all: after all, at all, indeed! The earth is about 4,600 million years old, and, oh, by the way, in celestial terms, this planet is a newborn baby.

THOREAU AND URBANATURE

Thoreau is the first urbanaturalist among American nature writers, even though he often works hard to keep his readers tied to a naturalistic—anti-urban—version of Romantic ecocriticism. *Walden* creates the illusion that Thoreau is living miles and miles from his nearest neighbor—my students often tell me that they think he is in the Tetons, or at least the Poconos—while, in fact, Thoreau was a mile-and-a-half from the town center of Concord, at that time, between 1840 and 1850, a town of slightly over twenty thousand inhabitants. As if to drive home this opposition between urban and rural, a great deal of Thoreau's writing—whether at Walden, in the Maine woods, on the Merrimack River, or at countless other sites scattered throughout his voluminous volumes and journals—emphasizes the feeling of being miles and miles from human habitation, at such a great distance back into the natural world that the culture of human society—especially urban society—seems to vanish almost completely; this tendency accounts for the common misreading of *Walden* that places its author in the midst of a wilderness. At the same time, however, Thoreau's central concept of *wildness*—"In Wildness is the preservation of the world"—has surprisingly little to do with geographical location, or with any aspect of the distinction between the "urban" and the "natural."

When the environmental historian William Cronon says that wilderness "is quite profoundly a human creation," he is noting that the spaces that many people want to call wilderness are "far from being the one place on earth that stands apart from humanity" (1). I have reversed Cronon's clauses here to emphasize the implications of one point of focus in the human-culture versus wild-nature distinction. The "Romantic" tradition in American nature writing—Thoreau, John Muir, John Burroughs, Aldo Leopold, Rachel Carson, and Edward Abbey, for example—stems, in part, from the idea that it is good to distinguish the pure "wildness of nature" from places that have been "corrupted and tainted" by humankind. I have no simple-minded, Romantic illusions about the world I now inhabit. Thoreau understood my point in the nineteenth century, when he compared the locomotive that thundered along within the sight of his cabin at Walden Pond to the beautiful sounds of nature. I now live in a world where six billion—and counting—members of one species, my own, exert a version of victorious dominance over millions of other species; science admits to having no precise idea of the accurate number of species that are still hiding in the treetops of Amazonia or the depths of the Marianas Trench: "Surprisingly, scientists have a better understanding of how many stars there are in the galaxy than how many species there are on Earth. Estimates of global species diversity have varied from 2 million to 100 million species, with a best estimate of somewhere near 10 million, and only 1.4 million have actually been named" ("How Many Species"). Now, however, it is time to admit that *Homo sapiens* (one single species) has "won" the 10,000 year war against nonhuman nature, so-called first nature. As a result of this apparent victory, humans and nature have merged wherever they are found: even in the condominiums and the skyscrapers, also in the parking lots and the city parks, in the oil tankers far out at sea and the space station that is circling high above us, in the waste materials that surround us—however we define "waste"—and in the human refuse we have left in space ("space junk") and on our only natural satellite: the moon.

This afternoon, from my pristine perch on the porch at the Roost, I can hear jetliners overhead on their approach routes to Dulles Airport. Crisscrossing contrails spread out in the sky above the hillsides. Townhouses smear the valley below me. Highways whine in the distance, just as they continue to whine whether I am on this mountain, or in a hotel in Manhattan, or in most of the mountain fastnesses of the world. It does not matter if there are still a few places, some lonely high peaks or wide ocean spaces, where the noisy highways and whining jets cannot be heard. Loud human sounds are roaring all the time, wherever I find myself, wherever I try to hide. When I was in the Alps near Chateaux D'Oex, Switzerland, four decades ago, in one of the most isolated mountain valleys I had ever seen, I heard these same human sounds. When I climbed to the top of Dun Cann that same year—on the remote island of Raasay in the Western Hebrides of Scotland—I could hear and see 1970s jets leaving their contrails in the wide northern sky above me.

Beyond such sounds, think of the impact of human beings on every inch of the planet. Mountain climbers now complain about the vast amounts of trash that litter Mount Everest: "With the debris of more than 50 years of climbing—oxygen canisters, tents, backpacks and even some bodies—Mount Everest has been called the world's highest garbage dump. [...] Last year, more than 40,000 people visited the mountain from the Chinese side, which is located in Tibet, the *China Daily* newspaper said. [...] environmentalists estimate they could have left behind as much as 120 tons of garbage, or about 6 pounds per tourist, the paper said" ("China Plans Mount Everest Cleanup"). How much particulate matter and CO_2 do airline passengers leave behind in the sky every time they make their way blithely from Philadelphia to Osaka, from Dulles to Beijing? Tons upon tons. However much airplane exhausts fill the surrounding atmosphere, however many smokestacks belch smoke into the sky, the scale of the earth's atmosphere still seems to defy humanity's ability to overwhelm natural processes. Humans may eventually alter natural systems in ways that will have irrevocable and destructive effects on human life and other life on the planet. The earth may indeed be small enough for humans to pollute—even its seas and sky—but it is big enough to *maintain* an atmosphere and a nonhuman ocean, however much humans may be able to alter them.

I may be sitting still on the porch at the Roost, but that is another illusion created by nature. The world, remember, is always spinning at approximately one thousand miles per hour, and yet each person is standing on the moving surface and so that person does not notice. This is a good model for the perspectival element of urbanature. When I am standing in what feels like wilderness, I cannot see how close the nearest city is; when I am standing in the heart of the city, I cannot smell the sweet fresh air of the nearest wild lands. When the first astronaut reached the surface of the moon, he had to import earthly nature there in the form of oxygen, water, and nutrition—the minimum requirements for life anywhere in the universe. If NASA travels to Mars or the moons of Neptune, the story will stay the same. Men and women in space will have to bring bits of earthly urbanature— tanks (urban) full of air (natural), plastic containers (urban) full of water (natural), and dehydrated (urban) apples (natural)—in order to sustain themselves anywhere they travel throughout the universe. Nature includes all of those substances that I did not make that allow me to live: apples, vitamins, eggs, and minerals. Nature also includes the rules of matter and energy in motion that keep us alive: gravity, evaporation, the speed of light, and photosynthesis. This is why the time has come to see beyond any Romantic view of ecocriticism that would describe natural life as one thing and urban life as another.

*   *   *

The first bat of the evening appears in the clearing in front of the Roost, close to sunset on the horizon, swooping and diving, in search of food. The sun is a fiery orange-red disk, growing redder and redder as it sinks toward the sharply outlined blackish-blue mountain ridge beneath it. The sky in the west turns a sudden scarlet red, then, just as suddenly, it all goes crimson. A fish rises, breaking the slick surface and, with it, the sun's flat shimmer. The sky light changes noticeably each moment, from silver to orange to red to darkening gray. Then the silver in the clouds turns a bright fire-red. The sun hits the horizon and seems to speed up its motion in a way that even the eye can see. First half-a-sun, then a one-quarter sun, then just a sliver and finally a tiny bright flash. In one instant the fast-falling sun is gone, but the clouds keep up their blazing, and then their fast-fading light show for several more minutes. A first star shines bright in the wide darkening, and light-swallowing, sky. I owe at least a part of this pristine scene to urban pollution. The sunset myth turns out to be true: "It is certainly true that the 'pollution' results in redder sunsets," says Craig Bohren, professor emeritus of meteorology at Pennsylvania State University (Ballantyne). Not long after the urbanatural sunset has finally faded, a female long-eared owl starts calling in the wide mountain hollow up the hill behind me. Her squawks, clucks, cackles, and burrs begin as soon as the first stars appears and last until well past midnight. The bird book says that this is a female owl, because only she makes this kind of a racket at her nesting site, but why? If she is trying to protect her nesting hole and her young ones from predators or other enemies, why set up a series of loud cries and screeches that must attract every creature within miles? If she is trying to be discreet, why holler? If she is trying to protect her nest, why squawk? The long-eared owl moves in mysterious ways, her wonders to perform. She keeps me awake, as if to remind me over and over: whatever dangers may threaten this wide, wild world and its inhabitants, a place like the Roost remains a haven for creeping, crawling, scurrying life.

5

JULY

What a place to live, what a place to die and be buried in! There
certainly men would live forever, and laugh at death and the
grave.

—*Thoreau, "Ktaadn and the Maine Woods"*

Consider the periodical cicada. This cicada has wings like a filigree
of the finest Belgian lace, crisscrossed and veined with hundreds of
tiny lines and flat crystalline chambers, each like a clear stained-glass
window. The cicada's eyes are bright red, as smooth as glass, and its
proboscis (mouthparts) are formed by a tiny pair of tubes that oscil-
late back and forth like the mouth of a manic mosquito. Its abdomen is plated and segmented, ready to receive sperm to fertilize its
eggs, and then to lay those same eggs that will lie in the ground for
seventeen years, in the cold and the dark, finally to crawl out, wet
and larval, and harden into a beautiful bug that will live for less than
one summer. The males will all die soon after they have mated, and
the females will then survive them, only to climb up and out onto a
million billion tree branches, burying the shafts of their ovipositors
deep into dry bark and pithy stems, expelling long lines of tiny eggs
that will hatch after one freezing winter. The hatched larvae will fall
to the ground, and then bury themselves deep into the earth for their
seventeen-year cicada sleep.

I remember waking early one morning, during a long-ago July at
the Roost, when the cicadas were coming out of the earth by the billions or trillions. I was lying under my bedcovers, where I could hear
them buzzing like tiny chainsaws in the trees outside my window.
They were climbing up the screens, smacking into the stone walls of

the cabin, smashing into the windows of countless cars that streamed across the valley below the Blue Ridge. It was early in the morning, so I dressed quietly and made my way out the door. Once outside, I literally fell to the ground I was so stunned by the number of insects all around me. I could see tiny pads of grass and earth pushing up as the cicadas' damp white heads appeared from deep underground and started to harden in the clear sunny air. Each emerging insect left a perfectly round hole in the dirt and a coiled pile of wet soil around the top of its burrow. My thumb fit almost exactly into one of these holes. I could feel the cool darkness even at that shallow depth. I was on all fours, peering into hundreds of abandoned cicada burrows, watching as the bugs crawled and scratched across the ground, each one looking for a tree or a low branch to climb. The huge tree in front of the cabin was covered with their crawling bodies. What had triggered the impulse that brought them all out of their burrows at the same time? How did they find those tall trees? What force inside each of their tiny cicada-brains sent them climbing up onto the leaves and the spreading branches above them?

That weekend these cicadas were everywhere, covering the forest as well as the water of the slow-moving river. Huge bass rose up from the depths of the Shenandoah, yanking their wide mouths open and swallowing three or four giant bug-bodies in a single gulp. Bugs clattered through the leaf mold and clamored across the rock walls. I followed them along their beeline-straight marches to the roots of mighty oaks and maples all around them. I watched them climb the bark of countless trees until they were way out of my sight. Their wing-beats filled the air like warm wind. I got my face close to the mated females laying their eggs, each one leaving tiny gashes in the delicate tree bark and shrubs, the stems and the branches. Each female's ovipositor would jab its way through the tough bark or tree stem. Then she would sit quietly, her body pulsing rhythmically, as the freshly fertilized eggs surged out from her spongy abdomen, flowing into the narrow cavity she had made. She would move along in a perfectly straight line, leaving six or seven evenly spaced gashes in each branch. When she finished, she would fly off in an erratic weaving path, back into the cool depths of the forest; or, she might stumble and fall exhaustedly to the ground, sometimes landing on her feet and crawling slowly away, sometimes landing on her back like a tiny insect-tortoise, her legs waving and flailing up at the hot, blue sky above her. Sometimes she was dying.

That night I stretched out and listened to the shrill and distant clatter as I fell asleep in my wide top-bunk-bed. I imagine a cicada:

digging her way out of a seventeen-year burrow, cracking her useless layer of larval skin, crawling into the sunlight, drying as she scaled the heights of a sassafras, flying high and wide in search of a mate, hunching together madly and wildly, then laying her eggs deep into the fastness of another living thing, only to fall exhausted and dying at the base of the tree from which her own young would be born, seventeen years later. Each incarnation may die within days of being born, but cicadas, as a species, go on and on and on. They sleep for seventeen years in the dark soil. Then they rise skyward with the warm days of one magical spring and summer. They are born with barely any capacity to eat, since their only goal is to mate and then to return the minerals of their own body-parts back to the earth to help feed the swelling, buried grubs of the next generation. Then they begin mating, within a day or two of hatching after seventeen dark years underground. They are dead within three or four weeks— but by then the males have deposited their sperm into the females, the females have laid their eggs in the delicate branch tips of trees all around them, and the future is secure.

These cicadas have risen four times during my own life: several years ago (most recently), when I watched them at the Roost for hours and days on end; in 1987, when I returned to the Middle Atlantic states after a brief sojourn in the hot, deep South (where the same periodical cicada takes only thirteen hotter-summered years for the brood to mature); and, in 1970, when a friend and I published a scholarly essay thanks to a Roost neighbor who let us dissect the cicada-filled copperhead he had killed. Oh, yes, I almost forgot; cicadas rose for the first time during my life the summer I was born. My parents lived in Alexandria, Virginia, where the cicadas were already flying and buzzing by the first day of June (my mother always said that she remembered them clearly). One morning in early June, my father took the wheel of their 1948 Plymouth Deluxe, and they raced to a hospital in Washington, D.C., so that I could be born while the cicadas were wildly emerging. There, on every tree branch outside my mother's hospital room—a room that, on that first day of my life, also became my room—were countless cicadas, cicadas by the billions, certainly the millions, buzzing and clattering, mating and already dying.

WILD ANIMALS HAVE NO SOULS

I have only looked wild animals in the eyes twice. The first time was in 1963. I was ten years old, and I was sitting on the wide rock below the cabin one evening with my mother to my left and my father to my right. I remember this scene like it was yesterday. We had watched the sunset in front of us and had stayed on the rock talking as the last long lines of red daylight gave way to stars and the black sky of night. By now it was pitch dark, and moonless, so dark that my father said he would walk up to the cabin and return with the flashlight we had forgotten. He wanted to light our way past the rock gardens, up the flat stone path to the house behind us. No sooner had my mother and I heard the screen door shut behind him than we heard a sound that has stayed with me for more than forty years. It was a yell—no, it was more like a scream—that sounded, as my mother said later, like a young woman being stabbed. The creature screamed once, and then a second time more loudly, and then fell silent. My father was, by this time, sprinting on tiptoes around the side of the house.

"What was that?!" I whispered loudly as he came up beside us.

"Bobcat, I think!" he whispered, as he motioned for me to follow him, down the narrow path that dropped off our sitting rock and into the dark woods to our right. Then we heard the scream again, this time closer but less loud, and we knew that this animal, whatever it was, was much closer than we had realized. We had gone only twenty or thirty yards, when my father suddenly pointed the flashlight down the open trail ahead of us, turned it on, and instantly, we saw the bobcat's bright eyes.

Yellowish grey-green, as clear as two reflective light spots in the dark of the pitch-black forest: the bobcat's eyes shone from the top of a large, diamond-shaped boulder, a rock on which I had carved all of our family initials the summer before. The flashlight beam was narrow and dim, so it was hard to make out anything except the piercing, stock-still eyes and a tufted corona of smoky fur around them. My eyes locked onto his eyes for what must have been two or three seconds, but it seemed much longer at that moment. Perhaps not surprisingly, I remember those eyes more clearly and distinctly than many other objects I have gazed on for hours on end since that night. I had never seen a bobcat before. I have never seen one since. Those eyes were the first eyes of any truly wild animal I had ever seen. They have stayed with me like a totem ever since, even though I did not know what they meant until my second sighting of wild animal eyes, forty years later and half a world away.

In 2003, a colleague and I took a group of students to Ecuador and the Galápagos Islands: *Los Encantadas*, the Enchanted Isles, as the Spanish sailors and whalers used to say. Our ship was motoring toward Gardner's Bay and Espanola one afternoon when we came upon our first full pod of Pacific bottlenose dolphins. We had seen single animals or small groups of dolphins in the wake of our bow throughout the week, but this was a pod of at least a hundred animals, adults and juveniles, swimming, leaping and rolling, not following our boat but making their way as an organized group around the northern edge of the island. We were just within sight of land when the captain sounded the depth for us. We had hundreds of feet of deep ocean beneath us. One of the students suddenly shouted, "can we swim with them!" and the captain told us to run and get our swimsuits, our masks, and our snorkels.

He maneuvered the hundred-foot-ship in a wide curving arc that intercepted the edge of the pod and cut off a dozen or so dolphins from the larger group. They seemed slightly disoriented at first, and their swimming slowed from a breakneck beeline to small circles, still rolling and surfacing, as though they wanted to stay in this area with us for a while. At that point the captain yelled "jump!" and we went off the starboard side of the ship into the sea. At that the dolphins spooked; after all, these were not tame, Marine-Land trained creatures; these were wild animals. As fast as we were swimming, they darted ahead of us and disappeared deep beneath us, until they rejoined the larger pod and continued swimming in a willful direction. The ship used the zodiac to pick up the dozen or so of us who had jumped and, once back onboard the main ship, the captain gave fast chase again. This time he broke the pod almost in half, as he carved a wide circle to the left side around a large group of the animals. This second time the hearty souls in our swimming group clambered into two zodiacs and gave quick chase until we found ourselves literally in the middle of the larger group of dolphins.

Once in the water what was most startling was the sound. I could hear clicks and beeps, and long drawn-out echo noises all around me, coming from every side except above, especially loud directly beneath me. I could see nothing except the sapphire blue water turning black in the depths and the distance. Then all of a sudden, a twelve-foot-long, six-hundred-pound *Delphinidae* raced up from directly beneath me and turned to show me his stomach, for just a few seconds, before he whizzed past no more than ten feet from my right side. My heart stopped, my breath caught, I spluttered into my snorkel and lost sight of him in an instant. Then I recovered and decided that I should stop swimming and just tread water. So I did. Dozens of dolphin vocalizations were fading and then growing stronger. The pod was clearly staying in our area. Perhaps they were as curious as we were. Every time I took a gulp of air and dove straight down as deep as my lungs would allow, the sounds grew louder and louder.

By using this method of falling and rising, I saw one bottlenose at a distance, rolling on the ocean's surface. Then I had two more animals swim up beneath me, this time facing stomach-to-stomach and slanting even closer to me than the large single dolphin before them. When this pair brushed by me, I could feel the pressure of their bodies against the water. If I had reached out my right arm, I could have touched them both. I was startled and elated—and even a little afraid—and I was breathing so hard that I began to feel light-headed. Suddenly, the clicks and beeps and the high whining stopped. I figured that I must be out of the pod now, so I surfaced to find the Zodiac. It was much farther away than I realized, so I decided I had better start swimming. My face down, I swam slowly and steadily, still using my snorkel, peering hard into the aquamarine blue sea fading to black in a wide circle all around me.

Without any warning, I heard the loudest dolphin sound I had heard in my life: a high whine, click-click, double-beep, double-beep-beep that rose once again from straight below me, but still I could see nothing. When the dolphin at last appeared, he was swimming much more slowly than the others. At first he scared me, since his motion seemed more like a shark than a mammal. But he rose beak-first directly below me, rolled slowly from one side to the other, moved literally beside me and turned his entire body to the right so that I could first see his blowhole, then his beak, and then his bold left eye, black as the night but shining brightly in the dappled water-lights only two feet beneath the ocean's surface. Once again, my gaze into his eye must have lasted only two or three seconds. We were both moving, he much faster than I, but this time it was clear that he was looking at me, and I at him, if only for one memorable instant. I will not say that our eyes met—that would be too melodramatic—but I will say that we were looking at each other, and I will add that we could see each other clearly. Then he was gone, and I rose to the surface, silenced and stunned.

Two years later I learned from a marine scientist that my swim with wild dolphins was not the wisest move I had ever made. The Ecuadorians, he said, have a different standard for safety than North American oceanographers. It turns out that wild bottlenose dolphins have been known to turn aggressive when in the water with humans. They can easily use their massive bodies to ram human swimmers to the point of serious injury. This is not the worst danger in the open ocean, however. When dolphins swim in pods, they take advantage of feeding opportunities along the way. This results in a steady trail of partially eaten fish, shimmering scales, and blood—a veritable chum-line of shark bait—in the area of any pod of oceanic dolphins. In fact, according to this marine biologist, schools of sharks have been known to congregate just below any fast-moving pod of wild dolphins, taking advantage of any opportunity, waiting for food. So there I was, in the open Pacific, living it up with a few curious dolphins, blithely unaware of the reef sharks, the hammerheads and, who knows, the bull sharks or tiger sharks (we had seen both during our expedition), swimming just below my new friends and me, waiting to see what might show up within, or just above, the swimming depth of these curious dolphins.

So what is significant about my two cases of eye-to-eye contact with wildness? The thing that has stayed with me most strongly, from that forty-two-year ago bobcat and that five-year ago dolphin was that I came eye-to-eye with magnificently beautiful creatures, but I was looking at animals without souls. So, what is the point? There was no need for a soul in the wide-alive eyes of those animals, so why do human beings persist in believing in the need for a soul in me? I cannot figure it out. This contact with wildness made me more sure than ever that I do not have—or need—a soul. Surely human beings can get along fine, as both of my wild-eyed creatures have done for millions of years, without a soul or the need for a soul. Why do humans have this need? What is its purpose? Is it just to assure humans that they live forever? Is it to make us feel superior to every other living creature? What function does the soul serve? No physical scientist can argue logically for the existence of a soul, since no physical scientist can believe in anything that is not composed of matter: of atoms, protons, and neutrons. Is there anything in the universe that cannot be understood in terms of the elements of the periodic table, in terms of quanta and atoms and molecules, in terms of matter and the forces that act upon matter? I doubt it. A person can talk about dragons, or Santa Claus, or souls, but beyond the need for imaginative beliefs like these there is little reason to talk about the need for a soul.

Keats did not believe in the soul either, at least not in an immaterial soul connected to an afterlife or any God-force. The lack of such a belief did not seem to bother him in the least. In the letter in which he publicly admitted to this belief, he said,

> The common cognomen [understanding] of this world among the misguided and superstitious is "a vale of tears" from which we are to be redeemed by a certain arbit[r]ary interposition of God and taken to Heaven—What a little circumscribe[d] straightened [limited or restrictive] notion! [...] It is pretty generally suspected that the chr[i]stian

scheme has been coppied [*sic*] from the ancient persian and greek Philosophers. [...] as one part of the human species must have their carved Jupiter; so another part must have the palpable and named Mediator and saviour, their Christ their Oromanes and their Vishnu. (*Letters* 288, 289)

No Ra for the Egyptians, no Zeus for the Greeks, no Jupiter for the Romans, no Yahweh for the Israelites, no God for the Christians: with all these fanciful gods gone there would be a world in which souls could be *made*—"Call the world if you Please 'The vale of Soul-making'" (288)—not born, a world in which people could live and let live, in which humans could love and be loved. The poet Shelley said much the same thing when he wrote,

> All that we see or know perishes and is changed. Life and thought differ indeed from everything else. But that it survives that period, beyond which we have no experience of its existence, such distinction and dissimilarity affords no shadow of proof, and nothing but our own desires could have led us to conjecture or imagine. [...] It is said that it is possible that we should continue to exist in some mode totally inconceivable to us at present. This is a most unreasonable presumption. [...] such assertions should be either contradictory to the known laws of nature, or exceed the limits of our experience, that their fallacy or irrelevancy to our consideration should be demonstrated. They persuade, indeed, only those who desire to be persuaded. ("Future State" 193–95)

Humans do not need a soul any more than any other sentient creature on the planet needs a soul. They do not need one to come to life or to depart from life, and they do not need one to be saved. Think of all that human beings have accomplished over the past four millennia, even if we remove the concept of an immortal spirit; or perhaps I should say, a "ghost." There are no ghosts. A soul, after all, is nothing but a ghost, an ancient worn-out idea that human beings should now be able to leave behind and live without. Whatever someone says they have heard ("I heard a ghost") was all in that person's mind. Whatever someone says they saw ("I saw a spirit") was a natural phenomenon, or a trick born out of human consciousness.

What does my wild animal, no-soul talk, have to do with urbanature or the argument of this book? Once I dispense with the need for even the idea of a soul, I am drawn closer than ever to the rest of the living world. How is my life different because I have decided that, just like bobcats and dolphins, I do not have a soul? What does it matter that this life I have been given on earth is the only life I have? It does not matter at all. Is not such a world sufficient? It seems so to me. Do I still want to be good? Of course I do. Do I still want to want love my neighbor, and also to love my enemy? Yes indeed, I do. The world I see outside the Roost's window this morning is the only world I need, the world in which I find my happiness, or—as the nature-poet Wordsworth said—not at all.

ECOMORPHIC URBANATURE

Ecomorphism is the antithesis of anthropomorphism. Instead of seeing myself at the center of my world, I can now help both myself, and the world around me, if I come to see my own activity—indeed, all human activity—in terms of its connectedness to nonhuman life. For centuries the poets have said, "that bird's song is sad in the same way that I am sad" or "that flower looks happy, just as I am happy." But the time has come to reconsider the tenor and the vehicle of such anthropomorphic metaphors. The vehicle is the personal subject—humans—from which the metaphor's characteristic (sadness or happiness) is taken. The tenor is the natural subject (bird or flower) to which the human characteristic is given. Poets, and other metaphor-makers, should now consider reversing this metaphoric order as often as possible in the interest of ecocentrism. No longer should ants be imagined to resemble humans: "The ant colony is just like the corporation for which I work; every ant is trying to work for the good of the whole, but individuals can often seem frustrated in their efforts to help others." The time has come to reverse this claim and point out that humans often act like ants, or birds, or even flowers, not vice versa. A bird does not build a house the way I build a house (anthropomorphism), but I now know that I can roost the way a bird roosts (ecomorphism).

My claim here is connected to David Orr's quotation—with help from Barry Lopez—in Orr's groundbreaking *Ecological Literacy*, as part of his own argument for a version of urbanature:

Ecological literacy also requires the more demanding capacity to observe nature with insight, a merger of landscape and mindscape. "The interior landscape," in Barry Lopez's words, "responds to the character and subtlety of an exterior landscape; the shape of the individual mind is affected by land as it is by genes." The quality of thought is related to the ability to relate to "where on this earth one goes, what one touches, the patterns one observes in nature—the intricate history

of one's life in the land, *even a life in the city*, where wind, the chirp
of birds, the line of a falling leaf are known." The fact that this kind
of intimate knowledge of our landscapes is rapidly disappearing can
only impoverish our mental landscapes as well…If we must live in an
increasingly urban world, let's make it one of well-designed compact
green cities that include trees, river parks, meandering greenbelts, and
urban farms where people can see, touch, and experience nature in a
variety of ways. (86, 89; italics added)

My own emphasis would replace "even a life in the city" with "especially a life in the city," since I want to emphasize that cities are where
most twenty-first century people learn their love of nature and their
desire to care for nature. The child growing up today in Manhattan,
who turns over a rock and finds a toad, is having the same experience
of nature as the suburban child who crawls through a drainage tun-
nel and finds a huge bullfrog at the exit (that was me in the 1960s),
or the rural child who lives by a creek where he finds a frog and a
toad. Orr is quoting from Lopez's *Crossing Open Ground*, the book
in which—as much as any other—Lopez writes about the human
animal as just one among the many species of animals and about
human culture as deeply intertwined with the flow of nature and
the rhythms of nature in the Southwestern United States and Alaska,
linking the cultures of humans to the nonhuman places they inhabit.
The places where human beings congregate are like the places where
animals live; that is why humans are like their nonhuman relatives,
not the other way around.

This difference between anthropomorphism and ecomorphism is
subtle but significant. Science has revealed that ant colonies are like
human communities, but equally important is the idea that human
colonies are like ant colonies. Both are adaptive responses to specific
social conditions. Likewise, butterflies do not use mimicry to dis-
guise themselves the way humans use disguises. Humans use forms of
mimicry—derived ultimately from mimicry in butterflies and other
"lower" creatures—to accomplish similar tasks. Humans gather and
store food the way squirrels do, not vice versa. Humans seek their
mates just as the rest of sexually selecting nature does, with many of
their traits in common. Humans are more like animals (they *are* animals) than animals are like humans. Humans should not look *down*
on the animal kingdom, saying, "Oh, isn't that sweet the way the
mother elephant cares for her young." Instead, humans beings need
to realize that the way humans care for their offspring derives directly

from parental behavior in the rest of the animal kingdom. Humans have inherited behavioral characteristics directly from earlier forms of life on the evolutionary tree, just as humans have inherited almost all of their physical characteristics (bilateral symmetry, oxygen-based physiology, expanded brain-case) from earlier forms that preceded them. Natural selection created mammals, creatures notable for the length and complexity of the care they give their offspring. Great apes, elephants, dogs, even mice: all are characterized by the time and the concern they lavish on their offspring. Ecomorphism reminds humans that, since they arrived on the scene millions of years after most of these creatures, it is more accurate to say, "we are like them," than it is to say, "they are like us." This is a key to my idea of "roosting"; if humans strive to live on the earth as other animals do, they will find themselves in closer connection to the forces that shape their lives, the factors that determine their destinies.

My brain at once creates the sense of what I have to fear and reconnects me to the wider world. Ecocentrism, like the related term "ecomorphism," emphasizes this need for humans to see themselves as determined by—while existing within—a world that lies beyond the boundary of the human body. The complex fact of consciousness is the condition that allows people everywhere to appreciate this truth about their surroundings. Humanity is a crucial part of every environment it inhabits. There is no absolute separation between a world outside (nature) and a world inside (the mind). Self-consciousness—as writers from Percy Shelley to Annie Dillard have reminded us—can give way to forms of unselfconsciousness that allow for fleeting moments of unification between individuals and their wider worlds. Mystics from every cultural tradition have recorded this truth. Such unselfconsciousness can also be described in terms of environmental ambience. The concept of ambience describes the unification of every element in a set of natural circumstances with the conscious mind that perceives those surroundings. In the ambient unity of self and surroundings lies one hope for a new ecocentric ecology, one version of the sort of post-Romantic ecocriticism I am advocating. As Timothy Morton—one of the architects of ecoambience—puts the problem, "Ecology may [now] be without nature. But it is not without us" (*Ecology* 205).

Progress toward this view of a link between the human and nonhuman worlds began with an emphasis on untouched nature and inviolable natural law during the Enlightenment. Romantic empathy toward animals began when Locke and Rousseau, among others, described a pristine, idealized natural state out of which all human beings emerged. Keats and Shelley then began to praise birds and beasts for their own sakes, not merely for their practical or pragmatic value to humans. By the twentieth century, such Romantic empathy merges with environmentalism, from Rachel Carson's *Silent Spring* (humans have produced chemicals that can end animal life and the life of human animals as well) to Bill McKibben's *Hope, Human and Wild* (humans have the capacity to live in harmony with their surroundings, as they do in surprising ways in Curitiba, Brazil; Kerala, India; and the Adirondacks in northern New York state). Modern "ecoempathy" has also evolved into what Carol Gilligan calls—broadly—an "ethic of care" (174). But any ethic of care also implies the need to share. Humans now need to share a world they did not create (call it "nature") with the world they have created (call it "culture"). These two worlds are really one; that is the emphasis of urbanature. From *men* with dominion over *nature*, society has evolved into a group of men *and women* who need to recognize their dependence on the whole human *and* nonhuman world around them: urbanature.

From the illusion of arbitrary control, humans have moved toward the idea of symbiosis. In the process, the biosphere (another twentieth-century idea) is now seen as a continuum of all living things and living processes. From Jaweh's monotheological rod of control, Western culture moved through Keats's anthropomorphic nightingale and Shelley's anthropocentric skylark, toward modern versions of ecomorphism, ecocentrism, and—most recently—ecofeminism. The ecofeminist ecocritic Nandita Batra has described this history as the long (and often painful) progress from dominion to empathy to symbiosis. Such symbiosis replaces dominion at the same moment that anthropocentrism gives way to ecocentrism. Batra points out the necessary progress from a masculine Romanticism, characterized by "the dialectic between the adult, male consciousness and its constructed Other" (168)—think Shelley's skylark and cloud, Keats's nightingale, and Wordsworth's daffodil—to a feminine version of Romanticism that consistently questions this duality. Such an ecofeminism offers, instead of patriarchal control over nature, a symbiosis that links human and nonhuman while subverting "the polarities of dualism," and helps to "dismantle the hegemony of man" (168). Batra's essay offers a crucial step in the movement from anthropomorphism to ecomorphism and from anthropocentrism to ecocentrism.

Blake's point-of-view in his lyric "The Fly," to choose one example of the progression described by Batra, puts the reader into an ecocentric (and ungendered) mindset by asking, to what—or to whom—do I appear to be a fly?

> Little Fly
> Thy summers play
> My thoughtless hand
> Has brush'd away.
>
> Am not I
> A fly like thee?
> Or art not thou
> A man like me? (1–8)

Such a dream of contact across the species boundary is the basis not only of all anthropomorphic thinking, but also of all ecomorphism. As almost comical as it sounds on one level—like a Monty Python skit—a fly's life does share characteristics with any human life: he respires, he eats, he finds a mate, he reproduces. More important than these shared characteristics is the subsequent metaphoric question: if a fly is *like* a human being, what might that comparison say about the human? That is Blake's question. Such species boundary-crossing is not simply a poetic metaphor, however; in the twenty-first century it is a scientific reality. All species are genetically related; they can all now be literally linked as well as metaphorically linked. I do have genetic connections to the fly that I can see on the windowsill. Humans have known about these metaphoric links at least since the time of Aesop (620–560 BCE), who said that the ant was industrious, the fox was sly, and the tortoise was patient. Now I know that such imaginative and metaphoric connections were based on literal links among creatures large and small. When science finds a cure for cancer or AIDS, it is likely that the cure will be based on the same sorts of physiological connectedness that cause vaccines to protect humans from pathogens and allow antibiotics to save us from scourges that once killed millions. Such medications work because humans have direct chemical links to countless plants and animals, links that emerge from our shared ancestors and ancestry.

The post-Romantic nature of urbanature is not the mysterious nature that earlier humans feared (wolves and thunder and winter), nor is it the pleasing nature that the Romantics taught their readers to love (nightingales and daffodils and springtime). Rather, urbanature offers a version of all nature that draws human beings closer to one another and also closer to organic, and inorganic, matter. Urbanature emphasizes concern for the whole planet, not just those parts of the planet that are up until now free from human harm. In 2008 the United Nations reported that there were twenty-two megacities with populations over ten million people each. By 2015, some of these cities will have populations of over twenty million human beings, and the conditions in many of these cities will be just those dreaded by the prescient urban planners of the 1990s and 2000s: "Unplanned and chaotic urbanization is taking a huge toll on human health and the quality of the environment, contributing to social, ecological, and economic instability in many countries" (Knickerbocker). The results of this urban population growth are as fearful as they are unpredictable. They will require serious concern on the part of those who see a connection between urban life and nature as well as those who believe that humans in the future will be able to roost on their planet without harming their surroundings. A 1970s study of a single roost of up to ten million blackbirds and starlings in Tennessee revealed that their economic impact on surrounding agricultural production was "minor." The study claims that "the strategy of reducing roosting populations with chemical sprays…needs to be reassessed" (White et al). Human beings should be able to imitate the effect of millions upon millions of roosting birds, by having an impact on their surroundings that at least does no harm. Urbanatural environments should not have to suffer just because humans live there.

In recent decades, environmentalists have targeted their primary concerns away from the urban centers of the developed world. Part of the reason for this attitude toward cities has been the understandable tendency of those in the vanguard of environmental preservation to say, "Yellowstone is safe; the Tetons are secure. We now need to identify more and more potential wilderness areas. We need to increase the acreage of the Arctic Wildlife Refuge. We need to expand the boundaries of the Everglades. What difference does it make what happens to South Central Los Angeles? Why should I, as a committed environmentalist, be concerned about the fate of the South Bronx? I am hard at work in the Everglades, saving the alligator and the tree cactus, the Everglades snail kite and the brittle thatch palm. Other people can care for the cities." Of course, these threatened wild species and spaces do need my concern, but not at the expense of the humans who can help to save these nonhuman creatures in the first place. Cities and wilderness "areas" need a new ethic that will unite upper-middle-class environmentalists with those people who first need a regular income, nourishing food, and secure places to live before they can begin to worry about peregrine falcons roosting on the residential towers of Central Park East. Once these two groups form an alliance—environmentalists and those who need healthy environments in which to live—society will be on its way toward urbanatural roosting, humans living together on the planet they share with the rest of nonhuman life.

*   *   *

The loudest sound before sunset last night was a wood thrush in the distance. Much closer and yet quieter, a pewee sang in time with the hum of the crickets. There was a hop-toad on the front stoop, a millipede under my bed, two camel crickets by the door of the porch, and a lone cicada carving tight circles in the clearing. The darkness fell fast, and the bird-song ceased suddenly, as the loud night-noises began in earnest in the hot, dry air. I saw a katydid on the rock beside me, as green as a spring leaf. His first hop carried him almost a yard down the rock, then again, and then again until he disappeared in the distance. By the time of darkness, the bug sounds in the trees were a loud and rhythmical lunacy: *jig-a-jig, jig-a-jig…jug-a-jug-jug, jig-a-jig*. There was no let up in this katydid chorus until just before sunrise. The trees were alive with sound. The whole darkness was singing. My heart was beating in time with the katydid as I spread out, without covers, on the rustic log-bed on the porch. I slept soundly and woke refreshed.

Then this evening, an even more wonderful experience occurred. The morning had dawned positively Wordsworthian, as he said, "one of those heavenly days which cannot die" ("Nutting" 2). All morning the sun and the clouds struggled for supremacy. The sky was bright; then the sky grew dark. The sky was dark; then the sky lightened again, then dark, and then light again. Turkey vultures turned slow circles above the river, all the way up the ridge into the clearing below me. A woodpecker *ham-hammered* in the distance. Two chipmunks skittered after each other in the leaf-mold beside the cabin. One chased and caught the other. They would roll in the leaves for an instant, then their roles would be reversed and the chaser would become the chased. They were not mating this late in the year. They were just having—nonanthropomorphic—fun.

Small birds hopped and bobbled in the wide stone-slab birdbath. A juvenile skink, with an iridescent and wriggling blue tail, scampered up the stones of the front stoop, flicking his tongue at gnats, scurrying erratically away from the slightest sound of rustling leaves. It dawned on me that I had not heard the sound of my own voice, or any other human voice, in three days; that is surely unusual in the twenty-first century. The afternoon turned hazy, hot and humid. The temperature pushed toward ninety-degrees in the shade on the worn thermometer by the side of the porch. A giant thunderhead rolled slowly but steadily across the valley beneath me. When the towering cloud reached the ridge behind the Roost, the rain broke in a torrent that thudded on the porch's tin roof and thumped on the shingles of the cabin for no more than twenty minutes. Suddenly, the sun broke through the western sky as fast as the massive cloudbank had arisen only moments earlier. As I stood in the rocky doorway, I could see each raindrop perfectly illuminated. They fell splattering on the rocky yard in front of me. Each shimmering, gigantic drop was lit up in rows, and then in sheets, by the blazing sun around the cabin.

Then I saw it: a rainbow had broken through these final raindrops and formed in the wet air in front of me, but it was not a rainbow in the sky; it was a rainbow arching brightly through the woods. All of its colors were clearly visible: purple and red, green and yellow gold. The brilliant colored light was all around me. It swept down from hundred-foot-tall oaks against the ridge line in the east, and it ended—yes—this rainbow literally ended, right in my doorway, right on the stone stoop that opened onto my front door. I was standing in the proverbial pot of gold. Soon the thunder thud-thudded off across the mountain into the wide green fields and hills of Virginia. Then the sky cleared quickly. Bright blue patches opened high above me. I was standing stock still and stunned. I was standing at the end of the rainbow.

6

AUGUST

The Tao that can be expressed is not the eternal Tao;
The name that can be named is not the unchanging Name.

—*Lao Tse,* Tao Te Ching

Last night I found a box turtle. I picked him up, turned him over, felt his shell top and bottom, felt the sharp claws of his hind legs scratching my wrist, looked deep into his bright red eyes, and then set him back down in the leaf-mold, watching him crawl off slowly into the darkening woods. That box turtle brought me pleasure last night, pleasure like the pleasure I felt when I picked up another such turtle—in 1960—that might have been his father or his grandfather (I do know how to sex turtles; males have redder eyes, longer and slightly flatter tails). This turtle was a male. I well remember the pleasure of picking up that other turtle four decades ago—perhaps it was even the same turtle; box turtles can live for eighty years—just as I now remember the pleasure of picking up that turtle last night. Pleasure taken from nature is often just this simple. You feel it right away.

THE LOVES OF PLANTS AND ANIMALS

What is it about this pleasure that humans take in the natural world? Why do some individuals take so much pleasure in nature? Why do others take so little? Why do almost all human beings take some level of pleasure in sunsets, flowers, chipmunks, and whale watching? Consider Walt Whitman; the pleasure he takes in his nonhuman kin is not only simple, it is also powerful:

> I think I could turn and live with animals, they are so placid and
>   self-contain'd,
> I stand and look at them long and long.
>
> They do not sweat and whine about their condition,
> They do not lie awake in the dark and weep for their sins,
> They do not make me sick discussing their duty to God,
> Not one is dissatisfied, not one is demented with the mania of
>   owning things,
> Not one kneels to another, nor to his kind that lived thousands of
>   years ago,
> Not one is respectable or unhappy over the whole earth.
> So they show their relations to me and I accept them (*Song of
>   Myself* 32)

"They show their relations to me"? Pleasure, indeed. How, in light of a possibility like Whitman's, can any human ever claim to find only a little bit of pleasure in nature. This Whitman sounds very much like Thoreau. "Demented with the mania of owning things," Whitman says; Thoreau echoes: "Superfluous wealth can buy superfluities only. Money is not required to buy one necessary of the soul" (*Walden* 221). So where do such pure versions of pleasure—nonmaterial, non-monetary pleasure—come from? Are human beings hard-wired, or genetically predisposed, to feel pleasure when confronted with their fellow creatures, or with all living things, and how might such pleasure link to my idea of urbanatural roosting?

Pleasure taken by humans in the natural world has not always existed. For much of history, nature was feared. Earthquakes and hurricanes and floods could kill; so could sharks and snakes and spiders: they still can. *Wild*-erness was originally that fearful place where the wild things lived. Such fear made a great deal of sense when nature was poorly understood; countless people got sick and died for reasons that not even the smartest Babylonian, Assyrian, Greek, or Roman doctor understood. Likewise, nature was terrifying when lions were on the edge of the encampment or wolves were literally howling outside the cabin door. Imagine a group of early humans watching a shark attack their companion while swimming in the shallows of some ancient sea. Not only the life-threatening, but also the vast and challenging aspects of nature, proved fearfully unpleasant to even the most thoughtful human beings.

In the seventeenth century, John Evelyn used the phrase "horrid prospect of the Alps" to describe the very same snow-capped peaks that most twenty-first century tourists currently describe as stunningly beautiful; Evelyn went on to note that these craggy summits looked "as if nature had here swept up all the rubbish of the Earth" (*Diary* 2: 506–07): not much natural pleasure here. Even the philosopher Immanuel Kant, as late as 1790, "asked impatiently, 'who wanted to call deformed mountain masses and the like "sublime" in the first place'" (Heringman 28). Geology, more than any other science, emphasized the nonhuman aspect of nature—and saw nature as distinct from human activity—since geological features seem so much less connected to human life or human lifetimes than lovely plants or delicate animals. The alien elements in geologic forms account for many of the most powerful Romantic encounters with the sublime fear and terror of natural "Otherness": Wordsworth on Snowdon and crossing the Simplon Pass, Shelley at the foot of Mont Blanc, and Thoreau on Katahdin all had a feeling clearly stated by Thoreau: "This was that Earth...made out of Chaos and Old Night. Here was no man's garden...Man was not to be associated with it. It was Matter, vast, terrific,—not his Mother Earth...[but] a force not bound to be kind to man" (*Maine Woods* 645). Here is proof that nature does not exist for the benefit of humankind and that "nature" is often what humans make of it in their minds. The domestic naturalist of Walden Pond is suddenly terrified by a rocky nature that has nothing to do with human life or human values; this mountain-top world is literally "inhuman."

So even the sense of nature as pleasing to the human senses is culturally created and historically conditioned. Such pleasurable responses in the modern world date primarily from the Romantic era in Europe and America. Indeed, the Romantic idea of nature is often based on pleasure, pleasure in the natural world and pleasure ascribed to or derived from the natural world by humans and other sentient beings. Six decades before Charles Darwin showed human beings that they were connected to every living thing on the planet, his grandfather Erasmus had said, "our intellectual sympathies [rest] with [...] the miseries, or with the joys, of our fellow creatures" (*Zoonomia* 1: 255). Or, as Percy Shelley put it as sweepingly several decades later: "I wish no living thing to suffer pain" (*Prometheus Unbound* 1.305). So, when Wordsworth notes his faith that "every flower / Enjoys the air it breathes" ("Lines") or when Keats describes an unseen nightingale pouring forth its "soul abroad / In such an ecstasy" ("Ode to a Nightingale"), a modern reader might think that these lyrical claims are poetic exaggerations, rhetorically suspect forms of anthropomorphism, overly sentimental and poetically overblown. Likewise, when Wordsworth's heart fills "with pleasure" at the sight of daffodils and

Blake says "How do you know but ev'ry Bird that cuts the airy way, /
Is an immense world of delight" ("Marriage of Heaven and Hell"),
the poet seems to be offering too much credit to the natural world
for a strictly human emotion. The idea of "animate nature," however,
included a belief that all living things—and perhaps even nonliving
things—are connected by the ability to please or to be pleased.

Pleasure in the natural world is also a concept that links Romantic
poetry to Romantic science in significant ways. Pleasure located in
the nonhuman world, and pleasure taken by humans in the natural world, are concepts that comingle in a whole range of Romantic
metaphors and writings: anthropocentric, ecocentric, and otherwise.
In fact, the anthropocentrism of much eighteenth- and early nineteenth-century scientific and poetic thinking turns out to be much
more securely centered on the nonhuman world than it first appears.
Discussions of plant and animal "pleasure" in the works of Erasmus
Darwin, and Georges Louis Leclerc, Comte de Buffon—often by way
of Oliver Goldsmith, who introduced many of Buffon's ideas to a
British audience—can be linked directly to the idea of "pleasure"
in poems by Wordsworth, Coleridge, Shelley, and Keats. This link
between the poetic and the scientific in Romantic natural history also
reveals direct links to the twenty-first century's sense of the interrelatedness of human and nonhuman nature.

Where does all of this Romantic talk about the heart filling with
pleasure like dancing daffodils, or a bird described as a "world of
delight," come from? It comes, to cite just one important source,
from an otherwise hard-nosed medical doctor and experimental scientist: Erasmus Darwin. Here is Darwin, in one of his characteristic
(and controversial) descriptions of the erotic love-life of plants:

> Hence on green leaves the sexual Pleasures dwell,
> And Loves and Beauties crowd the blossom's bell;
> The wakeful Anther in his silken bed
> O'er the pleased Stigma bows his waxen head;
> With meeting lips and mingling smiles they sup
> Ambrosial dew-drops from the nectar'd cup;
> Or buoy'd in air the plumy Lover springs,
> And seeks his panting bride on Hymen-wings. (*Temple* 2.263–70)

Darwin was criticized, as his predecessor Linnaeus had been, for his
tendency to sexualize the life of plants. "Linnaeus's [sexual system
of classification] amused some of his contemporaries but scandalized
others [...] 'To tell you that nothing could equal the gross prurience

of Linnaeus's mind is perfectly needless,' wrote the Rev. Samuel Goodenough, late Bishop of Carlisle, to that devoted Linnaean scholar J. E. Smith in January 1808: 'A literal translation of the first principles of Linnaean botany is enough to shock female modesty'" (Stearn 248). Sten Lindroth is more complimentary of Linnaeus: "How close he stands to traditional wedding poetry in the admired opening to the dissertation on the nuptials of flowers [...] The same applies to the actual message of the work, the description of copulation, the nuptials of flowers in matchless bridal beds. With his hot sensuousness the young Linnaeus was as though obsessed with love, the mysterious drive that kept all living things in motion" (10). How else to describe the life force but as the sex drive?

For Darwin, erotic descriptions of plant love (and plant lust) were analogues for human sexuality as well as accurate descriptions of the way flowers actually lived and reproduced. Almost all of Darwin's claims about plant sexuality were based on his own direct observations. He expanded his poetic rhapsodies on the sex life of plants with prose footnotes that ascribe a wide range of intention and emotion to the plant kingdom: "The vegetable passion of love is agreeably seen in the flower of the parnassia, in which the males alternately approach and recede from the female; and in the flower of nigella, or devil in the bush, in which the tall females bend down to their dwarf husbands. But I was this morning surprised to observe [...] the manifest adultery of several females of the plant Collinsonia, who had bent themselves into contact with the males of other flowers of the same plant in their vicinity, neglectful of their own" (*Botanic* 197n.). Claims such as these about plant life consistently suggest that willfulness, intention, and pleasure all extend—albeit in somewhat diminished forms—from humans to animals to plants, and perhaps even lower on the Great Chain of Being.

More important than Darwin's descriptions of the sex life of plants are his views, clearly summarized in the poetry and footnotes of *The Temple of Nature* (1803), about natural pleasure. In this work, Darwin describes pleasure in any part of animate creation as an aspect of pleasure extending through the whole of the terrestrial biosphere: "From the innumerable births of the larger insects, and the spontaneous productions of the microscopic ones, every part of organic matter from the recrements [remains] of dead vegetable or animal bodies, on or near the surface of the earth, becomes again presently re-animated; which by increasing the number and quantity of living organisms, though many of them exist but for a short time, adds to the sum total of terrestrial happiness" (160n.). Pleasure in the entire biotic realm is increased not only by the prolific reproduction of "insects" (the word means "small creatures" to Darwin) and microscopic organisms but also by the death and organic regeneration of larger creatures: "The sum total of the happiness of organized nature is probably increased rather than diminished, when one large old animals dies, and is converted into many thousand young ones; which are produced or supported with their numerous progeny by the same organic matter" (*Temple* 162n.). Reanimation, for Darwin, means simply the return of motion and sensation to inorganic elements that came back to life after having decayed out of the bodies of other living things. Mary Shelley's fearful reanimate—Victor Frankenstein's nameless monster—is not far off.

Darwin also notes that the Pythagorean belief in the transmigration of souls derives merely from the organic and "perpetual transmigration of matter from one body to another, of all vegetables and animals, during their lives, as well as after their deaths" (163n.). This chemical and organic movement of elements through the bodies of living creatures leads, over eons, to a unified and complete "system of morality and benevolence, as all creatures thus became related to each other" (164n.), at least in terms of the matter that composes them. What Darwin calls the "felicity of organic life," is a function of the "happiness and misery of [all] organic beings"; this felicity, he says, depends ultimately, on "the actions of the organs of sense" and on "the fibres which perform locomotion" (165n.). Every living thing, Darwin concludes, is subject to "immediate sources" of "pains and pleasures," the encouragement or avoidance of which might "increase the sum total of organic happiness" (166n.). Pain and pleasure, he goes on to argue, are entirely a function of the expansion and contraction of nerve and muscle, fibers of sensation, organic elements which exist in all living things, albeit in diminished forms and intensities as one moves from more complex to less complex creatures. All emotional responses—pleasure, pain, happiness, and sadness—are thus based entirely on the actions of material parts that can be found in each life form. This version of philosophic materialism accounts for all emotions and feelings without any need for an immaterial part, such as a soul.

Finally, and perhaps most dramatically, Darwin's understanding of geology leads him to conclude that the planet earth itself is a record of the pleasures of earlier ages of animate beings: "Not only the vast calcerous provinces [...] and also whatever rests upon them [...] clay, marl, sand, and coal [...] gave the pleasure of life to the animals and vegetables, which formed them; and thus constitute monuments of the past happiness of these organized beings. But as those remains of former life are not again totally decomposed [...] they supply more copious food to the successions of new animal or vegetable beings on their surface [...] and hence the quantity or number of organized bodies, and their improvement in size, as well as their happiness, has been continually increasing, along with the solid parts of the globe" (*Temple* 166n.). More dry land over eons, more living things century upon century, more happiness produced from millennium to millennium. At this point, Darwin breaks down the boundary between the organic and the inorganic as part of his wider economy of nature, what scientists would now call his "ecology." Material processes, compounds, and elements—which Darwin always describes in fundamentally chemical terms (clay, sand, coal, heat, oxygen, hydrogen, carbon, phosphorus)—compose, decompose, and recompose, first into inorganic, then into organic, and finally into animate creatures, including human beings.

Darwin similarly argues that the plant and animal kingdoms are connected by the possibility of sensation. In *Zoonomia*, he describes "Vegetable Animation": "The fibres of the vegetable world, as well as those of the animal, are excitable into a variety of motions by irritations of external objects. This appears particularly in the mimosa or sensitive plant, whose leaves contract on the slightest injury" (1: 101). Darwin discusses such "sensitive" plants at great length. He notes that "many vegetables, during the night, do not seem to respire, but to sleep like the dormant animals and insects in winter. This appears from the mimosa and many other plants closing the upper sides of their leaves together in their sleep" (*Botanic*, "Economy of Vegetation" 205n.). He also classifies the mimosa in terms of its polygamous behavior: "Mimosa. The sensitive plant. Of the class Polygamy, one house. Naturalists have not explained the immediate cause of the collapsing of the sensitive plant" (*Botanic*, "Loves of the Plants" 32n.). He also comments on a recent plant "lately brought over from the marshes of America" that is even more remarkable: "In the *Dionaea muscipula* there is a still more wonderful contrivance to prevent the depredation of insects: The leaves are armed with long teeth, like the antennae of insects, and lie spread upon the ground round the stem; and are so irritable, that when the insect creeps upon them, they fold up, and crush or pierce it to death" (*Botanic* 15n.–16n.). So the Venus fly-trap suddenly leaps out of the system of traditional cosmic order by preying on creatures that are supposed to be found "above" it on the Great Chain of Being. The once-fixed chain of being is becoming a much more organic and dynamic tree, or a web.

But all of the "fibres" responsible for such sensation are also related to pleasure: "When pleasure or pain affect the animal system, many of its motions both muscular and sensual are brought into action [...] The general tendency of these motions is to arrest [i.e., stabilize] and to possess the pleasure, or to dislodge or avoid the pain" (*Zoonomia* 1: 45). The conclusion Darwin draws is obvious: "The individuals of the vegetable world may be considered as inferior or less perfect animals" (1: 102). This belief that sensation might spread throughout all of animate creation was widely discussed in Europe and America throughout the eighteenth century by natural scientists, natural theologians, and poets, among others. As Christoph Irmscher has written, this was an era "that ascribed sensitivity, even souls, to plants" (31). But as Erasmus Darwin suggested, the point was not simply that plants might have souls, but that what we call "souls" might turn out to be nothing more than complex combinations of material (i.e., muscular, nervous, electrochemical) motions: no soul but one that could be described in material, mechanical terms. The naturalist John Bartram (father of William Bartram), writing to Benjamin Rush, noted that there was much to be learned about "sensation" in plants, even though many animals were already known to be "endowed with most of our [that is, human] faculties & pashions [*sic*] & ... intellect" (*Correspondence* 690). Bartram's attribution of passion and intellect to animals indicates that such a view was widespread by the late eighteenth century.

Buffon likewise describes many of the animals he catalogs in terms of human passions and feeling. Buffon's marmot "delights in the regions of ice and snow" (*System* 121). His elephant is "susceptible of gratitude, and capable of strong attachment" (152) and "loves the society of his equals" (153). If "vindictive," the pachyderm "is no less grateful" (159). Numerous writers were likewise willing to extend pleasure into the realm of lower life forms. A 1792 compilation by several natural historians of insects includes comments such as the following: each insect, no matter how small or seemingly insignificant, is "adapted for procuring its particular pleasures" (*Insects* 2); indeed, every insect "was formed for itself, and each allowed to seize as great a quantity of happiness from the universal stock [...] each was formed to make the happiness of each" (6). "The butterfly, to enjoy life, needs no other food but the dews of heaven" (75) and "it is impossible to express the fond attachment which the working ants shew to their rising progeny" (125). Animals, of course, had been described anthropomorphically in relation to human capacities and emotional response since ancient times: loyal dogs, wise owls, and busy bees were all staple figures in beast fables from many cultures. What was new by 1790 was the sense that these were not just rhetorical comparisons of behavior between human and animal realms; rather, such observationally supported comparisons reflected a deeper—and organic—unity of all living things. Ecomorphism was replacing anthropomorphism.

Eighteenth-century talk about emotion and sensation in "lower" life forms was related to an underlying philosophical monism, well articulated by Johann Wolfgang von Goethe. In "The Experiment as Mediator between Subject and Object" (1792), Goethe offers a holistic critique of "living Nature" that was designed to counter the fragmentary quality of empirical science: "Nothing happens in living Nature that does not bear some relation to the whole. The empirical evidence may seem quite isolated, we may view our experiments as mere isolated facts, but this is not to say that they are, in fact, isolated. The question is: how can we find the connection between these phenomena, these events" (*Science* 80). Likewise, Goethe is willing to include "joy and pain" among categories that are applicable to any organism: "Basic characteristics of an individual organism: . . . as living things tend to appear under a thousand conditions . . . Genesis and decay, creation and destruction, birth and death, joy and pain, all are interwoven with equal effect and weight; thus even the most isolated event always presents itself as an image and metaphor for the most universal" (52). "Joy and pain" are among the categories applicable to any living "organism." So, while observational science is suggesting that expansion, contraction, attraction, and repulsion of tiny material parts are physical properties of all living (and perhaps nonliving) things, the metaphysics of Romantic science argues that characteristics found in one part of nature are likely to exist throughout the entire natural system, admittedly in differing and modified—reduced or expanded—forms. A dog's pain is not my pain, but it is pain nonetheless. A skylark's pleasure is not Shelley's pleasure, but it is pleasure just the same. This is no longer anthropomorphism but rather a recognition of likeness across the species boundary.

ROMANTIC POETRY AND THE PLEASURES OF NATURE

Just like the natural history of the Romantic era, its poetry revealed a belief in the pervasiveness of natural pleasure. Percy Shelley's quintessential skylark sings consistently with "shrill delight" (20), while his sensitive plant (*Mimosa*) once "trembled and panted with bliss" (9). Shelley's poem on the sensitive plant derives directly from Erasmus

Darwin's reflections on the tropical *Mimosa pudica* as a curious bridge between the plant and animal kingdoms. Shelley goes beyond mere ascription of sensation to the plant. In fact, he provides a direct analogy between this reactive plant and certain human emotions and perceptions. Not surprisingly, his real subject in this poem—ostensibly about a plant—is actually a "sensitive" poet, one not unlike the sensitive poet Shelley, himself. This affinity of plants for other plants, and this image of plants as sharing in forms of attraction that exist throughout the material universe, reaches its apotheosis in the poem's most Shelleyan lines. These mimosa flowers,

> Shone smiling to Heaven, and every one
> Shared joy in the light of the gentle sun;
>
> For each one was interpenetrated
> With the light and the odour its neighbour shed,
> Like young lovers whom youth and love make dear,
> Wrapped and filled by their mutual atmosphere. (*Shelley* 64–69)

This idea, that aspects of the rest of nature might be analogous to human nature, is as old as poetry itself. What is new in a poet like Shelley is the sense that an emotion like pleasure might organically link human beings with the nonhuman world.

Consider, from this same perspective, "The Cloud" (1820), Shelley's paean to a natural entity whose nourishing waters offer sustenance for "thirsting flowers" and provide shade for delicate leaves in their "noonday dreams" (lines 1, 4). In a powerful proto-ecological vision of the hydrological cycle—"I pass through the pores of the oceans and shores; / I change, but I cannot die" (74–75)—Shelley elaborates electrical attraction between the ground and the cloud, only recently described by Benjamin Franklin and by Shelley's own science teacher Adam Walker (from Syon House Academy and Eton), as a kind of "love" between earth and sky. Shelley also says that the "moist Earth" is "laughing below" (72) while the cloud brings various forms of pleasure to each part of this natural cycle. So the science of meteorology offers Shelley the precise facts he needs to make "love" between earth and sky a version of the force of attraction that draws lightning to earth. Science now knows that the bolt is actually drawn from ground to sky, but the force of attraction remains the same for Shelley, and for science.

Even a satiric and imaginative flight of fancy like Shelley's "Witch of Atlas" is shot through with accurate details drawn from the natural science of his time and linked to a direct "sympathy" between natural and human realms: "Vipers kill, though dead" (2), "a young kitten" may "leap and play as grown cats do, / Till its claws come" (6–7). Wordsworth, in a famous passage from *The Prelude*, links a similarly scientific form of observation to a pleasure that is essential to the definition of the "poetic." Wordsworth most often sees this link in much more psychological terms than Shelley: "To unorganic natures I transferred / My own enjoyments, or, the power of truth / Coming in revelation, I conversed / With things that really are" (1805 2.410–13). Wordsworth sees this interaction as more than a merely symbolic representation of his inner states in the outer world. Rather, he links feelings of pleasure in himself directly to emotions he ascribes to the rest of the material world: "From Nature and her overflowing soul / I had received so much that all my thoughts / Were steeped in feeling" (2.416–18). The grammar in the conclusion is undeniable: "I at this time / Saw blessings spread around me like a sea" (2.413–14). The editors of *The Prelude* say that Wordsworth here perceives "the existence of a shared life-force" (86). I would only add that these "blessings" are shared and shared *alike* by the poet and by *all* of nature. As a result, this is not just a thin-gruel, watered down, Wordsworthian pantheism: his 1805 description of the unity of natural process owes as much to the "hard" natural science of his era as it does to his own emerging eschatology:

> I felt the sentiment of being spread
> O'er all that moves, and all that seemeth still, [...]
> O'er all that leaps, and runs, and shouts, and sings,
> Or beats the gladsome air, o'er all that glides
> Beneath the wave, yea, in the wave itself
>   [...] in all things
> I saw one life, and felt that it was joy (2.420–21, 425–27, 429–30)

The passage reflects the natural science of Wordsworth's time while also connecting his emotional—and poetic—powers to similar powers in plants and animals (and even the "waves") around him. His daffodils are perhaps the most famous example of this recurrent tendency: "A Poet could not but be gay / In such a laughing company" (9–10), another image which leads directly to more feeling, "And then my heart with pleasure fills, / And dances with the Daffodils" (17–18). Whatever the positives and negatives in nature, the Wordsworthian life force is "joy" (*Prelude* 2.30).

A rarely discussed manuscript fragment from 1798 reveals just how far Wordsworth is willing to go to link his own sentiments to the natural science of his time, a science that often associates animate and inanimate objects into a naturalistic unity:

> There is an active principle alive in all things;
> In all things, in all natures, in the flowers
> And in the trees, in every pebbly stone
> That paves the brooks, the stationary rocks,
> The moving waters and the invisible air.
> All beings have their properties which spread
> Beyond themselves, a power by which they make
> Some other being conscious of their life. (*Wordsworth* 676)

In this attempt to describe one source of consciousness itself, Wordsworth imagines an "active principle," yet another version of the life force, that exists in rocks, in water, and in air. This property, rather like the Buddhist idea of varying levels of consciousness in all objects (animate or inanimate), spreads beyond the border of each entity (the skin of a human, the bark of a tree, the surface of a rock) in order to allow other objects or organisms to know that each other "thing" exists. The passage confirms "unity in multeity"; the smaller things are always part of one big "thing."

Coleridge well understands this same connection between pleasure within the self and pleasure drawn from the external world, although he describes the link more dispassionately, and more ambiguously, than Wordsworth. We might call Coleridge's version of this process "transference": that is, he transfers his own emotions onto nature, usually for complex psychological reasons. Here is Coleridge's clearest example: "A child scolding a flower in the words in which he had been himself scolded and whipped, is poetry,—passion past with pleasure" (*Anima Poetae* 8). The child transfers his enjoyments, or his miseries, onto objects of nature that surround him: flowers, birds, trees. The process is as simple as the simplest of childish experiences: "the child collecting shells and pebbles on the sea-shore or lake-side, and carrying each with a fresh shout of delight and admiration to the mother's apron, who smiles and assents to each. 'This is pretty!' 'Is that not a nice one?'...Such are our first discoveries both in science and philosophy" (*Anima Poetae* 250). I would add poetry to Coleridge's list of adult activities spurred to life by recollected pleasures of childhood experience in nature. Once the child's pleasure is echoed in the pleasure of the mother, then the value of the experience is confirmed by another person; at that moment a bit of science, or philosophy (or poetry) is born. Subsequent lyrical naturalists—Aldo Leopold, Lewis Thomas, Stephen Jay Gould, and Edward O. Wilson—all report versions of such childhood experiences in their own accounts of biophilia, Wilson's word for our innate—but experientially reinforced—love of living things. Coleridge's earlier phrase "passion past with pleasure" beautifully echoes Wordsworth's well-known description of the origin of poetry as "emotion recollected in tranquillity" almost directly: "the emotion is contemplated till by a species of reaction the tranquillity disappears, and an emotion, kindred to that which was before the subject of contemplation, is gradually produced, and does itself actually exist in the mind" (*Wordsworth* 611). My first emotional response to the natural object is reinforced—by the voice of the mother or the power of recollection—until the original pleasure returns to my mind.

Finally, consider the naturalistic emotions of Keats. Keats's grasshopper, in "On the Grasshopper and Cricket," is as full of the pleasures of life as any creature that Buffon or Erasmus Darwin might imagine: "he takes the lead / In summer luxury, he has never done / With his delights; for when tired out with fun / He rests at ease beneath some pleasant weed" (*Keats* 5–8). Likewise, Keats's hummingbird from "Sleep and Poetry" is a small bundle of similar satisfaction: "What is more soothing than the pretty hummer / That stays one moment in an open flower, / And buzzes cheerily from bower to bower?" (2–4). These anthropomorphic organic beings, however, are not merely hyperbolic flights of imaginative or lyrical fancy. This is Keats describing the natural world as he has experienced it. My suggestion is born out by a reference in Miriam Allott's note on the "choir" of "small gnats" mourning in "To Autumn": "Then in a wailful choir the small gnats mourn / Among the river sallows, borne aloft / Or sinking as the light wind lives or dies" (27–29). The lines echo, almost word for word, the 1817 natural history written by the greatest nineteenth-century British entomologists, William Kirby and William Spence: "tribes of *Tipulidae* (usually, but improperly called gnats) assemble [...] and form themselves into choirs, that alternately rise and fall [...] These little creatures may be seen at all seasons, amusing themselves with their choral dances" (*Keats* 653n.).

The naturalistic rigor of Keats's approach in such examples is confirmed by the opening of his nightingale poem, perhaps his most famous "nature" ode, when a pleasure so sweet as to be painful derives from another organic being (a bird) and nevertheless echoes the unity of all life, human and otherwise, past and present. The speaker's heart literally aches. He is at once drowsy and numb. He feels drunk on an emotion as powerful as that produced by a natural intoxicant (hemlock: the herb that killed Socrates, not the North American evergreen of the same name). We should think back at this point to Erasmus Darwin, who describes a chemical affinity between human beings and the opium poppy—"dull opiate" (3)—that can transport any person out of ordinary sensory pleasures into pleasures of a different, but no less powerful, kind (*Botanic* 57n.). How can plants produce such powerful narcotic (and emotional) effects unless there is some organic sympathy—Darwin calls it a chemical "affinity"—between human bodies and these plants. Science now knows that Darwin was right; molecules from the opium literally bond to receptors in the human nervous system and brain to produce effects that soothe pain, produce euphoria, and can lead to psychological, or chemical, addiction. All human beings are made of the same stuff as the flowers.

Crucial to this poem's power is the fact that Keats was not in any rustic wilderness when he wrote this immortal nature poem. He was warbling his woodnotes wild in the back garden of a house called Wentworth Place in the middle of a suburban neighborhood, in a street now known as Keats Grove (John Street in Keats's day), on the southern side of Hampstead Heath. The poem was penned just about a mile from Abbey Road, two miles from the Marble Arch at Hyde Park, on the outskirts of the largest conurbation on the planet in 1819. Keats's house and grounds were a long way from wild nature, even in the early nineteenth century. Wentworth Place was not surrounded by sprawling urbanity at the time Keats lived there, as it is today, yet "Ode to a Nightingale" is still a suburban nature poem if ever there was one.

Here on the southern edge of Hampstead Heath, Keats is happy in an almost excruciating way—"too happy in thine happiness" (6)—but this is a pleasure that is ordinary for this bird. The bird is simply singing the bird's song. The poet, by contrast is literally astonished, stopped in his tracks, struck dumb until he recovers himself sufficiently to write a poem that tries, in some sense, to copy the singing of the bird, or, as I noted earlier, at least to convey the emotion produced by the bird's singing to his readers. This bird's "happy lot" makes the poet's lot in life somehow diminished. What would an ordinary human give to sing with such "full-throated ease" (10). Having heard this one bird singing, human mortality seems like much less of a problem to the observant poet. There is nothing sentimental here, nothing overstated or hyperbolic. From such a purely observational, naturalistic perspective, there is also no death-wish in the poem: "Now more than ever seems it rich to die" (55); rather, the poet's final claim is a simple one. Having heard such a song, and having felt organically connected to such a fellow creature, death seems like much less of a curse. Human mortality now feels like part of something much greater, even if the greater something is "merely" organic and material, like a bird. I have lived to hear this song, the poet says; now it is all right if I die. The bird's song dies away as the poet's voice will soon die away, literally; Keats would lie dead of tuberculosis in Rome within a year of the publication of this poem.

Organic life expressed through song—bird's or poet's—is the one thing that most clearly distinguishes both this bird and this poet from the "Cold pastoral" aesthetic image of Keats's equally memorable Grecian urn. The urn is beautiful and long-lasting, but it will never be alive. Keats's living human happiness, the pleasure taken emotionally from one nightingale, recalls the fact that science can be linked to pleasure in a way that connects directly to the writing of poetry. John Herschel, the nineteenth-century astronomer, described the "great sources of delight" that might be derived from the study of natural sciences (Richardson, *Emerson* 123). Likewise, Goldsmith justified his own "popularizing" version of natural history—first published in 1774 and running to over twenty editions during the nineteenth century—in terms of its ability to provide pleasure:

> Natural History, considered in its utmost extent, comprehends two objects. First, that of discovering, ascertaining, and naming, all the various productions of Nature. Secondly, that of describing the properties, manners, and relations, which they bear to us, and to each other. The first, which is the most difficult part of this science, is systematical, dry, mechanical, and incomplete. The second is more amusing, exhibits new pictures to the imagination, and improves our relish for existence, by widening the prospect of nature around us. Both, however, are necessary to those who would understand this pleasing science in its utmost extent [...] From seeing and observing the thing itself, he is most naturally led to speculate on its uses, its delights, or its inconveniences. (1. iii)

So science is pleasing to the observer and to the participant. Nature possesses its own delights, and the elements of nature can provide delight to the natural scientist and his readers. Even the often staid and somber Wordsworth comments on this emotional connection between poetry and science: the poet "considers man and nature as essentially adapted to each other, and the mind of man as naturally the mirror of the fairest and most interesting qualities of nature.…The knowledge both of the Poet and the Man of Science is pleasure;…Poetry is the breath and finer spirit of all knowledge; it is the impassioned expression which is in the countenance of all Science" ("Preface," *Wordsworth* 606). Take a little bit of science, add a bit of "impassioned expression": the result? Poetry.

The pleasure human beings take in metaphor derives from just such observations of likeness. I see that my love is like a red, red rose, and that sense of similarity gives me pleasure. I see that a lobster is like a spider but not like a jellyfish. I see that a lion is more like a lamb than like a lammergeyer (a seabird). In each case, the perception of similarity leads me to be interested in, or attracted by, the objects I am observing. Pleasure results when I realize that two apparently dissimilar things are much more closely connected than I have hitherto realized. Of course, the element of dissimilarity—similarity in dissimilarity, Coleridge called it—also produces pleasure. A new object appears before me. I have never seen anything quite like it before, but now I need a way to explain it, to make sense of it. The unusual is linked to the usual in my mind. The unknown has passed into the realm of the known. The result might be science: look, this strange new lobster reminds me of a spider; I shall now describe this lobster anatomically and physiologically, and I shall also study its life cycle. Or, if not science, the result might be poetry: oh, look there, that moon dim glimmering behind the window-pane reminds me of a long ago night from my childhood. I think I will write a poem: "The Frost performs its secret ministry, / Unhelp'd by any wind. The owlet's cry / Came loud—and hark, again! loud as before" (*Coleridge*, "Frost at Midnight" 1–3). I see the moon, sense a connection, recall a memory, and then—suddenly!—a new poem.

Let me end with Erasmus Darwin, the grandfather of the man who would put all this talk about pleasure to rest for a century or so, but only until current thinkers (Steven Pinker, George Lakoff, and Mark Turner) helped science to realize that pleasure, like love, might be an emotion forged in material brains by organic molecules, not a divine process produced by spiritual "minds" and immortal "souls." Here is Erasmus Darwin linking every human being emotionally to ants [which he calls "emmets"] and worms:

> With ceaseless change, how restless atoms pass
> From life to life, a transmigrating mass;
> How the same organs, which to day compose
> The poisonous henbane, or the fragrant rose,
> May with to morrow's sun new forms compile,
> Frown in the Hero, in the Beauty smile.

Whence drew the enlighten'd Sage the moral plan,
[That] man should ever be the friend of man;
Should eye with tenderness all living forms,
His brother-emmets [ants], and his sister-worms. (*Temple* 4.419–28)

"Eye with tenderness all living forms": that is the goal. A world full of animate creatures described in terms of their ability to feel pleasure or bestow pleasure on other parts of nature. A world of living things bound together by forces that act and react on all such creatures in similar ways. A biological world shot through with the possibility of pleasing or being pleased, all creatures at once interrelated and interdependent: not such a bad idea after all.

FALL

—AUTUMNAL ROOSTING—

URBANATURE

THE TEMPLE OF NATURE.

Pub.ᵈ Feb.ʸ 1ᵗᵈ 1803 by J. Johnson, London.

Unveiling the Secrets of Nature. The frontispiece to Erasmus Darwin's *Temple of Nature.* The muse of poetry pulls aside a curtain to reveal the many-breasted Artemis of Ephesus, goddess of wild nature. Anthropologists now believe that these were bull's testicles rather than breasts, signaling the singular fertility of the goddess of wild nature. Drawn by Henry Fuseli. (London: Joseph Johnson, 1803).

7

SEPTEMBER

The happiness of solitude is not found in retreats. It may be had even in busy centres. Happiness is not to be sought in solitude or in busy centres. It is in the Self.

—*Sri Ramana Maharshi*

There was a full-grown black bear on the move by the cabin this month. I did not see him, but my only neighbor did, the first bear ever reported in these woods, at least since my parents began coming to this mountain after World War II, in the late 1940s. This bear lumbered up the rock-strewn hill below the cabin, clambered onto the wide, flat rocks to the left of the porch, stood up on his hind legs to smell the downwind breeze, and then made a slow beeline toward the ridge, as though he knew where he was going, as though he had passed this way many times before. I now think of this great bear often, even though I have not yet seen him, heading off up the mountain to find the cave or hollow in which he will curl up and sleep soundly for the duration of winter.

This afternoon I saw no bear, but I did watch an epic cicada-killer battle over the body of a single yellow-jacket. Cicada killers are among the largest wasps in North America, members of the order *Hymenoptera*, of the genus known as solitary wasps and a species name that means "showy": *Sphecius speciosus*. They do not build a communal nest. They do not swarm together. Instead, they live in their burrows alone, for reasons that are as unsettling as they are remarkable. This afternoon I watched as one cicada killer, over an inch-and-a-half long, grabbed an unsuspecting yellow-jacket right out of the hot dry air in front of me. No sooner had this waspish monster grabbed her prey than a second cicada-killer appeared out of the bushes and buzzed into the clearing, dropping down like a yellow-rocket on the first assailant and her hapless prey. The two gigantic wasps rolled together through the air, with the yellow-jacket still between them, still struggling, still alive. All three combatants fell to the ground in a clump of waspish legs and bodies, not three feet from the spot where I stood transfixed. Then they rolled and rolled in the dust like a manic ball of waspness for at least five seconds, until one of the wasps was victorious and the other flew off into the pale sky above me.

I still do not know if the first assailant or the second assailant won, but the winner stumbled in the dry grass for just a moment, and then she grabbed her yellow-jacket prey tightly in her forelegs and regained her hind footing. She flew a few feet to the nearest branch of sassafras and grabbed on tightly as I stood by, still staring at this drama in stunned silence. She turned the yellow-jacket over and over again with her spindly segmented legs, holding on tight, stinging and paralyzing her prey again and again with a thick stinger full of venom. A wasp stinging a wasp: "go figure," as my daughters might say. The yellow-jacket quickly stopped its frantic struggle (paralyzed, not dead), and the cicada killer clung onto the thin sassafras branch by her two back legs, grabbing the now-rigid prey tightly in her four front legs. Finally she flew off in a straight line just beside my head, off to her burrow in the thick woods beyond me. If she had any idea that a six-foot-four-inch tall human giant was watching this heroic battle with rapt interest, she never let on, at least not to me.

Once the female cicada-killer gets to her burrow, she drags the yellow-jacket's body deep into a long tube she has already dug in the ground, where the new victim joins the bodies of a long stack of already paralyzed prey: mostly cicadas, but also other wasps, bumblebees, and large insects of various kinds. The cicada-killer fills her burrow, which can sometimes be up to a foot deep in the hard mountain soil, until she is ready to lay her annual brood of eggs. She then lays them on top of this food supply. When these eggs hatch several weeks later, the otherwise helpless young will have plenty of nutrition provided for them by the preserved bodies of the hapless—living, but still paralyzed—victims of their industrious mother. These young cicada-killers literally eat the living bodies of their mother's victims, nourishing themselves on that yellow jacket I saw being captured today. Within only a week of hatching and gorging, the cicada-killer larvae will be full-grown, at which point they will weave loose-fitting cocoons in which they mature. The developing brood of larva then live on in the deep burrow, with the desiccated bodies of this yellow-jacket and the mother's other victims, until the entire brood wakes up next summer and crawls from the ground. When they hatch, each one is full-grown, each one now a ruthless new cicada killer, ready to fly off and start killing, just as their mother killed before them.

FROM NATURAL PLEASURE TO NATURAL PAIN

Having considered the link between pleasure in the human world and the possibilities of pleasure in the nonhuman world, a related problem for all post-Darwinian naturalists is that such pleasures are always matched by a parallel set of pains. Here is how Alfred, Lord Tennyson saw the issue in 1850, nine years before Darwin published *On the Origin of Species*:

> Are God and Nature then at strife,
>   That Nature lends such evil dreams?
>   So careful of the type she seems,
> So careless of the single life;
>
> That I, considering everywhere
>   Her secret meaning in her deeds,
>   And finding that of fifty seeds
> She often brings but one to bear (*RNH, In Memoriam* 54.41–48)

Tennyson has done his scientific homework here, as his note to this second stanza reveals: " 'fifty' should be 'myriad' " (Bradley 247) he wrote, revealing that he knows all about nature's ruthless waste and profligate expenditures. No doubt it would be more accurate, if somewhat less poetic, to say that for the thousands upon thousands of seeds that fall to the ground—think of maple-tree whirly copter seeds every spring—only two or three make it to become full-fledged, spreading maple trees, able to reproduce and send out countless new seeds of their own. Just like Darwinian codfish: millions of eggs are required to produce just a few dozen reproductive adults. Tennyson continues,

> "So careful of the type?" but no.
>   From scarped cliff and quarried stone
>   She cries, "a thousand types are gone:
> I care for nothing, all shall go." (55.57–60)

It is now clear how right Tennyson's intuition was in the mid-nineteenth century. Of all the species produced by the evolutionary process over countless millennia, the hundreds of thousands of species alive today probably represent less than a tiny fragment of one percent of the total number of species that have ever existed. Nature is "careless" of everything, as careless of the type (species) as she is of the "single life." Just as all individuals will "go," so all species will "go."

Tennyson ratchets up his rhetoric until he produces a powerful phrase that has become a byword for the modern world:

> Who trusted God was love indeed
>   And love Creation's final law—
>   Tho' Nature, red in tooth and claw
> With ravine, shriek'd against his creed— (55.69–72)

Red in tooth and claw, indeed. Picture Blake's "tyger," his slathering jaws dripping with the blood of the helpless prey he has just slaughtered, life's juices and gore draining away from the kill, lapped up by the ravenous big cat. But that tiger, remember, is simply procuring food for its ever-so-cute tiger babies. What Tennyson wants me to consider in his famous phrase ("tooth and claw") are the long fangs and claws of a mother saber-toothed tiger, standing over the limp body of the Cro-Magnon man she has just killed, not the tiny red teeth of my little house-kitty poised over the blood-soaked body of the baby robin she has just slaughtered in the backyard. This is the story for Tennyson and many scared Victorians: "Nature" as a shriek. Blood and gore as all that humans get. "Ravine": the word from which come the words "ravenous" and "raving," as in "raving" lunatic. There is nature for you, a raving lunatic bent on nothing more than conspicuous consumption of others and compulsive gratification of all of its numerous lusts in all weathers. Blood now, pay later. As Annie Dillard says in her discussion of insects and deciduous trees, "Nature is, above all, profligate...the brainchild of a deranged manic-depressive with limitless capital...No form is too gruesome, no behavior too grotesque" (66).

But Tennyson also knows, a decade before Darwin and a century before Dillard, where "nature" originated and where it is likely to be going:

> No more? A monster then, a dream,
>   A discord. Dragons of the prime,
>   That tare each other in their slime,
> Were mellow music match'd with him. (55.77–80)

Ancient reptilian dragons—Tennyson did not use Sir Richard Owen's word "dinosaur," which Owen had coined around 1841—were more in tune with the order of the universe, and the laws of nature, than that self-deluded dreamer known as man. Until the British Victorians, no group of people on earth had ever even known that dinosaurs existed. Millions upon billions of remarkable creatures, living tens upon hundreds of millions of years ago, some taller than houses with claws as long as carving knives, others longer and heavier than any other land-animal that has ever existed: nothing left, all now dead, all gone, all as extinct as all of their successors will one day be extinct. So where was the solace for those many Victorians, the ones who, like Tennyson—at various points throughout *In Memoriam* (I am not concerned with his concluding outlook in the poem)—suddenly realized that they had no souls? Such thinkers claimed that they had never possessed a soul, nor had any of their fellow human beings—or ancestors—possessed a magical spirit beyond the physical body. It was a bitter pill for thoughtful Victorians, and their thoughtful successors, to swallow.

Here is a famous passage of late Romantic natural history, drawn from a Victorian novel, Thomas Hardy's *Tess of the D'Urbervilles*, which tried to set forth an answer to the question, "where is your 'soul'?": "Amid the oozing fatness and warm ferments of the Var Vale, at a season when the rush of juices could almost be heard below the hiss of fertilization, it was impossible that the most fanciful love should not grow passionate. The ready bosoms existing there were impregnated by their surroundings" (116). What more might I ask than to be impregnated by my surroundings? What incubation could be better than an incubation amid oozing fatness and warm fermenting? Hardy understood, better than most thinkers then or now, that humans care so much for nature because they are so much a part of nature. When Hardy wants to write about sex in the 1890s, he has to write about animal sex and plant sex instead of human sex, but it is all the same; that is precisely his point. Do not tell Hardy that his own rush of juices is any different than a bull's or a bee's. Do not pretend that flower fertilization, or bee fertilization, or snake fertilization, is finally any different than royal fertilization, aristocratic fertilization, or farmhand fertilization. Who needs a soul when the "rush of juices" (need I say "hormones") will do precisely all of the work required to start a love affair, grieve at a funeral, or feel the hormonal rush of "soulful" emotions spurting straight from the glands into the human blood-stream, where they suddenly lead to "feelings."

Earlier in the same novel, in a passage as beautiful as it is scientifically accurate, Hardy cannot quite abandon Romantic natural history completely, as he presents his readers with Darwin's ultimate conclusion:

> The season developed and matured. Another year's installment of flowers, leaves, nightingales, thrushes, finches and such ephemeral creatures, took up their position where only a year ago others had stood in their place, when these were nothing more than germs and inorganic particles. Rays from the sunrise drew forth the buds and stretched them into long stalks, lifted up sap in noiseless streams, opened petals, and sucked out scents in invisible jets and breathings. (*Tess* 101)

For Hardy, all human beings are just another year's installment of life, another chance for the womb of the world to send forth a seed that may sprout or may not, that may grow or may die, that may reproduce or may fail to find a fertile mate. If I am reading those words, Hardy implies, then I have made it; I am "fit." I have found my Darwinian niche. Germs and inorganic particles: that may be me, but how wonderful to be germs, how remarkable to be inorganic particles gone organic. Stay alive as long as you can; that is Hardy's message, just as much as it was Darwin's message. Survive to find some food and a mate. Struggle to keep yourself alive as long as possible and maybe, if you are lucky, you will help to produce the next generation or help the next generation along in their lives. Here is another example of the concept I call ecomorphism. Hardy reveals, not that the nonhuman world is like the human world (anthropomorphism), but that the human world is like the nonhuman world.

The natural world without humans is little different, for Hardy, from the natural world populated by humans. The secret to human happiness in Hardy's ironic and seemingly pessimistic depictions of life is the recognition that there is only the slightest of separations between cow udders and human breasts, dying pheasants and dying humans. Likewise, the blood of the horse Prince spurting arterially (almost sexually) on Tess's dress, anticipates the blood of Alec D'Urberville, staining the hem of her blood-red dress and the wide spot on the landlady's floor and ceiling: pints of his blood have seeped through an upstairs rug, floorboards, timber-framed lathe, and horsehair plaster before dripping from a heart-shaped stain on the ceiling into the landlady's prim Victorian parlor below. What made Hardy's work so upsetting to many of his contemporaries was precisely this sense that human life was merely the Darwinian extension of nonhuman life. Humans see their own lives as vastly superior to all other lives, says Hardy, only because of the petty, paltry, and temporary systems that humans have constructed: religion, politics, art, and social norms. These fleeting systems and empires—Assyria, Babylon, Egypt, Greece, Rome, England, America (?)—always describe themselves, during their ascendency, in ways that make each culture seem more significant than any other culture in history, or than the rest of organic life. For Hardy, however, such human egotism is simply unwarranted.

This is the same truth described less than a century later by John Fowles in *The French Lieutenant's Woman*, "In a vivid insight, a flash of black lightning, he saw that all life was parallel: that evolution was not vertical, ascending to perfection, but horizontal. Time was a great fallacy; existence was without history, was always now, was always being caught in the same fiendish machine. All those painted screens erected by man to shut out reality—history, religion, duty, social position, all were illusions, mere opium fantasies" (165). Darwin told the truth, Hardy and Fowles assert; human beings are just another species in a long line of species. They came into being the way all other creatures did, and they will go out of being via extinction, just the way all other species eventually do. Humans have different feelings about themselves than most creatures. Thanks to self-consciousness they have ethics, morality, and powerful personal emotions. None of that, however, will influence their biological destiny, at least not beyond their ability to influence that same destiny for their own good (or ill), or for the wider good (or ill) of the entire planet.

Of course, this seemingly pessimistic outlook—Hardy always said that he was a "meliorist": a person who believed that things can improve, but only as a result of human effort—had important consequences for any view of divine omnipotence. Hardy could not believe in the God of his fathers because he could not imagine a Judeo-Christian God who allowed all of the evil and suffering in the world: the pain, the bad luck, the accidents, and apparently limitless agony deriving from illness, disease, and death. In a similar way, Charles Darwin lost the last trace of any religious faith he had possessed with the "random" death of his beloved daughter Annie at the age of ten (Keynes). For Darwin, no God worth believing in could have allowed the death of Annie. For Hardy, human life only amounts to what each human makes it. As a result, *Tess* tells the tale of a godless, Darwinian world of personal and hereditary decline. Tess's rape triggers her evolutionary descent into an unfit status: her child (Sorrow) dies of illness; she cannot find the right mate, and she thus becomes as "extinct" as those Norman families of England who once ruled a mighty empire and—by the Victorian era—were merely mouldering in their graves. Throughout the nineteenth century, Burke's genealogical publishing house produced volumes with titles like *Extinct Peerages* and *Extinct And Dormant Baronetcies Of England, Ireland, And Scotland*. Hardy must have appreciated the Darwinian irony of these descriptions of such great British families as "extinct." As species become extinct, so with families. Once my family ceases to fill its niche, it becomes extinct, no different than the passenger pigeon, the great auk, or the dodo. Hardy describes a Darwinian world, one in which a great deal of human pain derives from nature.

A PERFECT BIRD, A PERFECT POEM

These September days I have taken to rising and setting with the sun. When I lie down on my bed on the screened sleeping porch, the only sound I can hear is the long-eared owl, moving around the mountain, squalking her curious calls. Is she lost? Is she looking for a nest hole this late in the season? There are great trees for her in the woods just around the Roost, huge dead or dying oaks with holes high up where branches once branched, where woodpeckers have worked their way through the bark and into the core of the dying tree. This particularly persistent owl has been here for over a month, starting her croaking, screechy call near dusk and keeping it up all night. Last night she was on the move, first above our neighbor's cabin to the south, then down into the deep stand of trees near a line of rocky ledges, and finally, when I woke at sunrise, right in front of the cabin, so close I could hear every quaver and click, but I still could not see her. Tonight I will get my flashlight and try for a closer look.

The mist starts rising off of the river by sunrise. It has formed there during the night like a coiled rope, a white snake of fog following every twist and turn of the bank sides, every curve of the stream. When this mist begins to rise, it looks at first like a cloud on top of the river. Then the sun hits it directly and plumes begin to lift up from the main band of steam, rising in stately procession and moving off slowly to the north; or, they simply disappear, delicate wisps of air floating straight up into the sky. On some mornings, when the atmospheric conditions are right, the river mist does not rise at all; instead, it spreads out over the land like a ground-hugging fog, moving like a giant amoeba, then dissipating slowly into the fields and streams, or heading out across the tall, single trees scattered widely over the valley. The river mist has formed because that is where the moisture is, and it dissipates because the heat of the sun dissolves its tiny particles. Even on the driest of days, however, the river makes a cloud blanket for itself each night, a blanket that hides billions of tiny insects from their prey, that keeps moisture on the rocks and trees to hydrate all of the rock and tree creatures, a blanket that rises and spreads out every morning, back to the sky from which it came as rain or out over farm fields and woodlands which it will once again nourish.

On the rarest of mornings, when the wind is coming gently from the west, the river-born cloud crawls slowly up the mountain toward the Roost. It moves so deliberately that I can see it coming up the hill, over the distant road, along the ridges and rock lines. Finally, it crests in the clearing below the cabin and blocks out every sight in the valley. On these mornings, it seems as though I am suddenly high above the clouds, as though I am looking out from an airplane window or standing on top of a peak many thousands of feet in altitude. Finally, the fog-cloud hits the cabin. I open the screened-window on the porch as the fog streams in like thick smoke. Even the screens cannot stop it. They grow gradually dripping-wet with moisture, but then even they have to admit this misty visitor. By this time, I can see its wisps in front of my face. It dampens my clothes. It leaves moisture on every chair leg and tabletop. Finally it moves through the cabin (I have opened the cross-ventilating doors), off up the mountain, and a startlingly clear view reemerges again below me; forty miles of valley and distant mountain ridges, now as clean and clear as a freshly painted canvas.

This morning I rose early because I wanted to see that owl up close. Most owls are as wary as wary can be. In my life, I have only seen three owls face to face: a barred owl on a branch in Virginia long ago, a tiny saw-whet owl sticking his head out of a hole a mere ten yards from the Roost porch, and once, in Montana, a beautiful pygmy owl, fresh from its kill, its beak still glistening red with blood, sitting on a dry snag, blinking and looking around as though my friend Michael and I were not ten feet away, as though we did not have our cameras clicking fast. We got that picture. But I know that this Roost owl on this particular morning does not want to be seen. Every evening in recent weeks I have walked into the woods at sunset when her call starts up in earnest. As soon as I step into the giant stand of oaks where she lives, the sound falls silent and stays silent until after dark and after I have gone. Today, I will try and catch a glimpse of her at sunrise.

The task turns out to be easier than I had supposed. I leave the cabin before seven, head up the abandoned road a short way, and then turn above our neighbor's cabin toward the tall trees. I have been confused some nights about whether this is a long-eared owl or a screech owl. The two look totally different—the screech owl is small, the long-eared is large—but their calls can be easily mistaken. One book says "screech owl: a quavering whistle (monotone or descending)" (Robbins 174) and long-eared "a variety of low hoots, whistles, and shrieks" (174). How to decide? My sentimental, old-fashioned bird book, from 1917, with its phrases like "these lovely songsters" and "as the poets said," is actually of much more help. It says "a weird, sweet, whistled shivering tremolo from under our very windows startles us" (175) describing the screech owl, and for the long-eared call it says that one "is a soft-toned *wu-hunk*, *wu-hunk*, slowly and several times repeated...Another is a low, twittering whistling note, like *dicky*, *dicky*, *dicky*, quite different from anything usually expected from the owl family," then, in "early spring they hoot somewhat like a screech owl" (179; no help!)—and finally "the most common cry of the long-eared owl, the one that has given it its popular name [cat owl], is a prolonged *me-ow-ow-ow*, so like a cat's cry that it would seem folly for a bird that lives chiefly on mice to utter it" (Blanchan 180).

Those older descriptions are more helpful, since they describe the numerous owl sounds I have been hearing so accurately, but by the time I reach the edge of the tall oak stand, I am still confused about precisely what sort of owl I am hoping to find. Then suddenly, without a sound, she drops straight down out of one of the tallest nearby trees and spreads her wings. They are four-feet across at a minimum, held in the perfect horizontal and flapped only once, again in utter silence. She disappears and lands out of my sight. Then, within seconds, she flies again, this time flashing her broad white underside toward me. With that, she is gone for good. I exhale in shock: long-eared owl, probably female—gone into the deep woods—beautiful. I hope that she returns to her own roost again tonight; I will still be here in mine.

Keats's poem on the month of September captures an afternoon not unlike the one I have just passed: clear, and crisp, and full of the promise of autumn.

1.

Season of mists and mellow fruitfulness,
   Close bosom-friend of the maturing sun;
Conspiring with him how to load and bless
   With fruit the vines that round the thatch-eves run;
To bend with apples the moss'd cottage-trees,
   And fill all fruit with ripeness to the core;
     To swell the gourd, and plump the hazel shells

With a sweet kernel; to set budding more,
  And still more, later flowers for the bees,
  Until they think warm days will never cease,
    For Summer has o'er-brimm'd their clammy cells.
                    2.
Who hath not seen thee oft amid thy store?
  Sometimes whoever seeks abroad may find
Thee sitting careless on a granary floor,
  Thy hair soft-lifted by the winnowing wind;
Or on a half-reap'd furrow sound asleep,
  Drows'd with the fume of poppies, while thy hook
    Spares the next swath and all its twined flowers:
And sometimes like a gleaner thou dost keep
  Steady thy laden head across a brook;
  Or by a cyder-press, with patient look,
    Thou watchest the last oozings hours by hours.
                    3.
Where are the songs of Spring? Ay, where are they?
  Think not of them, thou hast thy music too,—
While barred clouds bloom the soft-dying day,
  And touch the stubble-plains with rosy hue;
Then in a wailful choir the small gnats mourn
  Among the river sallows, borne aloft
    Or sinking as the light wind lives or dies;
And full-grown lambs loud bleat from hilly bourn;
  Hedge-crickets sing; and now with treble soft
  The red-breast whistles from a garden-croft;
    And gathering swallows twitter in the skies. (1820)

The poem had just been composed when Keats wrote to his friend Reynolds from the cathedral city of Winchester on September 21, 1819, saying: "How beautiful the season is now—How fine the air. A temperate sharpness about it. Really, without joking, chaste weather— Dian skies—I never lik'd stubble fields so much as now—Aye better than the chilly green of the spring. Somehow a stubble plain looks warm—in the same way that some pictures look warm—this struck me so much in my sunday's walk that I composed upon it" (*Keats* 650). The matter-of-fact way in which Keats describes his inspiration here belies the rhetorical power of a remarkable poem.

Is there a more perfect poem in the language, at least in the sense of perfectly clear, perfectly transparent? I doubt it. Insofar as possible, the poem offers no subjective perspective from the poet, no point of view that the reader needs to intuit or uncover in order to make sense of the words on the page. Instead, Keats does what all great poets in any language have done; he takes an ordinary day in a September field in rural England, and he gives that day back to his readers. He allows his readers to share in an experience; he makes readers feel as though they have participated in a moment in Keats's own life. That is all this poem does, but what an achievement. Keats puts words on a page that have the power to return a lost world, a world that has been lost to readers' own worries, to the flood of ideas, images, and words that crowd out reality from their busy—often overworked—minds. As Shelley says so well of all great poetry, Keats's poem "reproduces the common universe of which we are portions and percipients, and it purges from our inward sight the film of familiarity which obscures from us the wonder of our being... It creates anew the universe after it has been annihilated in our minds by the recurrence of impressions blunted by reiteration" (*Prose* 533). Adults sees things so often that they begin to ignore them. The mind grows familiar with ordinary sights and sounds to the point that it forgets their value. Unlike children, who retain a sense of wonder and amazement for all of the objects around them, the adult grows detached, disconnected from the world. "To Autumn" uses language to return its readers to an ordinary—but wonderful—autumn day they have lost. What a gift.

Keats's poem achieves this goal by offering a unifying and synthetic view of natural process, even in light of death and the recognition of decay. His active verbs begin the process: a nature that can "load," "bless," "bend," "fill," "swell," "plump," and "set budding" is not the theocentric "fallen" nature of Milton—or even of Blake—but is closer to "nature" as it was described by Erasmus Darwin, where every living thing contains the legacy of its biological origins ("the living filament") as well as indications of its connectedness to other living things. The nonspecific vital energy implied by Keats's verbs is as abstract as the concept of a "season." The poet personifies "autumn" in part to suggest that the power that loads the vines and swells the gourds is identical to the life force heard in the bleating "lambs" and whistling "red-breast" at the poem's close. Keats makes no reference to his own mind amid all of this organic life; part of the rhetorical power of the poem lies in the way it links human consciousness to a natural world that can be described so unselfconsciously. There is no monotheistic divinity invoked in the poem; instead, the natural processes described here are all self-sustained and self-sustaining. Keats's "nature," like Erasmus and Charles Darwin's, exists without the need for, or appeal to, any form of nonorganic "super-nature."

As is so often the case in Romantic writing, natural creatures in "To Autumn"—wailing gnats, bleating lambs, singing crickets, whistling robin, twittering swallows—all seem to speak a language that the human observer cannot quite understand. Keats is at no point anthropomorphic about his creatures or anthropocentric about himself. It is not that these creatures know something unknown to the poem's speaker, but rather that they seem, by their very existence, to partake of a unity that the human observer can hardly imagine. Blake describes a similar longing in "The Book of Thel," where the self-conscious Thel—unlike the cloud, lily, or worm to whom she speaks—is unable to accept her position in an organic cycle that will require her to suffer and die. Thel smells the flowers and hears the birds, but she takes no pleasure in them because of her worries about herself: "But Thel delights in these no more, because I fade away, / And all shall say, without a use this shining woman liv'd, / Or did she only live to be at death the food of worms" (*Blake* 2.21–23). The sense of impending death in "To Autumn," the same sense that so terrifies Thel, is countered by Keats with forceful images of ripeness and completeness that pervade the poem. "Where are the songs of Spring? Ay, where are they? / Think not of them, thou hast thy music too" (23–24): "songs of Spring" are not needed in this lyric because images of annual renewal fill these lines with their own cyclical promise, based on the season of autumn.

In biological terms, most of the plants and animals mentioned in the poem did not exist twelve months before the autumn day that Keats is recalling, nor will they exist in a matter of a few weeks or months after the moment the poem describes. Hardy echoes an identical ecology in his own description—in *Tess*—of that one year's "installment of flowers, leaves, nightingales, thrushes, finches and such ephemeral creatures," all of which take up their positions "where only a year ago others had stood in their place" (101): this year's blossoms and babes will replace last year's—again and again—in an endless cycle of organic renewal. "Ripeness is all" in "To Autumn" precisely because ripeness invokes the clearest "message" the poem contains, a biological one: living things reach their fullness, and then they die, but only after having prepared the way—organically and reproductively—for new living things, new forms of cyclical life. As I noted earlier, Keats's powerful language at the close of "To Autumn" has been linked to the less exalted, but no less accurate, scientific imagery of the entomologists Kirby and Spence. Human fascination with choirs of "small gnats" like these was based—in poetry and in science—on the brevity of their existence. Such species, for the most part, live long enough only to mate and then die; some do not even have mouth-parts. Kirby and Spence were particularly struck by one species that did not survive overnight: "It is still more extraordinary that these *Ephemerae*—which, appearing after sun-set, and dying before sun-rise, are destined never to behold the light of that orb— should have so strong an inclination for any luminous object" (*R NH* 359). The entomologists never consider the possibility that the moon might be the source of the drawn-to-light flight patterns of these *Ephemerae*; moon-attraction would surely be the most poetic option for these gnats.

*   *   *

Tonight I lie still on the screen porch and prepare for a windy night's sleep. I can hear the wind whistling through the drying autumn leaves and the pine needles just beyond the screens. The lights in the far off valley twinkle out beyond the flood plain, glistening and glittering like stars.

8

OCTOBER

*For I have swift and nimble wings which will ascend the lofty
skies,*
*With which when thy quick mind is clad, it will the loathéd earth
despise,*
*And go beyond the airy globe, and watery clouds behind thee
leave.*

—Boethius

The woods take on a new beauty when the summer is dying, when autumn arrives and a first hint of winter is in the air. The leaves—especially those of the quaking aspen—change almost overnight. One morning the branches are covered, green and dry, not shiny and shimmering as they were in June and July, still pale green, but now clearly dying. The next morning, scattered yellow blotches appear on the leaves, and brown streaks unroll amid black stains along the veins. Within days these leaves are falling, first in a slow trickle like snow flurries, then faster and more steadily, and finally a flood of yellow, brown, and faded green, covering the forest floor, landing silently on rocks, grass, and fallen tree branches. The woods themselves open up to view as the leaves fall. Rocks unseen all summer loom suddenly in the distance like crouching giants, silent sentinels on the hillside. New shafts of light cut along wide trunks and narrow branches, shining on hitherto unseen spots of forest floor, glancing off dead branches and live branches, shining away into the distance.

Down in the valley, the river's summer algae green has turned a dark grey-brown and blue-black. I can still see concentric circle-rings of fish jumping when the early evening light hits the water at a steep slant from the western sky. The crickets keep chirping, and the katy-dids keep *katy-diding*, well into these cold nights and cool days, but their sounds grow fainter and less frequent until one day, this year late in October, I notice that the woods are almost silent—except for the rustling sound of hanging dead leaves and dry branches in the soft breeze. The woods seem less friendly now, not exactly fearful, but much less warm, much less welcoming.

HAWKS I HAVE WATCHED

The sky overhead is full of birds during these early autumn days: grackles and starlings, robins and finches, a few fall and winter war-blers, and, of course, lots of hawks. Nothing is more noble than a hawk or an eagle in flight, nothing as heroic as a raptor high up in the cloudless sky, searching the airspace and the ground beneath for even the slightest sign of a small bird or a rodent's movement. A peregrine falcon can drop out of the sky like a blunt-ended bullet, reaching speeds of over 180 miles-per-hour, then somehow knowing how to pull out of such a death-defying dive without hitting the ground and dying. This morning a bald eagle came soaring up from his perch on a dead branch above the river, up the slope toward the clearing below the Roost, arching and curving with his long, slow, seven-foot wing beats, spiraling into the sky and then back into the clearing, finally disappearing in the treetops, down toward the wide bend in the river and the dam below it. I looked up above him, as he soared out of sight, and there they were: first three hawks, then five, then eight at least, stretched out at different altitudes but all moving together, all soaring and then flapping, all moving along the ridge together, all headed south. Here at the Roost, they are coming down the broken spine of the Blue Ridge by the thousands, along Catoctin Mountain, across the Kittatinny Ridge.

On Hawk Mountain, in Pennsylvania, I saw mostly hawk watch-ers. The wooded mountaintop parking lot had almost one car for every person: urbanature? The crowds of watchers were so thick that I could barely find a place to sit on the rocks. I had arrived on an October morning when the wind was steady from the north—and the west—and the leading edge of a high-pressure system had moved through the night before. Hawk Mountain is, along with Cape May, among the most famous hawk-watching spots in America. High up on a rocky outcrop of the Appalachians, not too far from the Delaware Water Gap, Hawk Mountain has been a sight of hawk-watching pil-grimages for three-quarters of a century. There is a hawk-watching building in the woods now, with hawk-watching displays and hawk-watching items for sale. There is also a big parking lot, often full of cars on cool October weekends, but there are still more hawks than hawk-watchers on Hawk Mountain on most autumn days.

On Waggoner's Gap I saw my first peregrine falcon. Waggoner's Gap is two hours down the ridge from Hawk Mountain and, unlike the more famous spot, Waggoner's Gap rarely sees more than a dozen pairs of binoculars at one time; there are always more hawks than people on this small rocky outcrop during migration season. My first peregrine came in low from the north and east at Waggoner's Gap and shot over my head like a feathery streak. His black eye-patch was unmistakable, as were his white-mottled wings and his torpedo-shaped body. He did not flap until he was almost out of sight down the ridge, and then he flapped only twice before his rocket-glide continued into the distance. The sight ended almost before it had begun, and none of the watchers on the rocky hill that afternoon said anything but "peregrine." I have seen other peregrines since, but never one that took my breath away with quite the same startling and concentrated falcon-force. That is why people go hawk watching.

On Virginia's Eastern Shore, several years ago, I saw more than eight thousand raptors in two-and-a-half days. That is correct: eight thousand. That particular hawk-watch broke records of all sorts. The conditions were ideal. The wind was steady and brisk from the north-north-west. The sky ranged from clear to broken clouds. Sometimes the cloudy sky made it easier to identify birds, because the clouds splashed their feathery silhouettes against a gray-white, mottled background. There were ospreys and bald eagles, merlins and kestrels, harriers and Cooper's hawks, sharp-shins and red-tails, and hundreds of songbirds as well, the latter apparently along as bait. The broad-wings came over as massive slow-swirling "kettles," twirling bundles that explained the origin of the hawk watcher's term "kettle": birds by the hundreds circling slowly in gigantic spirals, not like geese in their perfectly sailing V-lines, but flying specks of migrating raptor-life, each kettle a small, slow-moving tornado of hawks, all spinning in the same direction. That week, at Kiptopeake, the total hawk-count reported almost thirty thousand raptors. The word speechless came to mind, even among the most seasoned of hawk watchers. For a novice like me, it was then—and remains—the literal hawk-watch of a lifetime.

At Kiptopeake, Virginia, from that September 30 to October 1, I saw 7,705 hawks in those 3 days: 15 bald eagles, 139 peregrine falcons, 140 northern harriers, 573 ospreys, 185 merlins, 971 kestrels,

2,668 broad-winged hawks, 16 red-tailed hawks, 2,590 sharp-shinned hawks, and more. Friday, the day before we arrived, had recorded the largest one-day flight in the history of hawk-watching at this famous hawk-watching spot: 8,757 raptors in a single dawn-to-dusk count. We had gathered on a beautiful spot overlooking the Chesapeake Bay. Twenty to fifty counters were with us at any one time. A merlin dove suddenly, like a rocket, out of the sky in front of us, snagging a mockingbird from a perch directly in front of our faces—no more than thirty yards away—then releasing the fluttering catch as the desperate mockingbird struggled wildly for his life. A peregrine falcon rocketed in a mere twenty feet above ground level, split a large flock of songbirds in half, just like a shark slicing through a school of bait-fish, and then soared directly over our heads with his throat-crop bulging with song-bird, so close I could see his drooping black moustache and every detail of his beak, its knife-like point glistening yellow in the early morning sun. Hawks stooped to baited nets set out by an organization known as K.E.S.T.R.E.L. (Kiptopeake Environmental Station, Research, and Education Laboratory): harriers, kestrels, red tails, and sharpies (sharp-shinned hawks) were all carefully disentangled from these catch-nets and then brought to the observation platform for close-up inspection and photography by curious older birders and young birders who still had wonder in their eyes.

The flight had to be literally constant on each day to produce unlikely numbers like these; on Saturday, the numbers were slightly lower thanks to a slower northeast wind. Overnight the wind shifted, and Sunday dawned with a stream of cloud-high peregrines (the second largest peregrine day on record, 81 compared to 89), merlins, kestrels, and eagles—almost all close up—almost all easy to identify. The eagles came so close that the experts were able to age and sex them through binoculars. Individual birds would occasionally drop into eyesight range, identifiable without any binoculars at all. They would hover, hunt the nearby fields and bayside shallows on both sides of us, sometimes heading north for awhile before turning south again and racing toward the last point of land at Smith Island Inlet and Fisherman's Island. Then each bird would set off on the long flight over the wide-mouthed opening of the Chesapeake Bay—twenty miles from tollbooth to tollbooth—on down the coastline toward Virginia Beach. Slow swirling, tornado-like kettles of broad-wings rolled by all day on Saturday, one after another, hawks, hawks, and more hawks, up to three hundred birds in each swirling batch. Each watcher would count the kettle as fast as possible, then we would average our counts quickly before the next kettle came in, trying to agree with each other's counts, trying for as accurate a number as possible. All afternoon, controversy swirled about a possible Jaeger sighting out over the sunken concrete ships that form a crumbling harbor at the now abandoned Kiptopeake Ferry slip. The Jaeger is a seabird like a skua or a gull that would be very rare to sight under these circumstances and at this location. My friend Bruce and I had joined a group of birders who were out in the middle of a heaven-sent hawk watch this weekend, even for hawk-watchers who do not believe in heaven. As we drove home up the Delmarva Peninsula, past abandoned farms and row upon row of soybeans, corn, and tobacco, we were almost silent, lost in our own thoughts of peregrine wings, bald-eagle eyes and beaks, and the talons of fast-flying kestrels, sights too seldom vouchsafed to even the most earnest of nature watchers.

These dramatic hawk-watching spots are literally in many people's urbanatural backyards. All of them are close to one of the most popu-lated megalopolises on the planet (Boston to New York to Philadelphia to Baltimore to Richmond). Most people are not even aware that the hawks are flying overhead or that these counting stations exist to keep track of this migration. But every year, like clockwork since time immemorial, hundreds of thousands of raptors have made their way down these ridges and rivers and coastlines, headed south to the Caribbean and the Mexican Yucatan until the weather warms again. Then they leave their wintering grounds to trickle north in spring. But *buteos* and *accipiters* can be seen here, at the Roost, along the Blue Ridge almost any day of the year: soaring high over the Shenandoah, curving great circles in the empty air below the cabin, swooping and diving to get away from the crows that chase and plague them relent-lessly. This is the hawk-world in earnest: birds searching the skies and fallow fields for prey, landing on river snags or cloud-high branches, roosting in dead-stands with skeletal branch-fingers that stretch toward the sun, flapping through the mile-wide clearing between my screen porch and the slow-moving river, feeding and mating, migrat-ing spring and fall, breathing their air and living their lives—free, and clear, and unencumbered.

Here is how the poet W. S. Merwin describes humanity's link to migratory creatures: "One of the things that we late arrivals on the earth sense, and in turn portray as legendary, is an awareness much older than our own. In each of the migrants we are afforded glimpses of beings in whom the turning of the earth, its axis and magnetic fields, day and night and the seasons, the winds and all that we call the elements, and the motions of the celestial bodies themselves are the pulse of a heart and the illumination of a consciousness" ("Foreword" viii–ix). This is not idle anthropomorphism on Merwin's part; it is merely the recognition that the whole world, and perhaps the whole universe, is alive with life. Each human being is no more or less a part of these pulsing, sensing, responding organisms of the eons than any other living thing: animal, plant, bacteria, virus, or quivering protoplasm. Why Western humans have thought that their own status was so central—why they thought they mattered so much more than other living things for all those centuries—is unclear to me. Why most of humanity has been unable to acknowledge the value of the living world for its own sake (until recently) is still confusing. No doubt selfishness and egotism of certain sorts have some kind of adaptive evolutionary advantage, but I still do not see the reason for humanity's need to see itself as constitutionally superior to every other living thing. For one thing, it simply is not true. The eagle has eyesight that makes mine look paltry. The whale and the giant squid manage just fine when they are two miles down in the ocean; I would be crushed like a bug. A hummingbird flies miles upon miles each year in order to find enough food for the winter, to find a mate, to guarantee his survival—and his species' survival—until the next year. I could not fly ten feet.

Today the red tails and the sharp-shinned hawks are moving south in front of and high above the Roost. They waited through the night for the thermal air currents to hit them on their forest perches in the bright October sun of early morning. A high-pressure front moved through last night from the west, clearing out all but a few scattered clouds and dropping the barometric pressure dramatically, optimal conditions for a hawk watch. The wind is blowing steadily and hard, tearing leaves from the brown branches, swirling maple seed-pods out of the trees. This day recalled the poet Shelley, in Tuscany, in October of 1819, composing his "Ode to the West Wind," as his own note tells us in accurate meteorological detail: "This poem was conceived and chiefly written in a wood that skirts the Arno, near Florence, and on a day when that tempestuous wind, whose temperature is at once mild and animating, was collecting the vapours which pour down the autumnal rains. They began, as I foresaw, at sunset, with a violent tempest of hail and rain, attended by that magnificent thunder and lightning peculiar to the Cisalpine regions" (*RNH* 311). Florence had been the home of the legendary Dante Alighieri, creator of *terza rima*, the verse-form of his magisterial *Divine Comedy*, the rhyme-scheme that Shelley would adapt for his own view of an autumnal and naturalistic paradise. Here is how Shelley sees the October wind that ushers in the new season:

I

O wild West Wind, thou breath of Autumn's being,
Thou, from whose unseen presence the leaves dead
Are driven, like ghosts from an enchanter fleeing,

Yellow, and black, and pale, and hectic red,
Pestilence-stricken multitudes: O thou,
Who chariotest to their dark wintry bed

The winged seeds, where they lie cold and low,
Each like a corpse within its grave, until
Thine azure sister of the spring shall blow

Her clarion o'er the dreaming earth, and fill
(Driving sweet buds like flocks to feed in air)
With living hues and odours plain and hill:

Wild Spirit, which art moving everywhere;
Destroyer and preserver; hear, oh hear!
[...]

IV

If I were a dead leaf thou mightest bear;
If I were a swift cloud to fly with thee;
A wave to pant beneath thy power, and share

The impulse of thy strength, only less free
Than thou, O uncontrollable! If even
I were as in my boyhood, and could be

The comrade of thy wanderings over heaven,
As then, when to outstrip thy skiey speed
Scarce seem'd a vision; I would ne'er have striven

As thus with thee in prayer in my sore need.
Oh, lift me as a wave, a leaf, a cloud!
I fall upon the thorns of life! I bleed!

A heavy weight of hours has chain'd and bow'd
One too like thee: tameless, and swift, and proud. (1839)

I want to forget about Shelley's sentimentality ("As thus with thee in prayer in my sore need") and set aside his characteristic overstatement ("I fall upon the thorns of life! I bleed!") and think instead about precisely what he achieves in these justly famous lines of poetry. The wind here is not merely moving air; it represents the life force itself: the *élan vital*, the *chi*, a vital energy that pervades the universe. Some critics have said that for Romantic poets, nature is God, but if nature is God here, it is God as pure power, not God as an entity. Shelley comes close to such a pantheistic claim in these lines, but such a God for Shelley is no *thing*; this divinity is pure *force*:

> V
>
> Make me thy lyre, even as the forest is:
> What if my leaves are falling like its own!
> The tumult of thy mighty harmonies
>
> Will take from both a deep, autumnal tone,
> Sweet though in sadness. Be thou, spirit fierce,
> My spirit! Be thou me, impetuous one!
>
> Drive my dead thoughts over the universe
> Like withered leaves to quicken a new birth;
> And, by the incantation of this verse,
>
> Scatter, as from an unextinguish'd hearth
> Ashes and sparks, my words among mankind!
> Be through my lips to unawakened earth
>
> The trumpet of a prophecy! O Wind,
> If Winter comes, can Spring be far behind? (1839)

The West Wind is precisely that force that brings about autumn in this poem. This force kills—by ripping leaves and seeds off of the trees—but in the same moments it gives new life, by planting some of these seeds and returning the dead organic matter of leaves that will nourish those seeds in the ground. The wind may destroy, but the identical force that destroys the leaves of last year also plants the guarantors of next year's life. This force, this "god," may be uncontrollable—tameless, swift, and proud—but these attributes are the very aspects that are the assurance of the unalterable cycles of the seasons.

An additional key is that the human speaker—the poet—is linked to the natural force he feels throughout these lines. He clearly does not feel connected to nature when the poem begins. By the fourth and fifth stanzas, however, his hypotheticals—"If I were," "If I were," "If even / I were"—give way to a declarative certainty that admits of no doubt: "make me," "be...My spirit," "Be...me," "Be through my lips." By the closing image of the poem, the force of nature (the air as wind) becomes the force of the poet's voice (the air as breath from the lungs into words). A powerful wind that pulls down leaves, and plants dry seeds, has become the trumpet of a literal prophecy: the sound of Shelley's voice. The prophecy itself is nothing more complex than a simple truth of material nature: spring always follows winter; it never has failed to do so. Every death contributes organic materials that help to guarantee new life. Shelley produces a resurrection poem without any link to the supernatural. He offers a promise of natural power and organic efficacy without any reference to a world beyond the physical world, beyond the world I can see and hear and feel outside my window every day, whether I am *Oltrarno* (across the river in Florence) or up at the Roost on the Blue Ridge mountains.

URBANATURAL ROOSTING ON DISPLAY

When I traveled to Florence recently, less than a month ago during my own roosting year—remember, I promised an urban component in *Beyond Romantic Ecocriticism: Toward Urbanatural Roosting*—I sat near the spot where Shelley composed his West Wind poem. We do not know precisely where Shelley was when he wrote these lines, except for his claim about being "in a wood that skirts the Arno." Was he east of the city, in Rovezzano out toward Arezzo, or was he west of the city near the Parco della Cascine and Badia a Settimo, headed toward Pistoia, Livorno, and Pisa? Wherever precisely Shelley sat to watch his clouds and leaves, he described a scene remarkably like the one I watched before me on that warm, autumn day in Tuscany. I had walked to the outskirts of the city on a blue-skied, cloud-scuttling October morning—Florence is still a small city even when full of tourists—to a wooded spot where I could look back toward Giotto's bell tower and Brunelleschi's arching dome. I could see the clouds that Shelley described and the first autumn leaves falling fast toward the ground and into the river. I could hear the wind whistling, whining softly through tall spires of cypress trees and still-leafy sycamores.

I was in Florence and in Italy to go to museums, but not to the museums full of painted canvases that countless tourists usually fill. I was in search of urbanature. I walked along the long line of humanity that snaked its way around the block, waiting to get into the Uffizi, hundreds of people still here even after the high-season hoards of summer tourists had departed. I was not here for the wide halls filled with portraits and statuary by every Italian master and many nonItalian masters. I was here for the plants and animals, botanical and zoological specimens that traced their history back to the beginnings of natural philosophy—the phrase that first meant "science"—in Western Europe. In the natural history museum halls that I wandered for days, I was often the only visitor, alone in rooms full of stuffed birds, taxidermied rhino-heads, mounted mammals of every description, some of the first specimen primates (gorillas, chimpanzees, and an orangutan—first called *Homo sylvestris*—man of the woods). These were among the earliest such creatures to have ever been brought back from Africa and Asia for exhibition, first to royalty and then to countless wide-eyed wealthy Europeans, from the seventeenth century, through the eighteenth, and on into the early nineteenth century: Romantic natural history.

When I stood in front of those centuries-old display cases full of higher primates and great apes, I felt just like those early European viewers (poets and natural philosophers, potentates and princesses) just as Byron and Darwin must have felt the first time they gazed on a stuffed chimpanzee or orangutan. As I looked at those preserved great apes in Florence, among the first such stuffed specimens in the world—now moth-eaten and dusty—I thought to myself, "if I am not closely related to this creature, then nothing is; I can see that this animal and I share a kinship. I can feel it." This must have been what Byron and Shelley, and Goethe and Galvani, and Erasmus and Charles Darwin, also felt. As I looked in these display cases, I could see fingerprints on this chimpanzee's hands, the creases in his pale palms forming patterns just like the creases in my own palms. This chimp has wrinkles on the backs of his knuckles, just as I do. He has fingernails and eyelashes. He is my relative, of that I am sure. All animal-rights talk begins in this sense of similarity, this sense of such close relatedness. My worry is not immediately about animal rights, however, as much as it is about animal connection. I want to argue that it is impossible to look carefully at such a creature and not feel this sense of kinship, a connection that goes further than mere anatomical relatedness.

In the great natural history museums of Italy—in Florence, Rome, Bologna, and Naples—I also saw narwhal tusks, one set standing six-feet tall in ornate wooden stands at the doorway to a great vaulted room full of skeletons. These "tusks" are actually one of the narwal's teeth, grown out of proportion as a sexual characteristic for fighting and establishing dominance. They were exhibited throughout Europe for centuries to prove the existence of unicorns—like the ones in medieval tapestries—mythical horse-creatures with long tusks

protruding from their foreheads. In fact, confusion about this mythical animal led to early natural history books that called the narwhal,
actually an ocean-going whale of the northern latitudes, a "unicorn"
well into the nineteenth century. Here is a perfect example of the way
"Romantic natural history" works: the science of narwhal tusks links
up with poetic myth to produce a fantasy (does this tusk "prove" the
existence of unicorns?) in close connection with scientific fact (this
tusk is a remarkable evolutionary adaptation in its own right, at least
as wonderful as any unicorn).

Along with narwhal tusks, I saw wide crocodile skins unfolded
and spread out as wall-hangings next to the plated shells of ocean-
going turtles as long as I am tall. I gazed upon stuffed and mounted
heads covering wall after wall: rhinos, lions, elephants, ibexes, dik-
diks, gazelles, and reindeer. I stared at mollusks and other soft-
bodied creatures in jars, taxidermied snakes posed as though ready
to strike, shelled creatures of every wild shape imaginable, and case
upon case of invertebrates floating in fluid. As Emerson said of natural history museums, "In a cabinet of natural history, we become
sensible of a certain occult recognition and sympathy in regard to
the most unwieldy and eccentric forms of beast, fish, and insect"
("Nature" 43–44). Emerson was right; long before I reached the
hall of great apes, I felt a clear recognition and sympathy with creatures both like me and not so much like me. That chimpanzee and
I share almost everything in common. That tiger and I have bin-
ocular vision. That lemur's teeth look like mine, except his canines.
That iguana and I breathe air through two lungs. Those fish and I
share a circularly ribbed spine. Even that jellyfish and I are largely
made of water.

The purpose of these early natural history museums—La Specola
in Florence, the museum of the Universita Federico II in Naples, the
Zoological Collection on the edge of the Borghese Gardens in Rome,
the Archiginnasio in Bologna—was the collection, exhibition, and
scientific study of plants and animals, including the vast numbers
of new species that were being discovered as European expeditions
returned from far flung destinations in the East Indies, the South
Pacific, Central and South Africa, and South America. La Specola,
in the center of Oltrarno—just down the wide-cobbled courtyard
from the Pitti Palace—contains a vast array of animals ranging from
the simplest mollusk to the primates filling that room I have already
described. The primate-room includes a modern display-case in which
visitors can stand and see themselves reflected in a large mirror alongside an orangutan and a chimpanzee. So there I was, just another

slowly evolving specimen among this wide variety of species; I took a picture of myself with my cousins.

This museum, first organized and opened to the public in 1775 by the Grand Duke Pietro Leopoldo of Lorraine, was designed to exhibit the collections of the Medici family and the holdings of the Hapsburg-Lorraine family, including remarkable human anatomical models fashioned from wax and used as tools for medical and obstetrics students. These life-sized wax models include full dissections of heads and hands and entire human forms: men flayed open to exhibit the complete body cavity, with all of the individual organs intact, women opened up to reveal a full-term fetus and also earlier stages of prenatal gestation, bodies skinned to show the nervous system and organs opened wide to unfold their inner secrets. These graphic wax models were controversial in their day. Since human dissection was still considered grave-robbing, these replicas served as among the first tools available to European doctors for the study of the intricacies of human anatomy.

Another of the most remarkable of all of these early Italian museums is the Archiginnasio at the Palazzo Poggi museum in Bologna, site of the oldest university in Europe, which dates its founding to 1088. Ulysses Aldrovandi (1522–1605), the founder of this collection, was the Leonardo da Vinci of Bologna. He brought together one of the largest scientifically organized collections of natural historical specimens of his time, over 18,000 distinct objects: plants (pressed and mounted), animals (skinned and stuffed), as well as rocks and minerals, stones and amber, and unidentified objects that were often linked to mythological beings: "unicorn" horns, "mermaid" fins, and the eggs and teeth of mysterious "monsters." Aldrovandi was also responsible for one of the most comprehensive early publication ventures in natural history, an effort to catalog each living thing on earth in writing, as well as the first public scientific library in the Western world (Simili). In this regard, he was the Edward O. Wilson of his era; Wilson has recently announced his intention to create a hypertext resource that will devote a separate web page to every species on earth. Wilson's plan calls for more than 1.8 million distinct URL addresses, each one dedicated to an individual living thing (www.eol. org). Aldrovandi would be pleased. His own sixteenth-century natural history collection (he died in 1605)—animals, plants, minerals, and fossils—has only recently been restored and returned to public display in the Palazzo Poggi on the Via Zamboni. It includes dozens of beautifully carved woodblocks, paper traces and sketches, and the resulting printed pages from his masterful and shelf-filling books of

natural history: separate volumes on plants, animals, mythical creatures, anatomy, medicine, anthropology, and travel—a Renaissance
man's collection, a virtual survey of what was then known about the
natural world.

These urbanatural European natural history museums, like the
ones I visited in Italy, had two main functions. One was to collect
and exhibit the holdings of powerful members of royal families and
wealthy collectors for the viewing pleasure of titled nobility, the landed
gentry, and traveling gentlemen. These collections were designed to
show, in part, how widely the family had voyaged and also to reveal
the remarkable range of rarities, curiosities, and oddities that existed,
all to satisfy the expectations of even the most knowledgeable and
well-traveled of gentleman scientists. Byron and Shelley, for example,
along with Mary Shelley, visited a number of these museums, as they
recorded in a letter of Shelley's from the Frankenstein summer of
1816:

> We dined at Servox...where we saw a cabinet [museum] of natural
> curiosities, like those of Keswick [in the Lake District] and Bethgelert
> [in North Wales]. We saw in this cabinet some chamois' horns, and
> the horns of an exceedingly rare animal called the bouquetin, which
> inhabits the desarts [sic] of snow to the south of Mont Blanc: it is an
> animal of the stag kind; its horns weigh at least twenty-seven English
> pounds. It is inconceivable how so small an animal could support so
> inordinate a weight. (RNH 305)

A second motive behind these collections was to offer a centralized
location for the display and academic study of such diverse collections of living, once living, and nonliving, examples of wild nature.
Museums like these helped to spread knowledge that was being discovered so fast that it could not be written down quickly enough for
distribution via publication. Materials were collected and catalogued,
or left in boxes and crates, for the benefit of scientists, universities,
and the general public. Medical students (like Victor Frankenstein),
botanical illustrators, zoologists, herbalists, explorers, historians—
natural and otherwise—and the merely curious: all such people came
to these museums to be educated and entertained.

So, for example, the Royal Mineralogical Museum of Naples still
houses large chunks of the 79 ACE eruption of Vesuvius, displayed
only yards from the skeletonized remains of the mighty elephant
given by the Ottoman Sultan Mahomet V to Carlo di Borbone in
1742. This great creature now stands in the hall of the Zoological

Museum founded in 1813 by Gioacchino Murat. When the massive pachyderm died, in 1756, his skeleton was preserved by taxidermists and finally went on display in the museum six decades later in 1819, precisely where he still stands, now with a beautiful painting of him, painted from life, exhibited between his front and back left legs. Here is material urbanature on display for all to see: the wonders of the nonhuman world—collected, archived, catalogued, and displayed in the great cities of Europe—the wildest bits of nature domesticated for the viewing pleasure of a cultural elite and the professional benefit of a growing class of socially esteemed scientists.

These great collections contributed to the development of the idea of evolution in much the same way that Linnean and other taxonomies did. When I looked, even now, at case after case full of pinned beetles and butterflies, or when I walked through room after room of articulated skeletons, stuffed birds, and mounted primates, I could not help but be struck by the remarkable similarities amid all of this dissimilarity. What is it that produces parallel and perfectly symmetrical shoulder blades and pelvis bones in creatures ranging from salamanders and moles to chimpanzees and orangutans? What could be more obvious than bird claws emerging from lizard claws, or whale fins evolving from earlier mammal feet and paws? Thousands upon thousands of different beetles, bugs, and moths—as Charles Darwin had in his own private display cases at Down House—but all with exactly six legs, all with similar eye-structures, all with comparable mouthparts for feeding, and all with reproductive organs that performed the function of delivering sperm cells to eggs cells in any one of a thousand different ways. Bilateral symmetry in almost every creature that evolved after a certain stage in the history of life: two eyes, two ears, two nostrils, and one mouth? How could so many creatures share structural similarities that crossed such obvious boundaries in all of these living orders, families, and species? The answer had to be evolution, a developmental model of creation that revealed exactly how I could have so much in common with my primate (prime—first level—the most developed), mammalian (fed from the mother's body, sharing mammary glands), and even cordate (spine possessing, as in "spinal chord") ancestors. I share obvious traits with each and every one of these groups: gorillas and gophers, goannas (a big lizard) and goldfish. Of course, evolution also explained how creation could still be happening. Creation was not then; it is now. My own species *Homo sapiens* is still evolving. Humans are not now what they will be in a million years.

Darwin himself was a great cabinet-filler and pack rat. I saw his barnacles and his bugs still lining cases and drawers in London's

Natural History Museum in South Kensington and also at Down House, where many of his greatest ideas came to him on the dusty Sandwalk behind his main house or in his small greenhouses that held row upon row of secret-revealing plants. In three months alone, from May to July 1860, Darwin made three discoveries that revolutionized botany and helped secure the truth of evolution: (1) first, heterostyly: sexual dimorphism (males are not like females) in the primrose flower; (2) second, the secret of pollination in the ornate flower-cups of orchids, and; (3) third, the necessary link between insects and plant sexuality (especially the remarkable adaptations and adaptability of insect-eating plants: Venus fly-trap, pitcher plant, and sundews), marvelous structures and behaviors that made each of these plants, as his wife Emma noted, "just like a living creature" (Morris, Wilson, and Kohn 56). Darwin said that he actually made only one original contribution to evolutionary science—that was natural selection; almost all the rest of his work was based on combining and synthesizing the work of many other researchers: natural historians, marine scientists, botanists, biologists, entomologists, herbalists, pigeon-fanciers, and dog breeders.

Museums like those I explored during my urbanatural year of roosting and roving provide one additional benefit; they convey a sense of scale in the nonhuman world. In the Museo Zoologico in Rome, in the middle of a modern room full of display cases, lies the nineteenth-century marble statue of a beautiful woman, presumably the goddess Flora herself. Under her these words are inscribed in Italian: "Un ambiente abbastanza insolito e molto…personale! È difficile convincersene, ma il corpo dell'uomo è una vera e propria 'foresta' in cui vivono altri esseri viventi, protetti, lontano dai preddatori e ben nutriti." In English I could say, "A rather unusual environment, and one that is very…personal! It is difficult to convince yourself, but the human body is a real 'forest' in which other living beings thrive, protected, far from predators and well fed." So the human body is itself an ecosystem: respiring, excreting, feeding itself as well as feeding countless living creatures that thrive within and depend upon it. There are more bacteria in each human digestive system—yours and mine, right now—than all the human beings that have ever lived on this planet. So a display like this one, in a natural history or zoological museum, creates a strange sense of scale for me, for scientists, and for the hordes of schoolchildren who make their way through these halls and display rooms. Here are a blue whale and a giant squid replica, these animals so large—hundred feet and sixty feet respectively—that it is hard to imagine them as living things. Here are skeletal mounts (original bones and reconstructions) of dinosaurs and fossil creatures of all kinds, stretching back to the origins of life, to those weird stromatolite domes and wavy limestone that still stand in the shallows of Australian and other seas, fossil remains of the earliest living organisms. I feel that I am in a different world, on a different planet, when surrounded by such remains.

Seeing all of this life displayed organ-to-organ, developmental part to developmental part—mouths and anuses opening at both ends of the simplest creatures, tentacles and dark blobs of optical-swellings leading to eyes in octopi, neural lobes giving way to brains in higher animals—it becomes impossible not to believe that all of these living beings are related to each other, difficult to convince myself that all of these beings do not belong to the same living system that I do. In the rooms of these early "Romantic" museums, scientists came to believe that the human world had emerged directly out of these examples of nonhuman life. It awaited only Charles Darwin to end Romantic natural history. He provided a systematic explanation for natural processes that had seemed enigmatic, cryptic, and mysterious: "Therefore I should infer from analogy that probably all the organic beings which have ever lived on this earth have descended from some one primordial form" (*Darwin* 171). With that one sentence Darwin revealed to the modern world just why visitors to natural history museums feel a sense of the "family of man" and the "tree of life." That family and that tree are on display here.

Just imagine the looks on the faces of the general public when the first rhinoceros ever beheld by any European was uncrated from his wooden cage in London or Lisbon or Rome. We do not have the historical image of this precise moment, but we do have a remarkable picture painted by Pietro Longhi (1701–1785), now hanging in the National Gallery in London: *Exhibition of a Rhinoceros at Venice, 1751*. This rhinoceros arrived in Venice in 1741, and he was exhibited during Carnival season ten years later and, no doubt, on many other occasions. Longhi's picture tells the tale well. The slightly benighted-looking creature stands quietly between the hay he is eating and a pile of his own dung. Meanwhile, his handler holds a whip and the creature's horn which has, apparently, been cut from the fearful animal's head in order to make him seem less dangerous; he is surely dangerous-looking enough even without his horn. Four carnival goers—three masked men and one masked woman—stand next to the handler, all safely protected behind a waist-high wooden wall that separates them from the alien animal. Behind them, on a second tier of the exhibition room, stand three more revelers: two women—only one of whom is masked—and a young girl. The handler's whip arm is drawn back, as though he is getting ready to strike, or at least threaten, the hapless beast.

The effect of this remarkable painting is one of spectatorial display. The masked faces, except for one woman and the young girl, do not let us see any emotion from the viewers. Two unmasked viewers are looking directly at the painter, or at least toward the painter's point of view. Even their faces seem flat, almost smiling, if they are conveying any emotion at all. Only the lone handler, raising his whip, has his eyes and his mouth wide open as he looks at the rhino; he might be saying something to the viewers or shouting something at the animal. Of course, the scene is set at Carnival, a time when the ordinary rules of society are put by, when excess of all kinds fills the streets, and palaces, and houses of the city. The picture represents the clash of two worlds: the sophisticated, jaded, slightly decadent world of mid eighteenth-century Venice and the world of the alien wilds from which this creature had arrived only a decade earlier. The relation between urban and natural was thus rendered problematic, even as the proto-urbanatural world began to emerge amid the carnival masks of Venice.

*   *   *

Henry Ward Beecher described the current month well: "October is Nature's funeral month. Nature glories in death more than in life. The month of departure is more beautiful than the month of coming— October than May" (11). Every dead leaf is that much more food for next year's plants and flowers. Each dead wasp adds its dry body to the nutrients needed to bring about new lives next spring. I can see the fresh, green buds of next year's spring forming on the branch tips here in October, before the really cold nights start falling; there are no beginnings or endings except the ones that human beings create for themselves. The long, low light of afternoon is lengthening in the valley. The cold is coming on as I gather twigs and pine cones and pitchy fatwood to start the year's first fire. Hot flames lick up around the kindling and crackle as I place the first large log of this autumn in the woodstove. As it begins to sizzle and pop, I think of those countless people over millennia who have relied only on flaming firewood to keep themselves warm. Fall is ready to fall. Winter is waiting in the wings. I can feel it coming. My woodpile is ready.

9

November

There can be no very black melancholy to him who lives in the midst of nature.

—*Thoreau*, Walden

These are dark days now, when the sun lies low against the valley and the dusk spreads out each late afternoon toward the horizon. There is nothing like arriving in a dark forest on a darkening night. The first sensation is the smell; almost like touch or sight, it comes out of the woods and fills the nostrils and the mind at the same instant: musty and cool but delicately sweet as well. It is the smell of drying and dying leaves, of green ferns turned brown, of countless newly dead insect bodies lying in the damp leaf-mold, cool damp fungus and mossy moisture behind thick tree bark, mouldering and melting. When I step out of the front door tonight, I cannot see my hand six inches from my face; that is how dark the woods have grown. The clouds cover the stars on this moonless night, while darkness fills up the woods like endless water in the sea. But even in this pitch-blackness, I can still smell that deep smell of autumn, that leaf-moss and mold-damp smell of the dying surface layer of the forest. It smells almost warm in this cold, almost light in this dark. I breathe it in deeply and slowly, again and again. Then I turn from the dark woods and go back inside the cabin.

In the city, or in the wild, paper-wasps builds their nests in the best places they can find. Often, at the Roost, these wasps are my nearest neighbors. I can hear them buzzing close by when I pour hot water to make my coffee. I see them climbing the stone walls or emerging from tiny cracks in the rocks when I light a fire in early spring or late fall. This summer one particular batch of wasps found a dark hollow, a womb-like nook around a squared box of light that they thought would be a perfect spot for their nest. How do they know? Which wasp decides? They chose the black-metal ceiling lamp on the Roost's screen porch. How could they have seen the ultimate effect of their careful choice? Day after summer-day they toiled, fashioning the hexagonal cells that would house the fertilized eggs that they hoped would be their future. They wound the base of their nest into a single strand, a tightly twisted thick thread hanging in the air, so that their unborn larval offspring would all have their heads pointing downward toward the porch floor: what careful planning. I watched these adult wasps work for hour after hour. They worked so hard that I could not bring myself to knock down their nest, even though they had chosen to make it indoors with me.

Each egg was deposited carefully, as carefully and as deeply as the wasps knew how. Each egg was distinct, each walled-off from the others, each a new chance for life in the making, all different but all identical. A wasp pupa takes exactly one winter to develop—new lives for old—old lives working to assure the genetic survival of the next generation. What determines this developmental duration is a precise combination of heat and light, stimulating just the right flow of nutrients and nourishment at just the right time. Antenna warmth surrounds the egg cases to make each antenna, abdomen warmth is required at just the right time to fashion each abdomen. Slowly and silently, stealthily and invisibly, each growth stage in just the right order, each precise detail of each growing wasp is fashioned perfectly: perfect eyes, perfect legs, perfect wings, almost every time. Then each tiny squirming blob of pure white protoplasm becomes a perfect wasp, wriggling its way out of its egg-chamber, bursting the chamber's cap, spreading its clear-veined wings as it crawls drowsily out of its perfect hexagonal home, dropping into the air and flying off instantly, each one a small wasp miracle. One winter for each generation, one fall to one spring, then a new wasp generation asserts itself onto the world: perfect.

What these diligent parental wasps failed to realize, however, was the nearby presence of humanity—and humanity's need for a light bulb—a little bit of urban life amid all the natural life around. So I became this new generation's downfall: unwittingly, unknowingly, until it was way too late. These wasps' safe and sane nesting place turned out to be the hot ceiling lamp at the center of the Roost's screen porch. Nightly, the hundred-watt bulb beneath their nest came on to illuminate my human world, at least it did so every time I flicked the innocuous wall switch. Night after night I sat beneath that light, reading or writing, talking to my guests or looking at the stars. Nightly that light bulb's heat rose steadily, hotter and hotter around those developing young wasps. Something was going wrong in wasp-world; or, if not wrong, at least this brood had speeded up its growth in a way that was about to produce a tiny wasp-tragedy. Perhaps you can see it coming. Neither the wasps or I knew; I suppose I should have known or could have known, but I did not.

Tonight—I am writing in early November—this night, right now, was the night when this small tragedy of wasp-life unfolded; it literally unfolded. Tonight these young larvae, reared in record wasp-time, burst from their geometrically perfect paper-wasp enclosures, hurried along by the bright light and the intense heat just beneath them. These baby-wasps were all born too early, many months before their due date, developed perfectly but rushed into life by a General Electric hundred-watt light-bulb that has been shining just beneath them since summer, forcing them to develop way too quickly. The materials of creation are ever-present, but the arrangements of creation are as potentially chaotic as they are ordered. Just ask this brood of paper wasps. They were born before my eyes tonight, born fast, but moving oh-so-slowly in this cold November darkness. The only warmth near them was—ironically—the very light bulb that had hastened their birth and would prove to be the cause of their deaths. Unable to fly, since their wings had not fully developed, the young unfolded their partial wings as they crawled from their tiny chambers, falling instantly out of their paper-wombs and then down to the cold ground to die. They dragged their damp but drying wasp-bodies around the porch floor, a floor that I had painted carefully—Battleship Gray, Sherwin-Williams, Heavy Duty Gloss—only one month earlier. That gray porch floor was now suddenly covered with dying wasps. These babies were banging into walls and screens, rolling onto their backs when the shiny paint proved too slippery. I watched them for over an hour. I was stunned and amazed to see them being born and then dying right away. At the same time, I must admit that I did not really know what to think. Should I try to save them? How would I? Tonight's predicted frost will kill them for sure. The light bulb that gave them this early life will surely be the cause of their early deaths.

Here is what Thoreau might have said to me tonight. This thought comes from the *Journal* in which he expressed so many of his clearest observations about nature:

> It is a rare qualification to be able to state a fact simply & adequately. To digest some experience cleanly. To say yes and no with authority—To

make a square edge. To conceive & suffer the truth to pass through us living & and intact [...] Say it & have done with it. Express it without expressing yourself. See not with the eye of science—which is barren— nor of youthful poetry which is impotent. (November 1, 1851, *Walden* 358–59)

So which eye is it, after all? Which "eye" should "I" see with when I try to describe these dying wasps? Thoreau understands, in this powerful passage, that it is neither science (a human construction) nor art: "youthful poetry" (another human construction) that will hand over the world as it is. The scientist renders the world barren in Thoreau's terminology, by which he means unproductive, unfertile, and unable to reproduce. The world of science is the world of practical rationality—the world of reasonable comprehension, perhaps—but, for Thoreau, the preferred world is always the world of wild "nature": a world of mystery, contradiction, partial truths, beautiful incompleteness, dynamic change: a world that can never be the world of static certainty.

This is what Keats meant by "*Negative Capability*," what he meant when he said, defining his famous phrase, that the mind should always be "capable of being in uncertainties, Mysteries, doubts, without any irritable reaching after fact & reason" (*Letters* 261). Each person should be happy to remain in this border—liminal—state between simple sensory experience and complete intellectual comprehension; that is where my wasps are tonight, poised between their own freezing to death and my ability to understand why such a thing has happened. Thoreau is likewise suspicious of youthful poetry, however, because he sees it as too idealistic, too full of wish-fulfilling, an art designed to replace the harsh realities of material experience with imagined visions, hoped-for outcomes, in short, a childish dream-world that does not exist. So I must find my place somewhere between middle-aged science and youthful poetry, between urban and natural, experience and innocence. Thoreau's sought-for position is always the hardest position to occupy, and that explains why it has been occupied by so few. Who wants to be told that their hard fought-for science is cold and lifeless (urban)? Who wants to learn that their poetry is "Romantic," escapist and unrealistic (natural)? Who wants to find out that those wasps were too close to the urban light-bulb, that all of that natural perfection—those beautiful hexagonal chambers and those perfectly formed pieces of wasp DNA—were all wasted, all for nought, and that they now lie cold and dying on the dark-gray porch, late at night, at the Roost, in late autumn?

SCIENCE AND POETRY

In 1802, William Paley offered a sweeping justification for an entire school of thought that grew from the title of his book and sought to reconcile all science with revealed religion: *Natural Theology: or, Evidences of the Existence and Attributes of the Deity, Collected from the Appearances of Nature.* "Natural theology," the idea that the living world revealed the glory—and characteristics of—God has been challenged and debated during more than two centuries of human attempts to explain how the same loving God who created daffodils and chocolate and kittens could be the very God who created—or allowed for the existence of—cancer, mentally deficient infants, and AIDS. Within a decade or so of Paley's book, the poet Percy Shelley weighed in on this contradiction, noting in *Queen Mab* (1813) that, while any God based on the evidence of nature might resemble power and beauty and light, such a God would also have to resemble death, destruction, and greed. This problem links back to my discussion of the frequent "Romantic" heresy that wants to "see" God in nature, but the Judeo-Christian God can *never* be *in* nature, since God is a perfect supernatural spirit and nature is the fallen material condition in which all physical things live and move and have their being. As a result, the need to explain all observable phenomena in terms of their divine origins gives way in a relatively short period of time (1802—c. 1900) to an empiricist set of rational conclusions. The result of this movement in intellectual history is that Romantic natural history, still bound up with spiritual thinking, is transformed into natural science as a completely materialist and religiously "neutral" activity. By the Victorian era, after Darwin's *Origin* (1859), it becomes clear that it does not matter if an atheist or a Hindu or a Buddhist develops a cure for scarlet fever (I might now say cancer or AIDS); the cure will still be the cure. Whatever the religious views of the person who cures any disease, that cure will make sufferers well. Religion will have nothing to do with it.

The thoroughgoing Romantic natural history that gives way to modern biology, zoology, botany, and field research rested on a wide range of texts and their connections: Robert Hooke's *Micrographia* (1665), the work that first revealed the wonders of the microscopic world; Edward Tyson's *Orang-Outang, sive Homo sylvestris* (1699), the first account of a creature that seemed too human-like to be classified merely as an animal; Thomas Pennant's *British Zoology* (1768–70), the Comte de Buffon's *L'Histoire Naturelle* (1780, 1785), Oliver Goldsmith's *History of the Earth, and Animated Nature* (1774 and after), and Erasmus Darwin's *Zoonomia; or The Laws of Organic Life*

(1794, 1796). William Blake draws his "tyger" more directly from printed texts such as these than from any personal experience with the creature. Shelley's skylark and sensitive plant, Keats's nightingale and John Clare's glow-worm, likewise owe their literary existence to complex combinations of personal experience and knowledge of "natural history" taken from books. Much of what the great "nature" poets knew about nature was drawn not from nature but from representations of the nonhuman world in natural history museums, books, illustrations, and paintings in an era before photography. In this "pre-two cultures" era, Blake, Shelley, and Keats read scientific texts as assiduously as they read poetry (Keats had completed the medical-school training for his time; he was ready to become a doctor before he wrote a single word of serious poetry). In addition, much of what people knew about the natural world had to come from books, since travel was often dangerous and prohibitively expensive.

The science of chemistry accounts for some of the strangest and most sudden changes in the way people thought about the world they inhabited. Doves died in bell-jars not because of the absence of some mysterious ether of life, but because a scientist has pumped out all of the purely material "dephlogisticated air," as Priestley called oxygen. Coleridge put the possibility of such serious links well when he wrote to Humphry Davy in 1801, "As far as words go, I have become a formidable chemist" (Dolan ix). This was the same Coleridge who, when asked why he attended so many lectures on human physiology in London said, "I attend Davy's lectures to increase my stock of metaphors" (*Notes upon Shakespeare* 353); indeed, Hartley Coleridge connected Coleridge's metaphor-making directly to the realm of science: "My father was fond of illustrating mental facts by physical analogies, of explaining and adorning metaphysical subjects by images obtained from the realm of Nature at the hands of the physical Sciences, especially chemistry" (353). The poet needs imaginative leaps in the mind to draw new connections; the scientist needs physical facts from the laboratory. The poetic-scientist needs imagination buttressed by facts, or facts fired by imagination, to make new metaphors.

Many influential modern scientists have acknowledged that metaphors and visual analogies (think of whirling atoms as tiny solar systems or the cone-shaped vortex of a black hole) are the means by which science represents its conclusions, moves forward into new modes of thinking, and makes its way into the wider culture. Copernicus had to imagine the sun as the celestial body at the center of things—just as a poet might imagine it—since all of the physical evidence about the sun, from ancient times until that day, had suggested just the opposite: the sun clearly moved around the earth, every day. Darwin used phrases like "imaginary instances" or "I should infer from analogy" throughout *On the Origin of Species*. As the historian of science Robert J. Richards has noted, "the central currents of nineteenth-century biology had their origins in the Romantic movement" (xix). Take that, C. P. Snow (the author who proposed the two-cultures—arts-versus-sciences—view of society). Indeed, many of the great advances in science throughout history have proceeded by analogy, metaphor, and the imaginative ability to describe a world that cannot be seen, to depict images that occur only in the mind but which nevertheless represent reality as it has been revealed to the senses.

When I was lucky enough to meet Stephen Hawking several years ago, he advanced the idea that his own career as a scientist had been fostered by the terrible disease that has crippled him—(A.L.S., a.k.a. Lou Gehrig's disease)—because this debilitating ailment has restricted the movements of his body so completely. Hawking told us (a small group of friends gathered around him at an art show outside of Cambridge) that he had been a pencil wielding, math-based, physicist before he was struck down by amyotrophic lateral sclerosis early in adulthood. He said that once he was confined to a wheelchair, his mind began to think more often in completely visual images. Instead of reaching for his calculator—as he might have done before full paralysis set in—the wheelchair-bound Hawking has been forced to let his mind roam in silence and in stillness, and it has often roamed to pictorial images. The first intuition he had of a black hole, he said, was a literal picture in his mind, not a formula, not a mathematical calculation. He saw the vortex of a swirling, whirlpool-like structure. Of course, once Hawking took his imaginative mental picture and applied it to the "pure" physics, the mathematics worked, and the calculations "proved" the image perfectly. An almost poetic metaphor—"well, it is like a hole, like a black vortex; it is like a *black hole* in space"—had become a scientific principle, one that has since been well established by much more pure mathematics and many more astronomical observations.

Beyond the niceties of interdisciplinary thinking lies a potentially more ominous link between science and literature. As Rob Iliffe has noted, "while Babbage [the mathematician and early "computer" scientist] and others extolled the apparently self-evident virtues of scientific and industrial progress, conservatives, socialists and writers as different as Wolfgang Goethe and Mary Shelley wondered whether the unstoppable juggernaut would leave more misery than benefits in its wake" (xxiii). Clearly such anxieties about science produced debates in which many people are still engaged. Is our society better off with or without the obvious benefits of technological and scientific advances? Are the obvious gains produced by antibiotics, the combustion engine, and genetically modified foods, worth the trouble caused by nuclear power, PCBs, and genetically modified foods? The issue is sometimes dispassionate, but it is always about power and control. Science gives humans power over their own lives and also over the lives of others, and much of that power is remarkably beneficial. At the same time, some of that same control threatens individual human lives as well as the lives of all living things on the planet.

In critiquing these origins of Romantic natural history, I do not want to overstate the desire of most humans—then or now—to get "back" to nature. To most individuals in the nineteenth century, and today, truly wild nature was and is still something to be feared, especially nature in the wildest of wild places: harsh, rugged, threatening, and potentially deadly. Even today, a life lived completely *in* nature is one that most humans would not choose. Human beings—past and present—value their creature comforts. Humans like to be warm when it is cold, and comfortably cool when it is hot. They like to have their appetite for food satisfied when it arises, not after having to catch and kill, or even to harvest, each meal. A life lived completely *in* nature is still the one that Hobbes accurately described as "solitary, poor, nasty, brutish, and short" (84). Human beings have turned to cannibalism (the whale-ship Essex in 1820, the air-crash of the Uruguayan soccer-team in the Andes in 1972) and various forms of savagery (1990s Liberia, the Rwandan genocide of 1994, North Korean atrocities of recent decades) in almost all conditions of extreme privation during the last century. Once the comforts of the city are removed completely, human beings can quickly revert to the animalistic modes of life from which they presumably emerged. One strong strain in the civilized history of human beings is—sadly, or perhaps not so sadly—the history of trying to get away from nature: away from dark forests that seemed alien and fearful, away from wild animals that could devour adults and children, away from freezing cold and fearful dark, away from blazing heat and blinding sun. The modern desire to get "back to nature" is a strange combination of Romantic dreams about a very specific kind of—pastoral—nature (flowers, birds, abundant fresh water, and healthful foodstuffs amid a comfortable climate) with a rugged version of American individualism (camping gear, tools for rock-climbing, a good pair of hiking boots, and a wilderness just far enough away from cities so that the cell-phone connection still works).

Like other creatures, I need to consider the impact of every altera-
tion I make to my surroundings. If my nest breaks the tree branch,
I made it too large. If my roost soils the ground beneath me, I need
to move away or clean up the mess. Of course, it is also true that my
personal link to nature is also a natural phenomenon, not just a social
one. I can, at certain times and in certain places, recall a closer connection to my surroundings that must come from an earlier time. In the
right temperature and in the right light, I am reminded of a time when
I did live both *in* nature and *of* nature. This feeling helps to explain
why so many people like to climb mountain peaks at sunrise, why
they like to spend several days in the inhuman forest, why they like to
row their ocean-kayaks way out beyond sight of land. This feeling can
feel almost like a genetic memory. I know that my ancestors walked
for miles in the dense forest. I know that they killed wild animals for
food and tended crops in rough soils in all weathers. Of course, this
link to "nature" also remains in certain ways in even the most socially
civilized person, in a skyscraper penthouse; this penthouse-dweller
cares about, engages in, and revels in—or suffers through—natural
eating, and sexual activity, and excretion. But now I am growing too
Romantic in my own ecocritical reflections. If I reign myself in at this
point (I only have three months of roosting left to go in this year), I
may reach a vision that makes sense for an entire human future.

Imagine urban, suburban, small town, and rural spaces in which
the air is clear and the water is clean, in which the food is fresh and
preservative free, in which the energy is used but also reused, in which
human spaces are built in ways that blend inner nature with the outer
world. Think of houses that bring the out-of-doors indoors, in which
the indoors also goes out-of-doors (in ways that link daily weather
with daily thoughts, growing plants and personal emotions, animal
health and human health): in all such connections—sky with kitchen,
stream with study, stars with bedroom—urbanatural roosters might
find new sources of sustenance, new sources of strength. The idea of
being a nature "lover" needs to give way to something more subtle
and sophisticated. Human beings now need to become nature "car-
ers" and nature "sharers": care about it, then share it. The implications of this change are also very practical. The time has come to see
the walls of buildings not as walls but as permeable membranes, the
windows as openings to let in the light but also the heat, the doors
as interactive spaces, not barriers to keep something out. Built spaces
need to become flexible borders that functionally link my life indoors
with my life in the outside world. Technology will be a major part of
this transition: every southern-facing wall needs to be made of glass,

just as every northern facing wall needs to keep out the cold. Every newly made home needs to hold in every calorie of heat, or every bit of cool, it generates. It is time to let the sun into our buildings (or keep it out in sultry climes), to capture the wind along the walls and rooflines of our homes, to capture rainwater and reuse it directly as wash-water wherever we live, to capture every blade of grass we cut as compost, and to eat and drink more of what we *need* and less of what we *want*. Without too much effort, with just a slight reorientation of priorities, human beings can begin to make all of this happen.

A HARD RAIN'S GONNA FALL

The cold November rain must have started well past midnight, but it woke me just before the first light of dawn. By sunrise the rain was falling in sheets. I could hear it *tink-tinking* on the tin roof of the porch, *thud-thudding* on the spongy moss-covered shingles above my head in my wide double-bunk. The sound of the wind swirling in the trees mixed with rain sounds to produce a gentle, but still rattling, roar that thumped along like a slow moving machine. The rain kept falling hard for a long time. The low-pressure system above me must have been a swirling big one—a mini cyclonic storm—since the barometric pressure dropped below twenty-nine millibars by dawn. But the rain kept thudding for several hours more. I slept fitfully until its noise woke me again. I looked out the window into deep woods that were still dripping wet.

A good sized rainstorm on the East Coast of the United States produces 145 million pounds of rainwater for every inch of rainfall over every square mile. That is 17–18 million gallons per square mile. I can see at least twenty miles to the next western ridge, roughly forty miles from the Pennsylvania border to the north down into the heart of the Shenandoah Valley to the south; that makes 14,400,000,000 million gallons of rain for every inch of rainfall (*Water Science*). This morning's news says that just over one inch of rain has fallen during the night. So I have watched and listened as 15 billion gallons of water have fallen from the sky onto my mountain and the valley beneath it. "These things are not well enough known," as an earlier anchorite—Annie Dillard—said before me (232). The rain begins as microscopic dots of moisture rising like steam from the teakettle, lighter than air, swirling upward into high-climbing clouds. Then it ends as untold drops and wide sheets of water, filling the streams and the river below.

Shelley was the first poet in English to describe the scientific subtleties of the hydrologic cycle in a poem, "The Cloud." The clichéd and typical image of the Romantic poets, the one that sees them looking at flowers and birds and sky, and then dreaming their imaginative fancies into lines of lyric verse, gets it all wrong. Shelley was reading reams of scientific data about clouds and meteorology at the same time that he was penning his poems about weather. Like the painters J. M. W. Turner and John Constable, Shelley had studied the material science of clouds and rainfall in precise detail long before he ever set pen to paper to describe a cloud accurately, poetically, in the first person:

> I bring fresh showers for the thirsting flowers,
>   From the seas and the streams;
> I bear light shade for the leaves when laid
>   In their noon-day dreams.
> From my wings are shaken the dews that waken
>   The sweet buds every one,
> When rocked to rest on their mother's breast,
>   As she dances about the Sun.
> I wield the flail of the lashing hail,
>   And whiten the green plains under,
> And then again I dissolve it in rain,
>   And laugh as I pass in thunder. ("The Cloud" 1–12)

Consider what Shelley knows, in this single stanza, about the science of rain. He knows that rain comes from vaporized molecules of H_2O drawn from oceans and rivers and streams. He knows that this water, falling on spring blossoms, swells them into new life, and that lower temperatures in the cloud can produce frozen precipitation, as hail, that melts as it falls. He also knows that thunder arises during both hailstorms and rainstorms. He knows a great deal.

The most powerful stanza in Shelley's poem, however, is the last one, not only for its accurate science but also for its recognition of the connection between natural processes and nonhuman cycles, a theme of which Shelley is the master:

> I am the daughter of Earth and Water,
>   And the nursling of the Sky;
> I pass through the pores of the oceans and shores;
>   I change, but I cannot die—
> For after the rain, when with never a stain
>   The pavilion of Heaven is bare,
> And the winds and sunbeams with their convex gleams,
>   Build up the blue dome of Air—
> I silently laugh at my own cenotaph,
>   And out of the caverns of rain,

Like a child from the womb, like a ghost from the tomb,
I arise and unbuild it again.— (73–84)

For Shelley, the true resurrection is never human but always natural:
out of the womb of natural process—born and then reborn in every
cloud, in every rain shower—comes a new version of a fully natural
cycle and the resulting new life. The human womb, as James Joyce
and Samuel Beckett both said, is also a tomb, but the tomb of natural
process is always also the womb of new life. It is easy to agree with
Shelley in every detail of this claim. Once humans move away from
their egotistical human need for personal immortality, the central
principle of all nonhuman nature is eternal life. Nature lasts forever;
whatever else might a human being want?

As I look through the soaking-wet porch screens, I notice that
yesterday's dry moss beds have literally greened overnight. The rain
finally slows, and then stops around midday, and the damp birds suddenly take up their singing again in earnest. A hawk screams overhead
once, then twice, and then three times in rapid succession. A fat blue-
jay squawks across the clearing and flies off down toward the river.
A bird I cannot fully see on the ground starts digging and cackling,
sending up small clumps of wet leaves, dripping-wet sticks, and small
damp branches. Somehow he must have found his food, or the nest
building material he needs, during the long storm. He keeps working
his wet patch of ground in earnest.

As the back edge of this twelve-hour front finally blows through,
I can literally watch the needle of the barometer rise. The wind picks
up as the billions of brown November leaves I can see shake their
water droplets off all around me. The topographic map shows that I
am at roughly 1,200 feet of altitude here. As the storm breaks, and
the low-pressure system rolls off toward the northeast, the cloud's
bottoms are scudding by just a few hundred feet above my head.
Gray and black and white and paler cream, these cloud-bottoms keep
puff-puffing down and swirling in tufted curls, sliding slowly in a
stately fashion along the ridge line and over the back of the mountain
behind me. The clouds turn ever-so-slowly at the sharp side of the
storm system, rolling south toward Ashby Gap on the edge of the
cyclone moving east, off toward Point of Rocks and Purcelville, out
into the rolling fields of Loudoun County.

WINTER

—HIBERNAL ROOSTING—

BEYOND ROMANTIC ECOCRITICISM

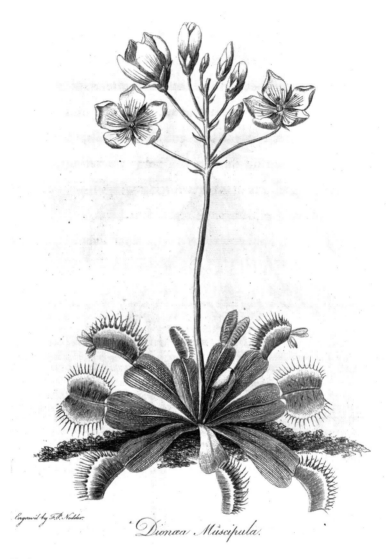

Engraved by F.P. Nodder.

Dionæa Muscipula.

The insect-eater, Dionea muscipula. The Great Chain of Being is broken forever when a plant can kill and consume insects. (*The Botanic Garden.* London: Joseph Johnson, 1791).

1 0

December

Then only will you see it, when you cannot speak of it; for the knowl-edge of it is deep silence, and suppression of all the senses.

—*Hermes Trismegistus* (Lib. 10.5–6)

How many humans in history have hurried—as I did tonight—trying to defeat the impending darkness. I arrived on the mountain at four o'clock this afternoon, and when I opened the cabin door, the inside temperature was thirty-six degrees. Before I started a fire, however, I realized that I had work to do, in a hurry. The sky was darkly overcast, the western horizon a deep purple red, and the light that remained to me was less than an hour's worth, at best. I had to move one pile of damp split-wood under the house in order to start it drying, and I had to get another pile from beneath the porch, under the eaves by the front door, to keep it dry and close at hand for at least the next twelve hours. The forecast is for snow. I did not want to have to transport armloads of wood in the snowy dark with only a flashlight, especially since I was alone on the mountain. I set to work immediately.

Just imagine all of those who have raced this same race against the growing cold and darkness: shepherds moving their flocks quickly from hillsides and pastures to the safety of barns or stony sheepfolds, children hurrying home from darkening rivers and streams toward cottages whose windows shine with only dim firelight, the emissaries of princes racing for the safety of the castle, travelers of all sorts in a hurry, lost or running late. In our own world of streetlamps, head-lights, neon, and fluorescent tubes, we have lost this sense of impend-ing nightfall almost completely. This is why that nighttime shot of the United States from outer space is so sobering. Civilization has replaced the darkness of night with the glaring brightness of well-lit skyscrapers, gleaming orange streetlamps, shining lights of all kinds, until now it is possible to trace the shoreline outline of almost every landmass on earth with lights that burn brightly all night long, every night. The one thing I can confirm about all of those people who ever hurried for the safety of a doorway as the night descended is that it was dark out there for them as well, dark and often fearful. Like true silence, that aspect of the natural world—real darkness—is almost gone now. Urbanature has ended it.

Romantic Rhinos and Victorian Vipers

Locked up in this cabin for a dark and snowy week in the middle of December has got me thinking about creatures locked up in cages of all types. Captivity represents another aspect of urbanature and calls for a different version of self-consciousness, a different aspect of awareness. I am initially less interested in the debate about whether zoos should exist than I am in the historical factors that led to the creation of zoos in the first place and the ecocultural factors that have sustained them for several centuries in the great cities of the modern world. To bring wild creatures long distances for spectatorial display, to keep wild animals captive so that they can be studied and allowed (or encouraged) to reproduce, to know that some of these wild species will become extinct except for the few specimens that can be kept alive in cages: all of these elements of zoos trace back to a fundamental form of pleasure that is derived from capturing and collecting wild nature.

> If you could have seen what it was like when I was a boy—half zoo and half museum, my father let us do anything we wanted. For a while we had a big tree in the corner, with live birds roosting in it. Aquariums, and an ant colony, and turtles and salamanders; and jars of preserved specimens everywhere, big slabs of fossil-bearing rock and mastodon bones and a plant press, books open on all the tables. A wonderful, fertile clutter. (260)

This passage from Andrea Barrett's evocative novel, *The Voyage of the Narwhal*, presents her main character, Erasmus Darwin Wells, reflecting on his childhood memory of the Romantic natural history repository his father had created in the early years of the nineteenth century. This image captures the mood of a moment that was particularly important in the history of humanity's relations to the animal kingdom. Natural history cabinets, like zoos and other forms of live or dead animal displays—as I have already suggested in my reflections on natural history museums—emerged out of precisely the combination of scientific curiosity and fascination with spectacle that is captured in this quote from Barrett's fiction. To see something new and amazing is often to learn something new, but the experience is also about being excited, titillated or amazed, in this case by captive animals of all kinds or by the material remnants of their captivity: stuffed specimens, skins, skeletons, body parts (claws, fangs, skulls, mounted heads) and the like. Captive wild organisms, whether dead or alive, represent a form of control over the natural world.

Zoological gardens in the eighteenth and nineteenth centuries developed as cultural sites with important implications for understanding the material aspects of nature and forms of imperialism that extended into the nonhuman realm. In addition, these sites embodied the relationship between ideas of spectacle and our treatment of other species, as well as members of our own species. The zoo chronicles an important history of the way humans seek to dominate their environment, often under the apparently innocent guise of expanding scientific knowledge. The first monarchs and potentates who assembled royal parks, menageries, and pleasure-gardens filled with living creatures made no pretense about their purposes. To fence or to cage other creatures was to control them for a number of related reasons: hunting, dining, entertainment, or mere diversion. The power of possession was justification enough for collections of lions, tigers, monkeys, giraffes, eagles, serpents, and other exotic creatures that date at least as far back as the Egyptian pharaohs. Kubla Khan's "pleasure dome," imagined so vividly by Samuel Taylor Coleridge, was an early European and Orientalist fantasy of just such a menagerie: "In Xanadu did Kubla Khan / A stately pleasure-dome decree: / Where Alph, the sacred river, ran / Down to a sunless sea" (*Coleridge* 1–4). Marco Polo had described the historical Kublai Khan's royal menagerie in Shang-tu in detail: it "included leopards, lions (they were probably tigers, since they were described as having black stripes), lynxes, and even elephants, as well as a variety of eagles and falcons used for hunting" (Hoage, Roskell, and Mansour 12).

By the nineteenth century, scientific knowledge had become a primary justification for private, and eventually public, gatherings and displays of a wide variety of creatures from around the world. It was ethically acceptable to cage other creatures, even human creatures, as long as the knowledge thus gained could be codified or organized as part of the great encyclopedic project that had begun as early as the fifteenth and sixteenth centuries throughout the civilized world. By the nineteenth century, the systematic collecting and classifying of nature was part of a combined imperial and scientific project that led directly to Darwin's *Origin of Species*. The *Beagle* expedition that carried Darwin to the Galápagos, and eventually around the world, was undertaken primarily as a hydrographic (water-depth) and map-making survey of South America, both crucial aspects of imperial activity. Darwin's role as naturalist and gentleman companion to Captain Fitzroy was a decidedly secondary aspect of the journey. Accurate oceanographic charts were essential for global exploration, and effective maps represented early forms of geographic control; the colonizer wanted to have a clearer picture of the land and water in question than the colonized peoples themselves. Collecting hitherto unknown plants and animals was an added benefit of such a voyage. In Darwin's case, the plants and animals (alive and dead) that returned from this journey proved to be the basis of his career as a scientist and of the theory of evolution.

Collecting wild animals was nothing new. Henry I had begun the first royal British menagerie; in 1252, Henry III moved this collection of live animals into the Tower of London where it remained until 1831 (Hoage et al 13). Stamford Raffles founded the Zoological Society of London on the edge of Regent's Park in 1826, but the grounds were not formally opened to visitors until 1828 and not to the general public (i.e., without invitation or subscription) until 1846. The immediate success of Raffles's venture, however, is indicated by a report from the government council indicating that 112,226 people visited the zoological garden during this first year of its public operation. William IV closed the Tower of London menagerie and presented the royal collection of creatures, along with those from Windsor Great Park, to the Zoological Society (Altick 317). This royal act suggested an important transfer of cultural authority. The collecting of captive animals, by the 1830s, was no longer a sign of the wealth and power of a single monarch but an added symbol of the domination of an imperial nation over the far corners of the earth from which these captive wild animals had originated.

In addition to zoos, of course, animals had been exhibited in a variety of carnivals, fairs, and "freak" shows since the Middle Ages. The first rhinoceros in Britain, for example, arrived in Restoration London aboard an East India ship in 1684 and was exhibited in numerous locales—at "Bartholomew Faire," at the "Bell Sauvage Inn at the foot of Ludgate Hill" and elsewhere—until its untimely death two years later; as Altick notes, "much of the charm of these show beasts resided in the aura of mystery or romance in which the show-men diligently wrapped them" (37). The curious—if not terrifying—sight of a rhinoceros must have been linked to the myth of the unicorn from the moment of its first arrival in England. Imagine the faces of those Londoners who witnessed the uncrating of this first rhinoceros or his early public exhibitions. Such a creature must have seemed like a beast from another world. "Sideshow" animal exhibitions like this continued unabated into the nineteenth century. Indeed, the ostensibly scientific objectivity of zoos shades over throughout their history into other less savory forms of animal exploitation: menagerie displays, circus performances, bear and bull baiting, cock fighting, and dog racing. As Randy Malamud says, "the Renaissance age of imperialism made it economically, historically, and morally possible to amass animals and squeeze them into the compartments people created for them. The Victorian age accelerated, institutionalized, and sanctified the processes of zookeeping and zoo spectatorship" (15). One dark side of urbanature began to emerge with the earliest establishment of urban parks designed solely for the purpose of displaying wild creatures. A captive world stood in for—and symbolized—a conquered world.

Zoos have had a special status in the history of human relations to animals because they offered not only the sensory *frisson* of live-animal display but also the satisfactions of imperial conquest (representatives of the viewers' culture had collected these creatures from every corner of the globe) and of scientific advancement (these specimens might be useful for taxonomic study, anatomical artistry, and even breeding purposes). Zoos, unlike other animal spectacles, helped to track and preserve records of the vast expansion of knowledge that accompanied global exploration and the subsequent return of living specimens to European and, later, American cities. One way of proving the importance of the voyage or journey an explorer had just completed was to bring back specimens, alive or dead, that confirmed the exotic aspect of the locales to which he had traveled. Thus an officer of the East India Company like Raffles might return with "Sumatran animals" at the end of his tour of duty, or "great white" hunters and collectors like Carl Hagenbeck and Frank Buck would trade animals the way other explorers and imperialists traded ivory, spices, or human slaves (Veltre 27). In fact, the trade in living animals was not as independent of the trade in human flesh as we might imagine; the same ships that trafficked in human cargo often transported "creatures" of other species as well. As a result, zoos participated throughout the century in a spectacle of animal capture, transportation, and exposition that was part of the larger discourse of domination that characterized nineteenth-century European imperialism.

As Harriet Ritvo notes of early nineteenth-century visitors to Regent's Park Zoo, "there was ample opportunity for visitors to enjoy simultaneously the thrill of proximity to wild animals and the happy sense of superiority produced by their incarceration. Only the exceptional visitor, such as the critic Leigh Hunt, found this relationship other than pleasant. He was struck by the animals' 'quiet...and the human-like sort of intercourse into which they get with their visiters [*sic*]' and ended his tour of the London zoo feeling melancholy about their captivity" (*Animal* 219–20). Hunt would eventually write movingly about the wrongs of animal captivity, "Why can we have Acts of Parliament in favor of other extension of good treatment to the brute creation, and not one against their tormenting imprisonment?" Animals' lives under such conditions, he concluded, "turned into lingering deaths" (Altick 318). One strain of Romantic ecocriticism would eventually link Hunt's reaction to caged animals to widespread twenty-first century debates about captivity and animal rights; during the Romantic era itself, however, his proto-ecocentric sympathy for captive creatures was clearly a minority viewpoint.

For most people then, and many people even now, the spectacular aspect of the zoo—the experience of looking at wild animals—was seen as innocent and entertaining. Sophisticated Londoners—like their counterparts in Paris, Berlin, and Amsterdam—would often travel to the zoo whenever a new animal had arrived from some far-flung destination. Exhibited creatures formed the basis for conversation, public lectures, scientific research, and artistic expression. Spectators were particularly drawn by those animal activities, such as feeding time, that were likely to produce the most active and energetic exposition of an animal's wildness or strangeness. In addition, the zoo created a very satisfying illusion about human control over nature. The captive python or rhinoceros assured the power of *Homo sapiens* over the rest of the animal kingdom. If representatives of the forces of social order could capture and cage creatures from throughout the global wild, then humans must also have the power to tame the natural world in general and, by extension, the human world in these same far-flung regions. During the century that saw the early ravages of the Industrial Revolution, and the first sustained assault on natural resources from South America to South Africa and South Asia, the artificiality of the lion enclosure and the reptile house suggested yet another way that human beings might transform, contain, and control nature for their own purposes. In many instances of animal captivity, urbanature took on a cruel, and often needlessly destructive, character.

A number of the motives for animal collection and display were legitimately scientific, taxonomic, and economic, but there were clearly more sinister sides to this activity. Blake reminded his society, as early as 1803, that "A Robin Red breast in a Cage / Puts all Heaven in a Rage" ("Auguries of Innocence" 5–6), much less a lion, or a bear, or an elephant. Indeed, the attempt to keep wild animals in captivity produced an immeasurable amount of disease, suffering, and death among the captives. Ritvo points out that the average large mammal lived for only two years in captivity by the middle years of the century. Live animals were treated in ways that suggest deep psychological undercurrents in all animal capture and display. When Queen Victoria visited the lion-taming act of Isaac Van Amburgh, the animals "had been kept purposely without food for six and thirty hours" so that the Queen might see them "in their more excited and savage state during the operation of feeding them" (Ritvo, *Animal* 224). The idea that humans might create their own versions of animal savagery with the help of deprivation or outright torture was confirmed by a London journalist in 1870 who reported, "how true the animals are to their savage instincts, even in confinement": the evidence for this savagery derived solely from the description of feeding time as the "crowning point of the show," remarking on the "bellowing, roaring, and growling" of the carnivores in conjunction with the excitement produced by the way "they drag and tear the big bone or lump of raw meat" (Ritvo 224). The apparent wildness of many of these creatures could thus be directly tied to the conditions produced by the humans in charge of their captivity. The animals were hungry, indeed, they might be starving; that was why they behaved in ways that excited their human— their human animal?—spectators. There was nothing *natural* in this process at all. Put a "wild" animal in a cage; deprive him of food, companionship, and his conditions in the wild. What result should then be expected? So even the animals' "wildness" was a creation of the human captors. Human keepers manipulated caged beasts like a stage show to produce the dramatic effects they desired.

One of the most widely known and public examples of cruelty to a caged animal was the 1826 execution in London of Chunee, a five-ton Indian elephant. Chunee began his captive life as a performer on stage and then went on to become a leading attraction at the Exeter 'Change [Exchange] Menagerie in the Strand at a site not far from Trafalgar Square and Covent Garden. Chunee was tame to the point of being docile for years but, as he matured, he became increasingly violent during periods of *musth*, those outbursts of completely natural male sexual excitement—described in powerful detail in George Orwell's essay "Shooting an Elephant"—that eventually became a threat to his keepers and to the general public (Flint 97). Chunee's final *musth* left him wild in his cage, banging his head and trunk against the walls and iron bars, trumpeting wildly at all hours of the day and night, lunging at his keepers and the public, endangering even those animal tenders who simply entered his cage to feed him.

His execution was not accomplished with ease. When he refused to ingest the dose of poison that had been prepared for him, his death required—by one account—152 musket balls delivered in over an hour, with the *coup de grace* finally accomplished with a sword. One witness reported that the sound of the elephant's "agony had been much more alarming than that made by the soldier's guns" (Ritvo, *Animal* 226). In addition, witnesses reported that gallons of elephant blood flowed deep on the floor of his cage before the great creature expired. Chunee's death was followed by illustrations in the popular press of the massive elephant kneeling on his hind legs behind bars while volleys of bullets were fired into his bleeding chest. Letters filled *The Times* to protest not only Chunee's death but also the conditions of his extended life in captivity. Poems appeared with sentiments on the order of "Farewell, poor Chunny! generous beast, farewell!" (Altick 314). The sad saga was even the source of a successful play at Sadler's Wells theater, *Chuneelah; or, The Death of the Elephant at Exeter-Change*. Of course, elephants had been used throughout Asia as tame work animals for centuries, but the idea of keeping a creature this large and this intelligent—elephants mourn their dead and teach their young—in a concrete room with iron bars where he could barely turn around has given ongoing pause to human viewers since the earliest days of zoos.

Another important aspect of animal captivity during the Romantic and Victorian eras was the extent to which animals—like Chunee— were anthropomorphized by spectators. Here is Lord Byron, recording a visit to the same Exeter Exchange in his *Journal*:

> Two nights ago I saw the tigers sup at Exeter 'Change. Except Veli Pacha's lion in the Morea,—who followed the Arab keeper like a dog,—the fondness of the hyaena for her keeper amused me most. Such a conversazione!—There was a "hippopotamus," like Lord L[iverpoo]l in the face; and the "Ursine Sloth" hath the very voice and manner of my valet—but the tiger talked too much. The elephant

[probably Chunee himself] took and gave me my money again—took off my hat—opened a door *trunked* a whip and behaved so well, that I wish he was my butler. The handsomest animal on earth is one of the panthers; but the poor antelopes were dead. I should hate to see one *here*:—the sight of the *camel* made me pine again for Asia Minor. (November 14, 1813)

As in Byron's witty descriptions, other writers praised chimps, orangutans, and comparably "sagacious" beasts for their intellect and for the strong appearance of human-like emotions that often characterized their behavior. Such humanization of captive creatures was part of a larger attempt to explain similarities between the animal kingdom and human life without the scientific evidence that would soon be provided by Darwin's *Origin*. Caged creatures, according to Byron and other writers, might look or act like prime ministers or presidents; these similarities could be instructive about both the animals and their human counterparts.

As in my earlier argument, Byron comes close to ecomorphism in his suggestion that, not only are they like us (anthropomorphism), but that we are like them (ecomorphism): Lord Liverpool is like a hippo, and Byron's valet is a veritable sloth. Thomas Hardy expressed one of the consequences of such early ecomorphism in his astonishment that modern humans could "tolerate such useless inflictions as making animals do what is unnatural to them, to drag out life in a wired cell" (Malamud 17). The question is clearly one of emphasis, but for Hardy, as for Byron, you and I are *like* these animals. Not a single human being wants to be caged; not one person would exchange lives with a zoo creature. By the time broadly evolutionary models began to have widespread influence during the Victorian era (after 1859), anthropomorphism would often be fully reversed, until Darwin himself was ecomorphically depicted with the body of an ape in the popular press. By this point, the early ecocentric human has become an animal in the public mind.

E. F. Benson, in an essay entitled "The Zoo" (1893), suggests a deeper, and ultimately more psychological, source for the spectatorial attraction—and repulsion—often associated with zoo going. Here he describes his own Victorian visit to the Reptile House—the world's first—in Regent's Park in vivid and memorable terms. Benson links animal spectatorship to a deep psychological truth about himself:

I once saw the snakes fed; the public are no longer allowed to see it, and quite rightly. There were about a dozen people in the snake-house, at the time, and I think we were all silent as we went out, when the feeding was over. The snake I watched was a live python from South America [...] and he was given a live rat, for they will not eat the dead food [...] it was horrible. It was many years since I saw that sight. It was, I think, the most terrifying thing I ever beheld. In sleep, the horror of it sometimes still reaches me. I am in a dim unfamiliar room, alone at first, but as I sit there, something wakes into existence which is horrible, evil, not understood, and I cannot get away. (232–33)

Malamud, who quotes this passage from Benson's essay, comments on the power of this observation and links it to the wider discourse of animal domination and degradation: the point "is not that animals eating is disgusting; obviously it is a fundamental facet of natural behavior. But something seems askew, inappropriate, about feeding rituals as they occur at the zoo, and about spectators' presence . . . what happens in zoos is essentially not about animals but about people . . . it is about us in disturbing ways" (233). What disturbs here is a sense of things that should not be seen, at least of things that should not be seen in the way captivity allows me to see them—that is—unnaturally.

Humans do not throw meat to animals in the wild. Humans do not make dolphins dance on their tails in order to be fed their fish in the sea. Just like those zoo-keepers who made an animal *act* wildly in order to be rewarded with food, the experience of watching a wild animal be fed in a cage unmasks a culturally constructed "wildness" that represents a human perversion of—or at least a corruption of—one small part of natural order. Zoo captives do not eat the way they do in the wild; the food is brought to them and placed on the concrete slab in front of them. My desire to see snakes or dolphins eating must be based on my desire for certain sorts of knowledge, knowledge of other creatures and their habits that is linked to my own identity-formation, my human self-definition. I watch a seal or a dolphin eating, and I feel better about my own carnivorous ways. Or, I watch a python or a lion eating, and I suddenly feel a sense of control over the life of these powerful, yet captive, creatures. When I would feed live mice to my eldest daughter's three-foot-long ball python, all of her sisters would gather and look on, their faces revealing a strange combination of fear, horror, power, and fascination. In such cases, Thoreau's sense of my own wildness seems somehow perverted, misused, even immoral.

Let me now turn briefly to the debate about whether zoos should exist in the twenty-first century. What does my idea of urbanatural roosting reveal about zoos and other forms of animal captivity and display? Nineteenth-century zoos participated in the tradition of Romantic natural history; they provided a subjective opportunity for the growing middle and upper classes to experience—and often record—their subjective reactions to wild animals. There have always been ostensibly "objective" and "scientific" defenses of captivity: why not keep wild animals in cages? What about the potential scientific benefits (medicines, transfusions, transplants, research) of studying and experimenting on creatures behind bars? In addition, the emotions conveyed to and by these creatures—both *their* emotions and *our* emotions—have provided additional defenses for their capture and sustained captivity: "This marmoset seems happy in his new enclosure; he always runs up to greet me, and he chatters when I give him food. He makes me so happy." Individual and species protection has been yet another defense: "This tiger (and his kind) would be dead had they been left in the wilds of Sumatra"—roughly five hundred Sumatran tigers do remain in the wild today.

In the twenty-first century, two defenses of zoos dominate the debate. One version of Romantic ecocriticism provides an argument that, no matter how much an anxiety I may have about zoos, they provide two undeniable benefits: a chance for young children to fall in love with the animal kingdom and the opportunity for adults to preserve the lives (and genetic inheritance) of threatened species. Both of these possibilities—falling in love with animals and saving endangered species—represent strongly Romantic desires. The scientific element of the modern zoo is its role as a site for animal research: species preservation, genetic experimentation, cloning, fertilized-egg cryogenesis (freezing), and the like. Behind such pragmatic concerns, however, the ethical dimension of zoo-keeping remains: humans should *care* for the animal kingdom; they need to help to *save* the nonhuman world. Humans only take care of those things they love. If caring for and saving the nonhuman world requires captive breeding, then so be it.

My idea of urbanature, however, suggests that cities (and urban dwellers) now need to move beyond the purely emotional aspects of captivity. The desire to domesticate the nonhuman world within the confines of city "parks" goes back—in Europe at least—to William the Conqueror and Henry I (Blunt 15–17). In the Middle East and Asia, this desire dates back even further (Hoage et al 8–11). Yet a strong conflict exists from then until now between celebrating similarities between animals and humans and, at the same time, keeping them as captives. In the twenty-first century, this emotional tension is also powerfully embodied in spectacles like Marineland (near St. Augustine, Florida), SeaWorld (in Orlando, San Diego, and San

Antonio), Ringling Brothers and Barnum & Bailey Circus (throughout the United States), and many of the world's great zoos. These
are modern urbanatural sites (human-fashioned "wild" settings) in
which many of the most self-conscious and intelligent of all animals
(elephants and apes, orcas and dolphins), as well as many of the most
fearful and dangerous (lions, tigers, and bears), are held captive and
displayed primarily to provide popular, public pleasure. This situation
should end.

Zoo owners—and their staff ecologists—should now move in one
of two directions. They should create opportunities for humans to
interact with animals in settings that are as fully wild as possible:
gorilla ecotours in Central Africa and birding expeditions to Costa
Rica are obvious examples; or, zoos should create environments that
are indistinguishable from the wild circumstances in which these
animals "naturally" exist. Hundreds of acres of captive-space should
be required for even the smallest of "caged" creatures. Wild animals
should be kept only in conditions that are as close as is humanly possible to their original circumstances in the wild. To the fullest extent
possible, caged animals should not know—or "feel"—that they are
captives. Urbanatural zoos need to leave off the emphasis on "urban"
that has characterized city-zoos for centuries: reptile houses, iron
bars, glass enclosures, garish signage, snack-bars, and shops. Zoos
now need to lean fully toward the "natural," the "nonhuman" aspect
of preserving the wild world. The urbanatural zoo should be a site
of captivity that does not feel like captivity, a place where cages have
no bars or obvious walls, a site that requires all humans to leave their
own environments completely behind to enter the wildest of possible
enclosures for lions, tigers, and bears.

*　　*　　*

The persistent cold outside of my warming Roost walls finally drives
me out of the cabin and back into civilization. I prepare to leave the
Roost two days earlier than I had planned. As I watch the end of
my morning fire die down in the woodstove, I wonder; if it takes
this much wood to heat my small one-room stone cabin for a week,
how much wood was required to heat a large, many-chimneyed house
with only fireplaces in the nineteenth century and earlier: a great deal
of wood for sure, cords upon cords of it. On my last December night
I find myself thinking about Coleridge again. Of all the Romantics,
Coleridge is the author whose images literally haunt my own mind
most often: "Shall hang them up in silent icicles, / Quietly shining

to the quiet moon" ("Frost at Midnight" 78–79). Where does a cold winter-week of roosting leave me? With quiet and then silence. Nature's quiet often ends in silence. Silence and cold. Cold, dark, and silence. The silence of this mountain on a night like this night. The silence of two voices that do not speak at the moment of pure love. The silence of death. Silence here. Silence now. Beyond sound. Beyond sight. Only silence. Beyond space and time. Silence.

JANUARY

In each atom a hundred suns are concealed.

—*Mahmud Shabistari*

Shabistari, from whom my epigraph for this month is taken, was a Sufi mystic of the 1300s. In this quotation, centuries before modern atomic theory, he intuited the precise truth that would lead to atomic energy and the atomic bomb. In some way he knew that the atom—the entity he believed to be the smallest building block of matter—contained the energy of "a hundred suns," the power of a force that humans had a hard time understanding, then or now. Yet he was right, as scientists learned when they split the atom and then harnessed its power in the 1940s, first for bombs and later for nuclear energy. As the socially conventional New Year—not my urbanatural year—begins: (I am roosting now in January; my roosting-year began in March), it seems appropriate to imagine a poet and mystic from seven hundred years ago who understood a truth of nature simply because he could imagine how much power every individual element of the nonhuman world must contain. His quotation might make human beings seem small—puny and very insignificant—by comparison. Yet every human being is also composed of atoms, so the energy of a hundred suns is lurking in each of my atoms as well.

All of that atomic energy does not help me much in a personal way. The Roost's weather is way too cold now for the good of any human being. As I sit by the blazing woodstove, and put my hands on the warm fieldstone around and above the narrow ledge of the fireplace-mantle, I wonder why humans ever moved toward the northern latitudes or stayed and settled anywhere except in the Mediterranean? If my primitive Norse ancestors could have gone south, why did they not move toward mainland Europe when the cold winds arrived? I am serious. Why did so many of my Viking ancestors remain up there, in the frigid land of the midnight sun? All of those Eskimos, those Inuit people and Laplanders, why did they not head south, looking for warmer climes? They must have known that there were places where palm trees were waving and clothing was optional. They must have heard stories from travelers about warm lands full of pineapples, mangoes, and papayas. Why would anyone stay in a land of cold and snow drifts and pack-ice when they could have headed south to sandy beaches, fresh fish, and coconuts every day, not to mention clothing made of palm fronds and a pale blue sea for swimming? On a cold winter morning I wonder: whatever kept human beings living in cold climates? I am clearly thinking of spring.

Displaying Human Beings

The nineteenth-century tradition of animal displays grows even more sinister with the reminder that "[z]oos, carnivals, freak shows and other traditions of human displays represent a continuum of spectatorial attractions with a related heritage" (Malamud 85). Human beings were, quite simply, put on display in precisely the same way as other members of the animal kingdom. The Victorian era saw the first widespread exhibitions of humans in public, as though they were little more than another wild creature, as though they represented just another species that other humans might capture and control. Richard Altick lists numerous exhibitions that blurred the distinction between human and animal: the famous "Hottentot Venus" in 1820 and a Botocudo Indian exhibited as "the Venus of South America" in 1832, groups of Laplanders (1822), African Bushmen (1847), American Ojibbeway Indians (1843), and "Aztec Lilliputians" in 1853 (270–80). The desire for spectacle sometimes led to the exhibition of humans mingled with animals in which all of the "creatures" from distant locales might be exhibited together.

Altick devotes an entire chapter, in *The Shows of London*, to forms of human display and captivity that were often linked to animal exhibition. The "Hottentot Venus" was a South African woman named Sartje, later baptized Sarah Bartmann, who was displayed in a variety of inhuman conditions between 1810 and 1815: she was, in the horrified words of the secretary of the African Association, "produced like a wild beast, and ordered to move backwards and forwards and come out and go into her cage, more like a bear in a chain that a human being" (Altick 270). The comparable "Venus of South America" was exhibited in Bond Street in 1822. As Altick notes, "she seems to have aroused no humanitarian emotions on the part of her beholders, only morbid (and latently sexual) curiosity and disgust" (272). The Hottentot Venus was just one example of a widespread practice that was not restricted to black Africans. During the first half of the century, Laplanders were displayed with reindeer and elk at the Egyptian Hall in Piccadilly, Ojibbeway Indians with horses at Vauxhall Gardens, and two bushmen children (8 and 15 years old) from South Africa, along with "the great ursine baboon" and "some exceedingly rare varieties of the monkey tribe" (280). Robert Bogdan notes the link between human and animal display in the rise of the "freak show" in America; he points out that the phrase "living curiosities" was often used during the nineteenth century to refer both to animals and to humans on display (26). Curiosity was clearly part of the story, but the real issue was a question of power and control.

This notion of exhibiting exotic humans along with animals (in the same spaces) suggests precisely the link between the privileged position of spectator (who is the looker? who, or what, is being looked at, and for what reason?) and the very definition of words like "primitive," "savage," "native," and "natural." My sense of the things I see depends entirely on the settings in which I see them. A lion in a cage is a very different creature than a lion on the African savannah. A person in a barred and locked enclosure is being represented—and exhibited—as no longer fully human. If I am the spectator or the creator of the display, then I get to say what it is that I see or what my spectators will see. The subject of my observation does not have the same privilege or authority, particularly if that subject is not human or not *defined as* human. "Spectacle," in this sense, is about self-definition ("who am I in relation to this spectacle?") and about my definition of the other: "who is this other (person or animal) in relation to me?" Do I feel superior to the animal or human, the other creature I am observing? Do I feel in some sort of control because my powerful culture has been able to provide this spectacle for me? Zoos *catch* (italics and pun intended) human beings in acts of self-reflexive looking with important implications for the definition of the "other." Creatures in cages exist, in one sense, for human consumption. Creatures in the wild, by contrast, do not exist for anyone's benefit.

ROMANTIC URBANATURE

Romantic ecocriticism arises out of the belief that human beings once existed closer to "the state of nature." Romantic writers, thinkers, and artists produced a view of the relationship between human beings and the natural world that was often interpreted as a call to "return to nature." These authors claimed that it was possible to *get back* to a nature from which civilized life and modern urban culture had removed humanity. Centuries, indeed millennia, had passed since humans had existed in this supposedly earlier version of harmony with the nonhuman world. This earlier state was sometimes represented as an Edenic, prelapsarian version of the biblical narrative: Adam and Eve existing in harmony with nature before the sin that constituted The Fall. The secular version of this Romanticized picture was Jean-Jacques Rousseau's account of the noble savage and the state of nature: life in a wild garden that was communally shared and always fully satisfying, one's physical strength fully at one's disposal for the tasks of living, conditions that produced nobility out of the rigors of a life lived in nature. Rousseau's conclusion is obvious: "most of our ills are of our own making"; as a result, "we might have avoided them all by adhering to the simple, uniform and solitary way of life presented to us by nature" (93). In just this way, Mary Shelley's wretched creature in *Frankenstein*—he never has a name—is evil only because of the way he is treated by humans, not because of anything "natural" or innate in his being. The closer all humans get to nature, the fewer the civilized ills will follow. Many of Rousseau's ideas were used as support for modern anthropological thinking that described "primitive" life as somehow more *natural* (and thus more pure and somehow more moral) than urbanity, more closely linked to the nonhuman world, more satisfying and fulfilling: Margaret Mead's sexy savages, Ashley Montagu's brotherhood among primitive peoples, Stephen Jay Gould's nonviolent ancients. The violence and pain of primitive life—the death, disease, destruction, and suffering of nature—is ordinarily overlooked in these accounts. Modern anthropology, like modern culture generally (with very few exceptions—see, for example, *Yanomamo: The Fierce People* by Napoleon Chagnon) has adopted a predominantly Romantic view of early humans and primitive peoples in our own times.

Numerous Romantic locales confirm this positive connection between humans and their nonhuman—"natural"—environments: Wordsworth's Lake District childhood ("Nor, sedulous as I have been to trace / How Nature by intrinsic passion first / Peopled my mind with beautiful forms" 1805 1.571–73); Coleridge's hope for his son Hartley's development away from the city ("For I was rear'd / In the great city, pent mid cloisters dim, / And saw nought lovely but the sky and stars. / But *thou*, my babe! Shalt wander like a breeze, / By lakes and sandy shores" "Frost at Midnight" 56–60); Keats's frozen world of aesthetic—and naturalistic—perfection on the Grecian urn ("Sylvan historian, who canst thus express / A flowery tale more sweetly than our rhyme!" 3–4); and even the formative experiences of Mary Shelley's nameless "Wretch," describing his own early life in "Nature" (quoted here from Charles Robinson's "earliest" edition of 1816–17, revised by Percy Shelley):

> The pleasant showers and genial warmth of spring greatly altered the aspect of the earth. Men, who before this change seemed to have been hid in caves, dispersed themselves, and were employed in various arts of cultivation. The birds sang in more cheerful notes, and the leaves began to bud forth on the trees. Happy, happy earth! fit habitation for gods, which, so short a time before, was bleak damp, and unwholesome. My spirits were elevated by the enchanting appearance of nature; the past was blotted from my memory, the present was tranquil, and the future gilded by bright rays of hope, and anticipations of joy. (*Frankenstein* 141)

All such powerfully realized nonhuman places present a picture of nonurban spaces where beneficial human contact with the natural world seems assured. Likewise, many "romanticized" descriptions of indigenous Americans, Amazonians, Africans, and South Asians have described cultures in which the gap between humans and animals, humans and plants, societies and landscapes, tends to disappear. When Alexander von Humboldt explored the wilds of South America, he noted that the indigenous, and "primitive," people "had the kind of local scientific knowledge that cosmopolitan transients like himself could only taste. They could cure fevers with roots and leaves; they could distinguish the water—by flavor alone—of several different rivers; and they could navigate rapids, thick jungles, dusty plains seemingly devoid of any landmarks, with startling accuracy" (Sachs 66). While admitting a dark side to such "primitive" cultures, Humboldt always distinguished "the contrast between the virtue of a savage and the barbarism of civilized man!" (67). Many European explorers described "witch-doctors," indigenous scientists who knew how to use biochemical and physiological connections between plants and the human body to cure disease. Pagan polytheists were similarly described as understanding the forces of nature in ways that linked them more closely to their nonhuman surroundings: ocean, earth, and sky. Tribal shamans influenced the human world of the tribe, and their local cultures, because of their knowledge of plants and animals as well as their appreciation of events in the natural world that could have a directly beneficial influence on human life.

Many nature writers, from Wordsworth and Thoreau to Peter Matthiessen, Barry Lopez, Terry Tempest Williams, and Bill McKibben, adopt elements of this Romantic perspective, describing nonurban locales where a beneficial link between the human and the nonhuman is likely: the English Lake District, Walden Pond, the Himalayas, Antarctica, Utah, and the Adirondacks. Likewise, the *ur*-ecocritic Lawrence Buell describes trying "to explain to a dyed-in-the-wool (sub)urban sophomore why Emerson was justified in thinking that country living stimulates the mind better than city life" (*Imagination* 15). Buell quickly admits, however, that this is one version of "the artificiality of American naturism," of the tendency of ecocritics and others to "imagine the heart of America as more rural than their own positions at the time of imagining" (15). Thoreau's Walden Pond and Dillard's Tinker Creek are not as far from the urban world as they often seem. In a chapter called "Pastoral Ideology," Buell admits the Romantic, or at least the pastoral element, in his own project: "Indeed this entire book, in focusing on art's capacity to image and to remythify the natural environment, is itself a kind of pastoral project" (31). The Romantic impulse at the root of Buell's powerful argument is evident when he says, "As this ecocentric repossession of pastoral has gathered force, its center of energy has begun to shift from representation of nature as a theater for human events to representation in the sense of advocacy of nature as a presence for is own sake" (52). Nature "for its own sake": what might that mean? Could nature ever be completely disconnected from human life? That is the question from urbanature. There was no "nature" before there were humans, since there were no words and there were no ideas. My answer is, therefore, a noncompromising and incontrovertible "no."

My own goal is to resituate advocacy of something nonhuman "for its own sake" in order to include the human—the city, the suburb, the urban, urbanature—in all discussions of ways that this planet (and its finite space) should be cared for and shared by human beings in the future. When an avowed Romantic ecocritic such as Jonathan Bate says that his goal is not to "return to the values of Jane Austen's English gentry or to propose that we should renounce our metropolitan modernity and become cider-makers" (23), I fear that his own valuable *Song of the Earth* cannot be sung without some hostility to the urban places that the Industrial Revolution in England turned into Blake's "dark, Satanic mills" (*Blake*: *Milton*, "Preface" 8). Hostility to industrial and urban wastelands is fine, but when it leads to those same wastelands being ignored by the very materially privileged people who could help to repair them, then an anti-urbanatural ethos results. The Australian ecocritic Kate Rigby sets out this dilemma clearly: "the challenge is not to flee to the country but to reinhabit the world as it is given to us…in the midst of those places, however urbanized, in which we dwell, tarry, or stray" (261). Once society moves in Rigby's "urbanized" direction, the results can be persistently positive: a "cherishing, beautifying, greening, and reenchanting" of all of humanity's places—urban and rural—not worrying about ultimate "place" value, but content to embrace "a resolutely countermodern ethos of conservation," and at the same time willing to live happily "amidst the elemental, the uninhabitable, and the incomprehensible" (262). I echo Rigby's call for this postmodern version of Keats's "Negative Capability," for a life "capable of being in uncertainties, Mysteries, doubts, without any irritable reaching after fact and reason" (*Letters* 261), a life amid the oxymoronic contradiction that is urbanature.

Many nature writers set out to describe places where an ecocentric view of nature links closely to the ordinary details of daily human life, urban and rural. After *Walden*, Thoreau's writing continued to be closely linked to other places that were described in ecocentric terms, whether he was revising his earlier *Week on the Concord and Merrimack Rivers* manuscript or describing his journey into the depths of the *Maine Woods*. Here is Thoreau, on a river in Massachusetts, making a day-trip to a blueberry patch seem like a journey to a terrestrial paradise: "we moored our boat on the west side of a little rising ground which in the spring forms an island in the river. Here we found huckleberries still hanging upon the bushes, where they seemed to have slowly ripened for our especial use. Bread and sugar, and cocoa boiled in river water, made our repast, and as we had drank in the fluvial prospect all day, so now we took a draft of the water with our evening meal to propitiate the river gods, and whet our vision for the sights it was to behold" (*Thoreau* 33). The blueberries are here for our beneficent use, Thoreau says, the way nature often seems to provide the precise gifts we need; we must therefore give thanks to the pagan riverine gods. Blueberries to eat, river water to drink, and the "vision" (the purely natural sights) that resulted; for Thoreau, the material world—no "spirit" needed—makes a fully human life possible, wherever it occurs.

Even more revealing than the riverside huckleberry feast, however, is Thoreau's terrifying moment on Mount Katahdin in Maine, the moment in all of Thoreau's writing when, for the first time, he feels a new version of nature, a nature that is not here for human beings. High up on the tallest mountain in Maine, Thoreau claims that the imagined Romantic "connection" between humans and a benevolent nonhuman world is the ultimate falsehood, the ultimate dream rendered impossible by the harsh, bare, inhuman, alien conditions of *natura*, or *res*: the thing in itself. Like so many Romantic ecocritics before and since, the Thoreau of *Walden* had offered up a version of nature with which readers feel at peace because they feel contented and connected. The Romantic Thoreau, like so many Romantic writers before and since, had claimed a comforting home in nature. But suddenly, at a place that has come to be known as "Thoreau Spring"—in sight of the terminus of the Appalachian Trail—Thoreau has a powerful and unexpected epiphany that literally changes his relationship to the natural world:

> I stand in awe of my body, this matter to which I am bound has become so strange to me. I fear not spirits, ghosts, of which I am one,—*that* my body might,—but I fear bodies, I tremble to meet them. What is this Titan that has possession of me? Talk of mysteries!—Think of our life in nature,—daily to be shown matter, to come in contact with it,—rocks, trees, wind on our cheeks! the *solid* earth! the *actual* world! the *common sense! Contact! Contact! Who* are we? *where* are we? (*Thoreau,* "Ktaadn" 646)

He is at once scared, and also overwhelmed, by the harsh materialism of the objects around him. Had he not left the small-town safety of Walden Pond for the jagged heights of Katahdin, his readers might never have been able to encounter this description of the fearful, the awful (in both his sense and ours—"awful" meaning both "inspiring awe or awesome" and "terrible or unbearable")—the truly terrifying (dare I say "nihilistic") aspects of the nonhuman world.

In this famous passage, Thoreau presents a view that counters Romantic ecocriticism completely and moves directly toward urbanatural roosting. He says that nature is not here for humans. The pure materiality of the physical world—"rocks [...] *solid* [...] *actual*"—leaves us distinct from (and distanced from) any determinate or stable meaning: "*Who* are we? *Where* are we?" (italics Thoreau's). Beyond this metaphysical anxiety—("*Who* are we?")—Thoreau's idea is that only the *social relations* of humans can give us a feeling of real connection to the world we inhabit: "*our* life [...] *our* cheeks [...] *we* [...] *we*" (italics added). Earlier, Thoreau has admitted—of this spot on the jagged mountain—that this "was a place for heathenism and superstitious rites" (645), linking Katahdin to the primitivist and idealized Romantic idea of the "noble savage." Likewise, the language leading up to this powerful moment is the language of a frustrated Romantic: "this was primeval, untamed, and forever untamable *Nature*, or whatever else men call it" (645). "Whatever else"? Who knows what [the hell!] to call it? It has no name; it is beyond naming. Meaning? Who knows from meaning? "Whatever else" men call it? Who cares about language; this is experience: the lived, true, REAL, the actual—NOW! Here Thoreau admits that he is up against the limits of language, the point at which even the word "Nature" may no longer suffice. This is the precise point at which another great master of language (the poet Percy Shelley) said, in a note to his prose essay "On Love": "These words are inefficient and metaphorical—Most words so—No help—" (*Prose* 504). In one of the great literary admissions of the limits of language, Shelley says that words do not finally work—they do not *do it*; they do not reach the heart of experience. They are "inefficient" (they waste semantic—meaning-based—space and energy), and they are "metaphorical" (they are parallel to—close to? nearby? not far from?—the thing they want to represent, but they do not fully represent it). They do not finally create an accurate or appropriate substitute, a verbal stand-in, for experience.

After admitting that the word "Nature" does not work to describe his own surroundings on top of Mount Katahdin, Thoreau, like Shelley before him, adds a point about the limits of awareness and expression: "It is difficult to conceive of a region uninhabited by man. We habitually presume his presence and influence everywhere" (645). This is a very strange statement from the Romantic naturalist who had said, "in Wildness is the preservation of the world." He concludes, "And yet, we have not seen pure Nature, unless we have seen her thus vast and drear and inhuman, though in the midst of cities" (645). This last ("pure Nature") is the strangest statement of all, linking, as it does, the idea of a drear (depressing) and inhuman aspect of nature with "the midst of cities": urbanature in reverse. "Nature here was something savage and awful, though beautiful" (645). The "Nature" that Thoreau finally finds on "Ktaadn" is thus a nature of which it is true to say that, "Man was not to be associated with it." When humans link themselves, their wishes, and their desires to "nature," they are often acting out a form of wish-fulfillment, not describing a state of affairs in the real world. I like nature when it makes me feel good,

when it makes me happy: birds, and butterflies, and flowers. The terrifying aspects of nature are a different story altogether; in fact, they
reveal the extent to which the very idea of "nature" is a creation of
the human-authored texts in which it performs certain functions (see
Wittgenstein). From the perspective of urbanatural roosting, "nature"
is not so much a cultural construction—or a "social creation" (Neil
Evernden)—as it is a textual one. Rousseau needed a version of nature
for his own specific purposes, and he *made* the "nature" he needed:
so did Wordsworth, and Shelley, and Keats; so did Thoreau. It is
revealing that, immediately after this powerfully threatening realization—"man was not to be associated with it"—Thoreau returns to
a mostly mundane account of a failed trout dinner—"we were compelled to make the most of the crumbs of our hard bread and our
pork" (646)—and the search for a "half-inch auger" to repair one
of the spike-poles with which they propelled their *bateau* down the
creek. Philosophical speculation gives way to the simplest of practical
details. Thoreau needs to repair his floating vessel so that he can flee
this world of "Chaos and Old Night" (645). He needs to fix his boat
in order to get out of this "awful" bit of "Nature."

Even a more recent anchorite naturalist—Annie Dillard—begins
the most transformative chapter of her *Pilgrim at Tinker Creek* with a
crucial moment during which the dislocations of a long highway journey prepare the mind for a new insight about the nonhuman world:
"It is early March. I am dazed from a long day of interstate driving
homeward; I pull in at a gas station in Nowhere, Virginia, north of
Lexington. The young boy in charge ('Chick 'at oll?') is offering a
free cup of coffee with every gas purchase. We talk in the glass-walled
office while my coffee cools enough to drink" (78). This traveler has
come a long way to reach this point, but now her traveling stops. This
moment of rest from her road-trip prepares her mind for a new awareness: "My mind has been a blank slab of black asphalt for hours, but
that doesn't stop the sun's wild wheel. I set my coffee beside me on the
curb; I smell the loam on the wind; I pat the puppy; I watch the mountain […] I am more alive than all the world" (79). A series of completely ordinary details—asphalt, sun, coffee, dirt, and puppy—clear
Dillard's consciousness as Thoreau's mind was cleared on Katahdin.
Then, suddenly, as if prompted by this momentary pause in the flow of
her own consciousness, Dillard's naturalistic writing turns into something else, a philosophical meditation on human awareness:

> This is it, I think, this is it, right now, the present, this empty gas sta
> tion, here, this western wind, this tang of coffee on the tongue, and I

am patting the puppy, I am watching the mountain. And the second I verbalize this awareness in my brain, I cease to see the mountain or feel the puppy. I am opaque, so much black asphalt. [...] It is ironic that the one thing that all religions recognize as separating us from our creator—our very self-consciousness—is also the one thing that divides us from our fellow creatures. It was a bitter birthday present from evolution, cutting us off at both ends. I get in the car and drive home. (80)

In this instance, a lyrical, nonnarrative, atemporal moment in the mind gives way to the literary (textual? linguistic?) need to describe her immediate surroundings. Once this description begins, the narrative flow returns, and the purity of a single observation becomes part of a larger verbal project: the need to explain what has happened, first to the self and then to others (her readers). The experience that the Romantics so often sought, the moment of unselfconsciousness that links the self ("me") to the external world (most often realized "in nature"), is the antithesis of self-consciousness, the experience "that divides us from our fellow creatures." Dillard loses herself when she finds the material world.

But Dillard is another closet urbanaturalist. Like Thoreau in his "hideaway," one-and-a-half-miles from Concord, she often creates a sense that Tinker Creek is miles-upon-miles from civilization, an isolated wilderness without any direct connection to human society. In fact, as Dillard knows well, the creek literally runs through the suburbs of Roanoke, Virginia. Her greatest moment of awareness in *Pilgrim at Tinker Creek* occurs neither in a wilderness, nor in a nonhuman world of flowers, and fields, and bristlecone pines. It occurs in a gas station on the roadside of a Virginia superhighway. She has been on the "blank slate of black asphalt for hours." The moment of pulling off of the interstate and stopping for a cup of coffee—even with Shelley's "western wind" invoked for the purpose—is the moment that gives way to the single greatest epiphany in *Pilgrim at Tinker Creek*. Without this ribbon of asphalt to prepare Dillard's mental state, there would have been no unselfconscious moment. Without this stop for gasoline and this domestic puppy, no chance to learn that self-consciousness is the curse of the city (but not the *urbanatural* city!), the curse that separates us from other people and other creatures. Shelley, recall, had said that to live for an instant—Dillard might add "for an unselfconscious instant"—is to live forever. At this point, Dillard (and her readers) should be pleased. They have learned that the urbanatural city will be one in which urban merges with natural, self merges with neighbor, and science merges with poetry in a vision of one world.

This is the idea that my book *Romantic Natural Histories* (*RNH*) and hypertext website (*Romantic Natural History* http://users. dickinson.edu/~nicholsa/romnat/) are working to develop. Once scientists more fully acknowledge the crucial power of the creative imagination, and once poets more completely recognize the essential importance of rational inquiry, humanity will be well on its way toward solving the last great problem of the species: how can human beings survive in sustainable ways on an increasingly populated—and warmer—planet, a planet with dramatically dwindling resources? My thinking here originates in an idea that I have already elaborated in this book, an idea that goes back to Romantic natural historians of the late eighteenth and early nineteenth centuries, the idea that all living things are related, that "animate nature" is a single and unified system. This idea is one of the major impulses behind Darwin's own thinking about evolution—the idea that all organic creatures are linked by a single, original germ plasm (we now know it to be a precise group of genetic markers) that stretches back to the origins of life on earth. This view of the ultimate connectedness of every plant, every animal, every protist, and every protein, continues to drive modern thinking about evolutionary complexities in each inhabitant of the biosphere. Current environmental problems (climate change, species extinction, over population) can find solutions by way of science and technology but only once people emphasize the familial and biological bonds that connect them all to all living things. The poetic imagination is required for individuals to envision the literal closeness of their connections to all living species. The rational sciences provide the method and the means to solve environmental problems, but the imaginative and the poetic arts provide the motive and the meaning needed to do so.

*   *   *

This morning the sky has dawned clear on the Blue Ridge. From my perch on the wide screen-porch, I can see individual windows and chimneys of houses five miles away as the crow flies. Every ripple on the river rapids below me is sparkling and shimmering in the cold, clear dawn light. A lone fisherman has paddled his canoe to midstream near a cluster of rocks; he casts his line slowly and methodically toward the gradual sunrise. With unaided eyes, I can see three mountain ridges in the distance: roughly fifteen, thirty, and forty miles away according to the topographic map, rolling out toward the west, out toward Western Maryland and Virginia, Ohio, and beyond. Middle Atlantic Indians saw versions of this sight from rocky outcrops on this ridge for centuries, for millennia, for eons. So did George Washington when he surveyed these acres or traveled from Alexandria to Winchester, and so did General Edward Braddock as he led his army through this wild, untamed mountain gap on the way to Fort Duquesne—near Pittsburgh—during the French and Indian War. I can see four states clearly: Virginia, West Virginia, Maryland, and Pennsylvania—all in one long glance along the western horizon.

The birds and the human world, in the brightening woods and out into the valley beyond, have fallen strangely silent in the clear morning air. No road sounds are making their way up the mountain this morning: no trucks are down-shifting on the hill below me, no engines revving, no motorcycles whining or gunning their way up the ridge. The barometer has climbed steadily during the night and is still rising. Yesterday's low-pressure system has vanished suddenly, the clear air of a high-pressure system taking its place. On the walls of the cabin, every shifting shine in the grain of the granite is visible. The rock looks solid gray from a distance, but up close, when I place my eyes next to the stony walls of the cabin, the truth about this solid rock-color is revealed: pure white flakes and jet black patches, rust-red flecks, even blue, and also yellow, red, and tiny sparkling crystalline flecks of gold.

1 2

FEBRUARY

There is in reality neither truth nor error, neither yes nor no, nor any distinction whatsoever, since all—including the contraries—is One.—

—*Chuang-tse*

February is the death-month in nature. I cannot find a single living thing in the cabin now: not a spider, not a beetle, not a wriggling bug. February reminds me that death is always part of the natural bargain. In a world where humans do not really know very much, they do know that they are going to die; that much is certain. Death is part of the deal. Life is much more valuable because each person is going to die. The bard knew this well: "This thou perceiv'st which makes thy love more strong, / To love that well which thou must leave ere long" (Sonnet 73). Love it well because you have to leave it before too many years have passed, Shakespeare says. No love without death. No life without life that is lost. "Not life, but a good life is to be chiefly valued," said Plato's master in the *Crito*. So once the good is gone, it is time to let go of the life. This is a lesson that the Romantics knew well in the nineteenth century and that the coming generations of twenty-first century human beings are going to have to learn as well.

Think for a minute about the full implications of this idea: things take on their value in large measure because they are going to be taken away. I love something all the more because I am going to have to give it up. This idea is at the heart of all nostalgia: the day is taken away from me (I will never get it back), my youth is taken away from me (it cannot return except in my memory), my loved ones are taken away from me (one by one, invariably, incessantly), and I will lose my own living self (of that I can be sure). In a Judeo-Christian culture like the West, it seems strange that death is still dreaded. After all, if my loved ones and I are going to a better place, why do so many people see this promised improvement as something to fear? If the unjust are going to receive their just deserts, then surely that process need not be delayed. For those who hold onto a literal belief in the Bible, as a result of which I am going to meet all of my deceased ancestors in a cozy afterlife, surely everyone should be ready to welcome this outcome, not to avoid it at all costs for as long as possible. So the modern Christian believer embodies a strange, yet powerful, contradiction. The obvious way to give life, and the reality around us, its greatest value is to say—as Shakespeare does—this is it, this is the end ("The rest is silence" *Hamlet* 5.2.345): one shot, no second chances, no life everlasting, no life to come for an ethereal misty soul-creature with a name-tag that says, "Hi, I'm Ashton. Welcome to Heaven (or Hell)." If the world as each person knows it is the entire story, the closed case—as I believe it is—then consider how valuable each moment becomes. Each time I see my wife or my daughters may literally be the last. Each day that I live gives me a unique and rare opportunity that will never come again, not ever. Never.

All of the arguments for euthanasia are based on the belief that there are worse things than dying, that it is not life itself, but rather a *good* life—*eudaimon*—that is to be valued, as Socrates said. Human beings have a relentless, almost universal, desire to sustain and continue life, all life, for as long as possible. Of course, when it comes to the animals that most humans eat, there seems to be no problem at all with the end of those countless lives for a practical purpose. How many billions of lambs die so that humans can eat lamb chops? How many trillions of cattle get shot in the head so that untold American children can sit down to their hamburger-based "happy" meals? The arguments in favor of vegetarianism are now too obvious to try and argue against them. When it comes to pets, most pet-owners have a line they are willing to cross when they finally say, "Well, Fluffy is clearly in a lot of pain; so, I think it is time we put her down," or, "Rover's back legs are gone; I don't see how it is fair to him or to us to keep him here, dragging his hindquarters over to his water bowl to drink. I'll call the vet this afternoon." Shakespeare got Rover's last day right: "love that well which thou must leave 'ere long." We love our pets enough to put them out of their misery when the pain gets too unbearable, or the quality of life grows too miserable. Why do we not love our human relatives in the same way, to the same extent?

Death and Dying

What terrified those early Victorians about evolution was not so much human descent from ape-like creatures. What unsettled them was not the thought that humans were just another species of animal. What terrified them most seems to have been death pure and simple, all of that earlier death that had to happen to allow a little bit of mature life to live. Here comes one single mother cod-fish, and she can lay five million eggs, and here comes one father cod, and he squirts out his cloudy semen—called "milt"—in such a way that maybe three-quarters of those eggs are even fertilized (my numbers are approximate because they vary so widely in nature). So of those 5,000,000 eggs, one quarter dies and rots before they are fertilized; that is a lot of death. Then of the 3,000,000 or so fertilized eggs, fewer than one third of this number manages to hatch. Life is rough in that part of the mid-ocean where this particular cod family spawned. On the day that those 1,000,000 little cod-fry finally hatch, well more than half of that number are gobbled up by predators, or they are born with severe "natural" birth defects: missing fins, blunted tails, and crooked spines. Then, these few hundreds-of-thousands (down from five million, remember) of fingerling cod—cute and shiny, perfectly formed—feed countless other fish and birds, and even large insects, during their early weeks of life. Lots of little cod babies, swimming around their bit of ocean, being gobbled up by the thousands: nature working its mysterious magic by offering untold deaths to help sustain a few larger lives. Dead cod all along the way, millions of dead, dead juveniles increasing in number until just a small school full of beautiful adult cod remain: the few who have made it, the lucky ones, the survivors. Five million eggs (five million possible cod-lives), honed away, hacked at, pared down by natural-selection, until just a few hundred, or a few dozen if it has been a ravaged batch, beautiful adult cod remain, the ones who will go on to mate, just as Darwin promised. Think, however, of all that death along the way: dead eggs, dead hatchlings, dead fry, dead fingerlings, dead minnows, dead minors, dead juveniles, dead young adults, dead sexually mature fish—all dying, all dead. That seems like a lot of death for just a little bit of adult life; a lot of creatures have to die so that just a few get to live. Here is Darwin down and dirty, always red in tooth and claw: and fin, and flipper, and feather, and fur.

In the state of nature, of course, these same challenges apply to humans. The only difference is that human beings are a bit better than most species at keeping themselves alive, better at fighting those forces—disease, disaster, accidents—that threaten every living thing along the dangerous road of life. This is the bleak news from the front-lines of evolution. This was the news that so terrified Tennyson—"So careless of the single life;…And finding that of fifty seeds / She often brings but one to bear…[Nature cares] for nothing, all shall go" (*RNH* 54.44, 47–48, 55.60). A hard pill to swallow, perhaps, but the one that makes lives like yours and mine—the lives of the few survivors—all that more valuable, all that more special: "Hey there, here I am. I was one of the lucky ones; I survived. I got to live!"

Here is how Tennyson's son, Hallam, describes his father's version of the nightmare: "he was occasionally troubled with the intellectual problem of the apparent profusion and waste of life and by the vast amount of…suffering throughout the world, for these seemed to militate against the idea of the Omnipotent and All-Loving Father" (*Memoir* 2: 78). The younger Tennyson quotes his father word-for-word: "An Omnipotent Creator Who could make such a painful world is to me *sometimes* as hard to believe in as to believe in blind matter behind everything. The lavish profusion too in the natural world appals [*sic*] me, from the growths of the tropical forest to the capacity of man to multiply, the torrent of babies" (2: 78). "The torrent of babies"?! That image, for the devout Tennyson of *In Memoriam*, is mostly of dead babies. "Blind matter behind everything?" Imagine what it must have felt like to be among the first Victorians to take such a sugges-tion seriously. In such a mood, Hallam concludes, his father said, "If we look at Nature alone, full of perfection and imperfection, she tells us that God is disease, murder and rapine" (2: 79). Once again, I am not worried whether Tennyson reached his own spiritual solution to the problem of the death of his best friend in his poem *In Memoriam*. I am much more concerned to show how Victorians were terrified by death as the "secret" of life in a Darwinian world: "God is disease, murder, and rapine": that is Alfred, Lord Tennyson speaking.

Consider nature's approach to death—it could not be more differ-ent from the typical human response. How many countless plants and animals die so that a few survivors make it? Tennyson and Thomas Hardy, Matthew Arnold—"we are here as on a darkling plain / Swept with confused alarms of struggle and flight, / Where ignorant armies clash by night." ("Dover Beach" 35–37), and even Darwin himself, "that he was a hypochondriac with a fear of death there is no doubt" (Speyrer): just four examples of Victorian fear of the simple fact of death, untold dead and dying creatures priming the pump of evolu-tion, death after death stoking the engine-room of life. Think of dead leaves falling from trees by the billions. Think of dead insects piling up each autumn by the trillions. Think of tens—maybe hundreds—of millions of dead human beings during the twentieth century alone, so that a handful of lunatic dictators could fight their wars for no good reason. The *Historical Atlas of the Twentieth Century* estimates close to 200,000,000 dead in wars and atrocities alone (White). Wasteful? Think how many thousands of millions of species have died forever— gone, extinct—so that the 1,800,000 or so species alive today might survive for awhile. But do not worry. Death is a healthy part of the story. That is the point; that is what Darwin makes clear. Death is the fuel, the immeasurable amount of reused and recycled matter that keeps the whole system of natural selection running.

In just such terms, Thoreau lavished praise on a dead and rotting horse by the cabin at Walden Pond:

> There was a dead horse in the hollow by the path to my house, which compelled me sometimes to go out of my way, especially in the night when the air was heavy, but the assurance it gave me of the strong appetite and inviolable health of Nature was my compensation for this. I love to see that Nature is so rife with life that myriads can be afforded to be sacrificed and suffered to prey on one another; that tender organisms can be so serenely squashed out of existence like pulp,—tadpoles which herons gobble up, and tortoises and toads run over in the road. (213)

If the ecocritic Simon Estok wants to argue that only vegetarians can legitimately be ecocritics or ethical environmentalists—since only they possess the appropriate morality on the animal rights issue—he needs to reread this passage by Thoreau. Thoreau also said that he "could sometimes eat a fried rat with a good relish, if it were necessary" (*Walden* 147). I do not mean to trivialize a very important issue. Although I was a strict vegetarian for a full decade in my own early adulthood, I now—like Thoreau—distinguish my own personal practice from best practice: "Whatever my own practice may be, I have no doubt that it is a part of the destiny of the human race, in its gradual improvement, to leave off eating animals" (147). Thoreau's thinking on this matter is complex, but explicit. Whatever Thoreau may eat himself, he knows that each human being in the nineteenth century "can and does live, in a great measure, by preying on other animals; but this is a miserable way,—as anyone who will go to snaring rabbits, or slaughtering lambs, may learn" (147); his own experience as a meat-eater has taught him that "the practical objection to animal food in my case was its uncleanness" (146), by which he means the general nastiness associated with killing, cleaning, gutting, packing, and then washing up the bloody messes of skin and guts—plus piles of fur and feathers and scales—that are essential to eating carnivorously. Animal food also does not feed Thoreau "essentially. It was insignificant and unnecessary, and cost more than it came to. A little bread or a few potatoes would have done as well, with less trouble and filth" (146). Finally, Thoreau asserts that "he will be regarded as a benefactor of his race who shall teach man to confine himself to a more innocent and wholesome diet" (147). Clean, innocent, wholesome, not filthy, not miserable: the goal of the species *Homo sapiens* should be to reach a diet that fits this description. In the meantime, the master says, humans should follow the "Hindoo commentator" who argues, in the *Vedas*, that a carnivorous diet should be restricted only to "the time of distress" (148).

My final point here is not about the vegetarian option. To end this discussion on death and dying, I only want to assert that nature clearly teaches that death is at the heart of the story of life. Only death and the return of life's organic and inorganic compounds to the cyclical system ("The circle of life," as the Disney film of *The Lion King* has it) will allow life to continue. Without lots of death and just as much rotting of organic life, nature would not have the raw materials for ongoing creation. Without death there would be no life.

ECOMORPHIC ECOCENTRISM

I need a few final definitions, and a few more new metaphors, to help me move beyond Romantic ecocriticism toward urbanatural roosting. Ecocentrism now needs to replace anthropocentrism, the idea that has—at least since the Renaissance—put human concerns at the center of all things. In a related way, the idea of ecocentrism reveals that everything can be imagined as part of a single global ecosystem: not only every tree, every river, every bird, and every insect, but also every house, every road, every computer, every human, and every object made by human beings. In some ways, the idea of an ecosystem, by itself, suggests that there is no separation between the natural and the nonnatural. Ecocentrism thus comes to replace anthropocentrism automatically, that centuries-old view that saw everything in relation to some image of mankind, some version of human self-description. A hitherto anthropocentric and anthropomorphic world needs now to become an ecocentric and ecomorphic one. This does not mean that humans are no longer a central concern of ethics, politics, social and family life, but only that humans need to see themselves less in isolation—"Is this good for me?"—and more in relation to their entire ecosystem: "Is this good for the ecosystem I inhabit?" Preservation of the self has come to include preservation of the self's physical place in the world: the environment, the ecosystem. It is merely a question of changing questions.

What about the new metaphors? Once ecomorphic ecocentrism is accepted, new metaphors will come easily. They will often be metaphors begun by those early natural historians I have discussed (and continued by their modern successors), metaphors in which science is more like poetry, in which the way writers describe one aspect of reality (facts, objective truth, a literal world) finds itself closely linked to the way they describe the other aspect of reality (feelings, subjective truth, the figurative realm). Similies and metaphors abound in science: every scientific truth is, in this regard, much like every poetic truth. The sun is *like* a bright yellow disk in the sky. My love is *like* a red, red rose. An atom *is* a tiny solar system made up of protons, neutrons, and electrons. My heart is a glowing coal burning with love for my beloved. The universe is bounded at the same time that it is infinite (Einstein). One thought from my mind can fill immensity, and so can one thought from your mind (Blake).

This new view has important practical consequences. Cities should naturalize their human spaces. Urban dwellers need to put plants on their roofs and walls, their decks, their porches, their window boxes, their rooms. Every urban space needs flowers and herbs and vegetables in containers of every description: green roofs, lawn-less yards, a new vision of the hanging gardens of Babylon stretching from Bethesda to Santa Barbara. All of the people in America could grow most of the green foods they need with only minimal effort, a few containers for soil, a few seeds, a bit of sun and water: lettuce, spinach, kale, chives, garlic, green peppers, and more. This is one simple example. If humans stopped eating meat, and stopped feeding their pets so much commercial pet food, and cut out the junk-food and processed sugar, and cut out desert except on special occasions, imagine the savings—economic and ecocentric—that would result from these relatively easy changes to life. The world needs more trees and shrubs everywhere that humans inhabit, and likewise it needs more urban and suburban wild species, especially predators—since we have killed so many off: more wolves and coyotes, raccoons and squirrels and hawks, more chipmunks and eagles and bats. "Bats eat as many insects at night as birds do during the day" (Kalka and Williams-Guilen et al): let them live.

This increase in nonhuman species of plants and animals in the midst of human habitation will first result in a more permeable barrier, and then no barrier at all, between the world described as *human* and the world once described as *natural*. In the old days, people thought that it was somehow them—the human beings—who were potentially unnatural and artificial. What nonsense! The Romantics, and the Romantic ecocritics fought against this, and many continue to do so; good for them, but now their time has come, too. It is no longer time to climb to the top of El Capitan and proudly say that you have therefore *returned* to some heroically pure aspect of nature. Yellowstone Park, where this great geologic formation stands tall, is a humanized invention; it was created by human logic and imagining, formed by master-planners with maps and plans for rearranging nature and reorganizing a lot of human beings, too, mostly Indians. Likewise, this beautiful geologic formation may have felt like nature when people said that it could not be climbed, but now this "natural" rock face has been speed-climbed, free-climbed, base-jumped, and used as the site for a powerful scene in the blockbuster film *Star Trek V: The Final Frontier*. Nature? Culture? I am no longer as sure as I once was; you tell me.

Even without an idea of *pure* wilderness (think of those Native Americans being relocated so that Yellowstone could be fashioned into "wilderness" by the US government), there is still a serious need for permanent preservation of many wild spaces, as well as regulations and controls in all sorts of locations. America now needs environmental care and concern for each and every ecosystem, all of the wild and all of the tame. By now my oft-repeated distinction between "wild" and "wilderness" should make sense. The "wildness" that Thoreau talked about was not only "wildness" as in "wilderness," but also "wildness" in the human mind: "in [my own mental] Wildness is the preservation of the world." By that wildness Thoreau means wild minds and wild places: "We are conscious of an animal in us...It is reptile and sensual, and perhaps cannot be wholly expelled; like the worms which, even in life and health, occupy our bodies" (*Walden* 149). There is, of course, a completely natural world *inside* of each human being as well. Recall that wonderful display in the museum of natural history on the edge of the Borghese Gardens in Rome (near the seated statue of Byron by Thorvaldsen): "the human body is a real 'forest' in which other living beings thrive, protected, far from predators and very well fed." That quote, as I noted earlier, appears under a marble sculpture of a beautiful maiden, reclining on her Grecian couch. The title above this odd description of the human body—a "forest" with its own ecology of wriggling parasites and countless other living creatures—reads: "An environment rather unusual and very...personal!" So nature does not even stop at the apparent border provided by my skin. Nature penetrates each person from without as it permeates each person from within. I am a bundle of cells as well as a bundle of other living organisms: bacteria and parasites, viruses and intestinal flora. Nature and culture exist in precisely the same relationship: no boundaries and barriers, all porous and intermingling.

This is why the term "wild" should also be a verb. I need to *wild* my mind, so that it can help to preserve the world—not just the wild world, not just the natural world, not just the human world—rather, the world, the whole world, all of it. Out of such thinking could emerge a new ethos of land preservation (preserving Detroit and the South Bronx as well as the Danube and the Southwest), new landscape art (think Andy Goldsworthy), urban landscape artists of all kinds, and new forms of architecture: organic, naturalized, houses *in* the hills, trees *in* the house, "usonian," as Frank Lloyd Wright once said, user-friendly, urbanatural architecture. Imagine organic buildings literally rising out of the ground they "inhabit." Imagine trees in our homes and homes in the trees. At the same time, as "eco-" becomes an ever-more widespread prefix, a new view of wilderness will also arise, one linked not to the Romantic idea of some pure, pristine, nonhuman—"inhuman"—space, but rather wildernesses linked to the humans who define and describe them, not the empty spaces cleared of human inhabitants by those nineteenth-century creators of wilderness parks, but rather new naturalized human landscapes and new humanized natural ones. Central Park is just as natural as Yellowstone when observed from outer space, or with a magnifying glass, or with a microscope. A child flipping over rocks to look for worms and bugs in any backyard or urban park is just as much at work in nature as an ecologist boring cores in Antarctica or the Sahara Desert. A teenager with her microscope examining drops of pond water from Rock Creek Park in Washington, D.C.—just like Edward O. Wilson did (see his *Naturalist*)—is just as much a naturalist as my friend Marcus and I were when we snorkeled with our students near the westernmost Galápagos Island, six hundred miles out in the middle of the Pacific. Look down on planet earth from Google Earth or MapQuest. Yellowstone is just as urban as Central Park when seen as part of a locale that includes Logan and Livingstone (Montana), Blackfoot and Billings, Butte, Powell, and Pitchfork (Wyoming), Cody, Cooke City, Cameron, Jackson, Big Sky, Bozeman, and Belgrade (these are all towns or cities "within" the park). Every one of these urbanized spots is part of a wider landscape that makes up Yellowstone's "wilderness," once the point of view moves back and glimpses the land from outer space. It is all a matter of perspective. From high above or face-to-face, it all looks the same; it all looks like urbanature.

Every landscape, from every perspective, is always mediated by human consciousness. Even my own neural network is not "mine"; it is a network that provides a connection, a web of interrelatedness between me and everything that lies around me: every bird, every building, every lizard, every lane of highway. Consciousness itself is no less a part of nature than is a sunbeam or a jellyfish. Every bit of nature is necessarily mediated by my senses, by my personal point-of-view. But that is not another problem; that is the clarifying solution. There is no "pure" nature within me or without me. There is no "pure" nature—period(.)—that is the lasting lesson of modern philosophy and cognitive science. What is now known, that was not known by those well-meaning earlier thinkers, is that "the meaning of a word is its use" (Wittgenstein 43). Consciousness plus language *makes* the world. In addition, modern science has revealed that the material objects of neural consciousness *are* a part of consciousness itself. There is no mysterious or mystical thought behind—or beyond—the brain that is doing the thinking. The related lesson, that reality is always mediated by a mind-brain, applies no less to our relationship to nature than it does to our relation to ourselves, to each other, to language, and to consciousness. An apple on the table, a light in the room, the transferred image of the apple upside-down on my eye's retina, my eye's version of the apple in my mind-brain: it is all one. The apple and my sensory perception of the apple are one "thing."

What we observe when we observe nature, is not some Platonically pure *nature* in itself, but a nature that is always changing, always determined by specific circumstances, by my consciousness, and by precise conditions in each contextual instance. Do I have my glasses on? If not, then the whole world to me is a confusing blur. Each experience of nature is conditioned by my asking certain questions, questions which themselves are always changing: ("Is that a female bluebird?"—since I am birding today), or by my temporary uncertainties, always subject to revision: ("I think it is a . . ."—I don't have my bird book), and my doubts, which always await clarification: ("if Roger Tory Peterson were here, I would have the answer"). *Beyond Romantic Ecocriticism: Toward Urbanatural Roosting* asks finally for a resituation of humanity's awareness of nature. The time has come to acknowledge humanity's position in a nature that is always urban, an urbanity that is always natural. The time has also come to roost on the earth as most birds roost in the trees, with care and concern for the site of each roost and for the resources that allow each roost to remain.

As long as the planet suffers under the shadow of environmental degradation, as long as individuals—and groups of individuals—remain concerned about sustainability, social justice, endangered species, and global warming, literary critics (and ecocritics) will debate the role of literary texts in the understanding of ecology and humanity's place in the nonhuman world. The importance of imaginative literature—poetry, fiction, drama, and nonfiction prose—to an understanding of human-ecological relations is crucial. In addition, ecocritical texts themselves have become part of the fabric of environmental awareness. These texts describe the nonhuman world and its connections to the human world, but they also remind individuals that they have an obligation to make themselves aware of ecological issues that confront them on a local and a global basis.

On the local level, poverty, ethnic conflict, and civil strife of many kinds are often the result of environmental factors: careless land use, resource degradation, social and ecological imbalances of many kinds. The blighted city of Detroit, as I have noted, has recently decided to reclaim the natural from the urban, to take the idea of urbanature to its logical conclusion, by turning vast tracts of the city from urban land back to rural land. The city plans that "Surviving neighborhoods in the birthplace of the auto industry would become pockets in expanses of green" (Runk). An area roughly thirty-five square miles in size (larger than many small cities) is about to be turned from city back into country. Detroit, ironically, may thus become one of the models for a great new urbanatural version of city space: "This continent has not seen a transformation like Detroit's since the last days of the Maya. The city, once the fourth largest in the country, is now so depopulated that some stretches resemble the outlying farmland and others are altogether wild" (Solnit 66). Such returns of natural wildness to urban spaces will become much more common in the future, as cities respond to environmental trauma (Katrina in New Orleans), or human trauma (industrial decline throughout the American rustbelt), that will require a literal greening of the shattered and rusted-out wastelands of post natural-trauma or postindustrial landscapes. Not "since the last days of the Maya": imagine green, urbanatural spaces rising from the ruins of districts in Pittsburgh (Pennsylvania) and Cleveland

(Ohio), Chicago (Illinois), Flint (Michigan), Stockton (California), Memphis (Tennessee). New living spaces will emerge where gardens come down into city center from the suburbs, where every house with a yard turns part of that yard into a garden for vegetables and flowers. Imagine neighborhoods in which fewer pets are shared among neighbors—uncaged—in which dogs and cats roam wild, fed and nurtured by neighbors, as is often done now on farms or in expansive rural settings. Consider the possibility that cites could integrate elements of traditional rural life into life in urban settings: sharing space, depending on one another, and caring for each other; these could all become ways of living in urban space as well. New ideas are needed from all of those thoughtful people who can imagine such blended ways of life. New thoughts are always required to make integration (of all kinds) a reality, but it is also just as easy as Blake promised: "What is now proved was once, only imagin'd" (*Marriage of Heaven and Hell*, "Proverbs of Hell" 33).

On the global level the problems may be even more severe, but they are also just as solvable. The seriousness of certain global environmental problems—climate change and species extinction first among them—have created a moment when many people are talking about the end of life as we know it, at least the end of the human species as it now exists. Such end-times talk now is not of nuclear apocalypse but of anthropocentric Armageddon; human impact on the rest of organic nature is increasingly seen as the factor that may cause the entire system to collapse: industrial pollution in the former Soviet Union, desertification in Africa, population explosions in South Asia and South America. Once a tipping point is reached—so the doomsday ecologists argue—a balance of nature that has sustained the planet since the world's oceans and atmosphere settled into their current form will be upset: the hydrological cycle will no longer function to draw moisture from the seas at current rates, photosynthesis will no longer operate as it has done for billions of years, and other essential systems will collapse, leaving humanity with a largely lifeless, uninhabitable planet. This scenario is one of the reasons that Stephen Hawking is seriously calling for humans to set off in large numbers to explore the solar system and beyond. "The long-term survival of the human race is at risk as long as it is confined to a single planet," he recently noted: "Sooner or later, disasters such as an asteroid collision or nuclear war could wipe us all out. But once we spread out into space and establish independent colonies, our future should be safe" (Highfield). Humans will need exploration of other planetary spaces in anticipation of a time when our own home—the "Third Stone from the Sun," as Jimi Hendrix so accurately called it—will no longer support human (or other organic) life.

What is called for is a new ethic, an ethic that worries less about those arbitrary lines of demarcation, between "human" and "nonhuman," that have existed since at least the Book of Genesis. It is no longer about preserving wilderness as distinct from human activity but rather about acknowledging how little difference there is between the natural and the nonnatural. Once I recognize my common destiny with every other creature and object on the planet, I have taken the first step toward ecocentric harmony, toward urbanatural roosting. The great cities in the world can no longer be seen as manmade—artificial—creations. When I drive into Manhattan from the west, I cross marshes filled with red-winged blackbirds and great blue herons stretching almost as far as the eye can see. In the capital at Washington, D.C., I witness the wide and muddy Potomac River, flowing through the heart of the city, filled with catfish, and crayfish, and water snakes. In San Francisco, the bay is as much a part of the city as any cable car or steep-sloped road. A Chesapeake Bay full of blue crabs and oysters comes within clear sight of Baltimore's Camden Yards ballpark and Hard Rock Café. The Front Range looms like a nearby shadow in sight of Denver, but its hawks and eagles draw no distinctions between Rocky Mountain fastnesses and the ledges of gleaming skyscrapers. Now, more than ever, New Orleans lies swallowed by the mouth of the mighty Mississippi at the edge of a marshy, egret-stalked delta that spreads out seemingly forever into the majestic Gulf of Mexico. The natural elements of these great cities are no less parts of the urban space than are gas stations, sewage lines, and sex shops. Do not tell me that nature stops at some invisible border and that something else—the city?—begins. Bill McKibben said, in 1989, that society's problem was the "end" of nature, brought on because human chemicals could be found in every sediment of every ocean trench, every snowdrift on every mountain peak. I say that the solution to the problem then posed by McKibben is a new and more accurately defined version of nature, a nature that appears once humans accept that they are part of those same ocean depths and mountain heights, and that those mountain peaks and ocean depths are also part of human life. The natural truth, like the human truth (as the Buddha said), is one. Wild nature and civilized culture represent—with only a slightly different emphasis—what the physicists call "a singularity."

Cities are most often located where they are because of natural forces. They tend to be placed in specific locations because of an ocean, a bay, a river, or a mountain range. Sometimes nature made the city, as in the case of New York (East River, Hudson River, a harbor), or Paris (the Seine, for river transport), or London (the Thames, a tidal estuary). Other times, nature stopped the city from expanding, or the city had to grow only as close to a natural boundary as it could, as in the case of Chicago (the lake), or Kyoto (the surrounding mountain ranges) or Key West (a tiny island). But nature is also in the heart of every city: countless trees, flowers, birds, and soils, and the untold trillions of living things that lie invisible beneath the surface of every square foot of soil, beneath the foundations of every building. The natural processes that control the life of forest, tundra, ice pack, and desert likewise control every town, suburb, highway, and cottage. I like being alone here on a Blue Ridge mountain where I can see no other human and no other human can see me. I like not speaking to another person for days. But why should I like this situation any more than I like standing in Leicester Square in London or Times Square in New York? I do not. Why should my life alone on this mountain be any different than my life in Calcutta or Cleveland? It is not. Eagles and falcons will not thrive in cities until the cities are cleaned up, too. Urban pollution will not end until city dwellers decide to save the lives of wilderness birds that share their global space. At this point in history, the significant distinction is no longer urban versus natural, nature versus culture. The meaningful distinction now is taking care of my spaces and place or not taking care, sharing my resources or not sharing them. The air that the city breathes is the same air that the wilderness breathes. It all needs to be breathable. The water in Calcutta is the same water that is on Mount Everest. It all needs to be clean.

Humanity now needs an idea of nature that reaches into the buildings that people inhabit, a nature that does not stop wherever a human hand intervenes. At the same time, humanity needs a human world that does not stop just because the wind howls outside the door or rain thunders on the roof. If humans could break down the separation between outdoors and indoors, then they would be well on their way to such an ideal of unity. To move in this direction would be like breaking down the philosophical distinction—in the Western world, at least, as old as Descartes—between outer and inner, what is within me and what seems to lie beyond me. The Romantic poems I have been critiquing often break down this separation between a world outside my window (wild nature) and the world inside my window (human culture). The nature/nonnature, natural/artificial, or human/nonhuman distinctions are all forms of Wordsworth's "meddling intellect" which "murder[s] to dissect." Jonathan Bate describes the collapse of this dualism perfectly:

> Is human consciousness part of nature? For the picturesque theorist, it is not: the perceiving, dividing eye stands above and apart from its "prospect." That strand of environmentalism which emphasizes the conservation of landscapes of "natural beauty" adopts the same stance. The converse position is that of Wordsworth's ecopoetic: the "mind of man" can be part of nature. "Lines written a few miles above Tintern Abbey" offers not a *view* in the manner of the picturesque, but an exploration of the inter-relatedness of perception and creation, a meditation on the *networks* which link mental and environmental space. (148)

The idea of such "*networks*" is crucial to the argument I have been advancing. The collapse of such dualistic oppositions, as Wordsworth and Bate suggest, is really not so difficult after all; it requires only a willingness to glory in the whole world—all of it, all of the time—to see the human world as an echo of the natural world, and vice versa, forever.

If humanity in the coming decades finds a way to reign in its materialistic excesses, if individuals agree to place fewer demands on the ecological systems that support them, if nations resolve to set aside their differences for the sake of survival, then ecological forms of literary criticism will turn out to have been prophetic in the positive sense, harbingers of an era of balanced living in which humans, animals, plants—and even the inanimate world—come to exist in harmonious and mutually beneficial ways. If, on the other hand, current trends continue—the world will get warmer, reserves of a wide variety of resources will diminish, and human culture will continue to swallow up the natural environment—then ecocriticism will turn out to have been little more than a hopeless warning to human beings about the unalterable errors of their ways. The assessment of these options is particularly relevant for the United States, a nation in which 20 percent of the earth's resources are consumed by 5 percent of the planet's population.

As an unsettling statistic like this suggests, one of the key roles for ecocriticism in the coming years—and for nature writers as well—will be the ability to translate what Scott Slovic has called the "numbing numbers" (47) of scientific data into emotionally charged rhetoric that can change the minds (of recalcitrant politicians and entrenched special interests) and alter the hearts (of wasteful consumers and thoughtless materialists). American ecocriticism emerged roughly two decades ago as a powerful new way of assessing humanity's impact on the global environment. It continues to flourish today as both a warning and a hope: a warning about the ecological damage that has already been done to this planet by human society, and a hope that it may not be too late for humanity to save the nonhuman world that makes all earthly lives possible.

*   *   *

I am cold, even though the thin flame on my own Roost fire is popping through the grate. April may be the cruelest month—if T. S. Eliot was right—but February is definitely the coldest month up here on my Blue Ridge mountaintop. In my little rock-walled room I can see my breath condensing, no matter where I stand in the cabin, no matter how hot my fire roars in the stove. The frost is forming on every one of my windows, as Coleridge knew it would. The air is icy. The room is cold. The night is dark. I am ready for spring.

EPILOGUE

SPRING, AGAIN

Fertilization of Egypt.

London. Published Dec.r 1.st 1791. by J. Johnson. St Pauls Church Yard.

The Fertilization of Egypt. The dog-headed god Anubis assures that life will always return, even in a desert culture. The deserts of Egypt are fertile because a god who is half-man (culture) and half-dog (wild nature) has assured that the floods of spring will bring water from the monotheistic face of a Yahweh-like Urizen (or perhaps The Ancient of Days) onto the flood-plain of the Nile. Drawn by Henry Fuseli. Engraved by William Blake. (*The Botanic Garden.* London: Joseph Johnson, 1791).

LIFE RETURNS WITHOUT BEGINNINGS OR ENDS

It is that first mild day of March, again, and for the second time during my year-long sojourn—after the coldest week of March I can remember—the frost is gone and the icicles have melted from the roof eaves. New buds are pushing out from thin stalks and branch tips. New birds are arriving every day along the forested spine of the Blue Ridge. I can feel the warmth of a new year coming. I feel life starting to move, and I see daylight growing longer. Spring is on its way back. What might feel like the end of my natural year is really no end at all. As always, it is only the human mind that creates this idea of beginnings and ends. The spring arrives long before the season called winter has ended. If I lift up a large rock and put my hand on the earth, the humus is much warmer to my touch than the cold air that surrounds me. This earth, just six inches beneath my feet, never really got cold at all. Early this morning two white-tailed deer come up to a rock below the cabin, one of them a large buck. When they hear me on the porch, they dash a few yards down the mountain where they freeze stock still, look directly at me, and then snort hard and release loud, camel-like bursts of air through their nostrils, drawing gulps of air in a hiss, snorting the steaming air in and out of their lungs like leather bellows.

* * *

The physicist Stephen Hawking suggested, as early as 1983, that one of the greatest of human errors—since the Enlightenment—will turn out to be the tendency to see time, human experience, and the existence of the universe itself, in terms of beginnings and ends. If Hawking is right, then the universe had no beginning and will have no end (Giorbran). This modern view of physics suggests that the traditional claim that "matter can neither be created nor destroyed" is literally true. The substance that makes up the physical universe has always been here and will always remain, just in occasionally altered forms. This radical model of time and creation still allows for the "big bang" theory of creation, but it sees that idea in relation to an infinite series of big bangs. The big bang that produced the current universe is just one among an infinite number of reorganizing moments, this current one—c. 12–15 billion years old—along with literally count-less others, coming into being in various steady or unsteady states, remaining forever or going out of one state to be replaced by other versions of the same substantial matter and energy in different states. Since Einstein, it has been clear that Newton's absolute separation between matter and energy was an error, or at least an oversimplifica-tion. In fact, the basis of Einstein's most famous equation was the idea that an equal sign ("=") could be placed between energy and matter ($E = mC^2$), a possibility that was utterly unimaginable in any strictly Newtonian universe. If matter and energy are nothing more than for-mal variations of the same "stuff" in different states—to oversimplify: matter is "slowed-down" energy; energy is "speeded-up" matter— then science can account for all change over time as different states of the same raw material. This view of matter and energy suggests yet another model of a universe—and a state of "nature"—in which everything is ultimately linked, a world in which all of the parts are completely interconnected.

If time is no longer a problem, then how does this book's empha-sis on literature link to my wider argument? Like Patrick Murphy, I do not want "the whole literary-criticism game" to be "transpar-ently irrelevant to events in the world" (x). Like Eric Smith, I do not want to be an ecocritic who takes "the distinction between 'culture' and 'nature'" for granted (30). Ecocritics and nature-lovers alike must be careful when their affection for one view of nature—often a "Romantic" view—allows them to ignore the dangers, limits, and potentially "false" presentations of such a perspective. Finally, like Dana Phillips, I seek an ecocriticism that challenges the pastoral impulse and admits that the current "idea of wilderness is plagued with contradictions too numerous to list" (147). I worry when an influential ecocritic (and nature writer) like John Elder claims that "To live in an urban world, cut off from tradition and nature alike, is to experience a life-threatening wasteland" (33). Contrary to Elder's claim, the "urban world" in the current century can be life-affirm-ing, life-sustaining, and beautiful; I have lived in such conditions on the banks of the Thames—in Hammersmith—in a London of twelve million people. "Tradition and nature," by contrast, can be dangerous, disease-ridden, and life threatening; my sister-in-law was rushed to a hospital with a dangerous case of enteritis (caused by *giardia*) while living traditionally (outhouse, no hot water) beside a crystal-clear Adirondack lake. These oppositions are tricky; they need to be discussed and debated carefully.

So, what has my urbanatural year of roosting taught me? I have learned that virtually wherever I am on this mountain, I can hear the noise of traffic on Route 9, sometimes the downshifting gears of tractor-trailers, sometimes the high whine of motorcycles. I have learned that W. B. Yeats was right when he sang about the death of the "woods of Arcady"; "their antique joy" is gone for good ("The Song of the Happy Shepherd" 1–2). I agree with those who have said that this old-world, Romantic dream of nature is gone. Artists may still be able to imagine those woods of Arcadia in their poems and paintings, their fancies and their fictions; meanwhile, humanity's actual relationship to nature has, for the past two centuries, been the tendency to carve it up, sell it off, categorize it, measure it, map it and mark it, until there is no spot on earth that is not a line of latitude or a mark of longitude, no place that has not been photographed from space, no square foot of land that has not been charted and captured in several human ideas or images: a piece of real estate, a bit of national park, someone's building lot, and some country's contested borderland. Every person on earth now lives in a world full of boundary lines and time zones, two tropics: Cancer and Capricorn, and two poles: North and South.

To the extent that human beings have destroyed the "antique joy" of those old woods of the world, they have remade them into little more than consumable objects for other human's use. A related problem emerges from the widespread historical lies that have been told in the name of both nature and culture:

> It is no secret that banning American Indians and appropriating their lands were deemed necessary for the initial establishment and continued security of Yellowstone National Park....When they imagined this Wyoming preserve into being, the park's conceivers projected themselves backward. They *reconceived* this environment as a natural Eden of pristine and pre-human existence...Although their heritage in the greater Yellowstone region has been established for at least nine thousand years, literally and figuratively Indians had to be "disappeared."...The answer to the question of whether Indians were to be considered part of the "natural" or "cultural" history of the park seems to have been answered by default...As long as Indians are seen as part of nature, they remain the one species who were not allowed to stay in their natural habitat. (Nabokov and Loendorf xi–xiv)

This description of the removal of the indigenous Indians to make way for the carefully crafted wilderness that would be Yellowstone, repeats the central premise of this book. All people on earth are part of the cultural *and* natural histories of the environments they inhabit. Urbanature reminds all human beings—from the few last stone-age tribesmen in the wilds of New Guinea or the Amazon to the most sophisticated urbanites on the Upper East Side of Manhattan or the Left Bank in Paris—of their vested interest in both realms.

Urbanatural roosting asks, simply, that the old lines of arbitrary separation—urban/rural, city/country, natural/artificial—be removed; the idea claims that the populous boroughs of Manhattan and the crowded neighborhoods of Los Angeles are not qualitatively different from the still lakes of the Adirondacks and the waving kelp beds off the California coast. All of these locations are equally worthy of human care and concern, all equally deserving of the attention needed to sustain them. Romantic ecocriticism tended to demonize the urban while idealizing the natural. Now that the Romantic world of nature has ended, urbanatural roosting asks that environmentalists and ecocritics embrace the new world they have made, glorying in the links between wide highways and wetlands, skyscrapers and sand dunes.

So how should I roost best? In rural isolation? Like many members of my generation, I was once a committed back-to-the-lander. I spoke out against sidewalks, shopping centers, suburbs, and streetlamps. Now, however, I seriously doubt the efficacy of the rural solution, at least on any large scale. The completely rural solution is no environmentally sensitive solution at all; it relies on automobiles full of petroleum products to get to isolated places, airplanes to take nature-lovers from one pristine beauty-spot to another, fossil-fuel powered machines of all sorts (tractors, chain saws, lawnmowers, weed-whackers, and hedge trimmers) as well as electrically powered wireless and wired technologies to keep rural-dwellers connected to utilities and information. What about thickly populated urban spaces full of antlike communal inhabitants; are they the answer for an urbanatural future? Some futurists and ecocentric thinkers think so. The great urban centers of the world, and their surrounding expanses, are humanity's most extensive and expensive contributions to the surface of the earth (at least in size and scale; they are clearly visible from outer space), but megacities are also humanity's most problematic contribution to planetary culture in terms of poverty, illness, overpopulation, and crime. What about suburban spaces and suburbanized sprawl? That culture is now the reality for increasing numbers of humans in all societies: vast expanses of undeveloped (or poorly developed) landscape that allow each person—each family—to gain a sense of independence (*my* house, *my* acre, *my* lot) without any real interdependence. Who are my neighbors? What are their names? How big is my garage? How many chemicals will I need to keep my artificially green-lawn green and dandelion-free?

What about ecoculture, a planning model that puts a premium on the ecology of smaller spaces, on a balance of human and nonhuman forces in civilized and civilizable places that human beings can manage best? Ecoculture suggests that small towns and decentralized urban spaces are probably the best model for roosting as I have described it, a new model for a new millennium. Small towns have shown their advantages since the Middle Ages, spaces that humans can manage while also understanding their surroundings, places that keep their occupants in close enough contact with earth and sea and sky, with the plants and the animals they depend on, and with each other, so that the separation between nature and culture does not seem so—well—*natural*.

It is also true that the solution to urban and rural planning in the current century will have more to do with the way different human lives are managed than with any single model for roosting. Bill McKibben examines this reality in *Hope: Human and Wild*, his response to criticisms of the pessimism of his earlier *The End of Nature*. McKibben's more hopeful book examines the Adirondack Mountain region in upstate New York, the Brazilian city of Curitiba, and the Indian state of Kerala as models for ecologically balanced living. The Adirondacks hold one hundred and thirty thousand human inhabitants, living in six million acres, in one of the most strictly controlled and regulated land areas anywhere in the United States, perhaps on earth. Curitiba is a city of a million and a half, yet it offers fifty-two square meters of "green" land for each inhabitant, more than three times the United Nations' recommended population density. The Indian state of Kerala, by contrast, has a population of thirty-two million and is three times as densely settled as the rest of India, yet its population growth rate is the lowest in India, and it is working to provide a model of balanced, environmentally sensitive, human life. A wasteful, thoughtless alternative to such "model" ecological places was the rule that characterized urban development around the planet for most of the twentieth century: urban centers that expanded with little, if any, form of control or planning, wide sprawls of humanity that left vast landscapes ravaged and left millions of people with limited, impoverished lives: Jakarta, Manila, Lagos, Sao Paulo, and Mexico City.

This history of urbanization created the need for these new ways of living more carefully on the world and off the land, ecosensitive to human impacts on the creatures, plants, and inanimate objects that comprise the environment, thoughtful about human connectedness to all of these resources. Urban ecology, and new concepts such as urban forests, transitional zones, reclaimed rural spaces, and populated wetlands, can help to transform the idea of roosting from a simplistic avian metaphor for the perch into a humanized model of living, not just lightly, but more thoughtfully, on the planet. If ecodevelopment can naturalize human spaces, then it can also humanize wild spaces in ways that will be acceptable to all but the most virulent of deep ecologists. Naturalized human spaces will include green-roof surfaces and organic walls, plant-covered decks and porches, windows that use multilayered glass with plastics and photovoltaic cells (or wind turbines and fans) to create more naturalistic models of harmony between buildings and their environments: structures open to the earth and sky, homes incorporating local water sources—think of Frank Lloyd Wright's "Falling Water"—public spaces that mix human and nonhuman uses in a new balance of shared purposes.

Roosting also includes more integrated ways of incorporating live creatures, as well as plants, into the human environment; it perceives pets as domesticated wild creatures sharing space with us, but it also emphasizes trees and shrubs to "green" our surroundings as well as urbanatural wild species—coyotes, deer, raccoons, squirrels, chipmunks, bats, and the like—as creatures with whom we share our space for pragmatic reasons, not just because we "love" nature. As Terrell Dixon has said of recent times, "urban nature has figured most often as an intriguing, if mostly marginal, oxymoron"; the result of this view is that, when "we assume that the city is apart from nature, we ignore how the absence of firsthand, place-based knowledge of urban nature has shaped a culture in which urban environmental degradation is the norm" (xi). Save the wilderness—ignore the cities! As long as environmentalists are busy saving unpopulated wild lands, they are wasting valuable resources that could help to save the whole world, not just those parts of it that are aesthetically pleasing to white, upper-middle-class nature lovers.

Where does my idea of urbanature lead? If every rock and every dark star, every swirl of galactic dust and every black hole, is completely natural, then so is each building and statue, every suspension bridge and Band-Aid. No rock was born (*natura*: to be born), yet it is just as natural as any part of the living world. The etymological source of *natura*, as "that which has been born," is part of the reason for traditional confusion about the word "nature." Urbanature moves from a history of "nature" as nonhuman toward a human history that is always natural, always inextricably linked to the sky and the sea, to the forests and the fields, to the animals and plants that have always surrounded human society and always will. The ideas of "urban" and "natural" thus represent one of the last great Western dualisms that needs to be bridged or dissolved: urbanature. This apparent opposition—nature versus culture, the natural versus the artificial, man versus nature—is all one and the same. Here is a final reason why. Urbanature already exists.

Central Park is full to bursting with life: chipmunks, chairpersons of the board, squirrels, stock brokers, birds and actors, bees and teachers, snakes and salamanders, sex-workers and snails, dragonflies and drycleaners, foxes and fish, lovers, paupers, writers, lizards, professors, wasps, ants, and invisible creatures beyond number. There are hawks nesting on the window-sills of penthouses. Birders watch them all day through binoculars and broadcast their antics on the Internet. A red-tailed hawk named Pale Male has become a local celebrity. The Hudson and the East River are clean and getting cleaner. They have the potential to be beautiful healthy rivers, full of fish and turtles and flocks of water birds. In England, efforts have been underway to restore salmon to the Thames since a nine-pound female fish was captured near London in 1974 (McCarthy). The Potomac River runs right through the pulsing political heart of Washington, D.C. The Chesapeake Bay (once bursting with crabs and oysters) is right next to Baltimore. San Francisco Bay sits close to Haight-Ashbury. The Chicago lakeside, Seattle's islands, and the beaches of Los Angeles: all of these natural features have the power to transform their urban surroundings if only they are allowed to flourish. When commercial flights fly into Denver, they descend, approach, and land through some of the most pristine wilderness that America has to offer. The Front Range spreads out nearby, to the west of the city, with the Flat Irons, Estes Park, and Rocky Mountain National Park reaching ever-higher to a snow-capped, elk-crowded fourteen thousand feet. This same link between the urban and the natural is evident when airliners fly over the top of the Everglades on the way to their Miami landings. There is no necessary separation between these "wildernesses" and the nearby human cultures, except for the sense of separation that human beings create. Thoreau got it right when he said that "Wildness" is not just about wilderness-lands. Wildness is about a wild-wilderness within each of us. Let it flourish.

The great cities of the world—New York, Paris, Rome, Cape
Town, Moscow, Mumbai, Beijing, Jakarta, Tokyo—are all as much
a part of nature as anything else on the planet. Look at these cities
in NASA's photographic images from outer space. They are just as
full of "nature" as Yosemite, the Mississippi Delta, the rain-forests
of Cameroon, or the Sahara desert. Even the world's largest cities
are full of a natural atmosphere, natural plants, and natural animals.
McKibben was mistaken when he said—in 1989—that nature had
"ended" because humans had left their toxic chemicals and residues
on the highest mountain peaks and in the deepest ocean trenches.
He was much closer to the mark when he said, in 1995, that humans
have already found ways—in places such as Kerala, Curitiba, and
the Adirondacks; I would add the villages of East Anglia (Norfolk
and Suffolk) in England, the Florida Keys, and Harpers Ferry, West
Virginia, among many others—to live in harmony with their surroundings. Nature has not ended because we have put our mark
everywhere. The Romans raised lead-levels in soils taken from wide
swathes across Europe because of their propensity for lead smelting;
that did not mean that the Romans had "ended" nature. That desire
of humans to control their surroundings will not end (it goes all the
way back to the Fertile Crescent between the Tigris and the Euphrates
rivers roughly eight-to-ten-thousand years ago). What might end, and
should end, is society's tendency to separate human creations from
those things that humans did not create.

We need a new ethic, not just Aldo Leopold's "land ethic" but an
even wider ecoethic. As Bryan Moore notes, "the term [ecocentrism]
came into use following the publication of [Leopold's] *A Sand County
Almanac* in 1949" (5). Leopold's ethic was almost a definition of
ecocentrism: "a land ethic changes the role of *Homo sapiens* from conqueror of the land-community to plain member and citizen of it. It
implies respect for his fellow-members, and also respect for the community as such" (*Almanac* 240). Leopold's "as such" provides for the
crucial transition to urbanatural roosting. Once the human members
of any community—urban, suburban, rural, wild—acknowledge the
intrinsic value of their fellow creatures (and also of inanimate nature:
water, air, even oil), society will be well on its way toward a more
balanced, holistic, and shared healthy life on planet earth. This new
ecoethic says that the most urban setting I can imagine is full of nonhuman life of all kinds: birds, rodents, snakes, insects by the billions,
worms, snails, microscopic creatures beyond counting. I understand
that some of this is life that humans do not particularly care about:
rats in the basement, bats in the attic, slugs in the garden, roaches in

the cupboards. But all of this life—even termites in the floorboards and mold on the bathroom wall—is life; it is all part of a complex ecology. This view of life proves that nature does not stop when people enter the city limits or the front doors of their homes. There is a seamless—I want to say "wondrous"—continuum that runs from the wildest wilds of north Alaska to the urbanest-urbs of South Boston, from the barest plain of Outer Mongolia to the most densely populated neighborhood of Manila. Humans need to recognize the relationships that connect plants to animals, humans to nonhumans, and the urban world to the nonurban world throughout this continuum. This ecoethic allows for the setting of rat-traps; I have set them, too, but it will ask that all people let the bats live in their attic; they eat thousands of mosquitoes in one night. I can kill a few slugs in my garden with jar-tops full of beer; that will help the plants. I can spray for cockroaches and termites, as long as I do so with organic pesticides (garlic, marigolds, baking soda, chrysanthemums, potassium). Roosting asks only that I think carefully and consistently about the relationships that link me to the entire world. Caring for the planet and sharing its riches: that is all that will be required.

The change I am calling for will not be so hard. Anthropomorphism was a bad thing—not artistically, but ideologically—because it imagined everything in terms of human beings. It assumed that "man" (gender-specificity intentional) was the measure of all things. A poet might say, "The willows wept for the day that was dying": there is nothing artistically wrong with this image; in fact, it makes a beautiful mental picture. But consider the implications of this simple statement. Willows do not really weep: they have no tear ducts, and they have no emotions, and days do not die. The "end" of any day is another human construction, based on where I happen to be standing. The sun moves around the sky constantly, and the earth keeps spinning and spinning; nothing "begins" in terms of morning sunlight or evening darkness unless you are standing still in one place. Point of view—my personal perspective—determines everything. So my poetic statement contains two lies: no weeping is going on, and no dying, and yet I have assumed these anthropomorphic metaphors to connect this tree and this day with two concepts my readers can easily understand: weeping and death.

So keep the anthropomorphism that the poets want as an artistic and aesthetic technique if it is helpful in those ways. The danger comes when humans take such anthropomorphism seriously and begin to see everything that is not human only in terms of human life and values. A willow tree has value in and of itself, separate from whether it weeps or not, distinct from anything a human might say about it or feel about it. It has value to the field it stands in, value to the creek it roots beside, value to the birds that nest in it, and value to the bees that feed on its blossoms. Many of those nonhuman values also produce value for humans, not just value to poets but also value to picnic-goers, beekeepers, birdwatchers, furniture makers, wood carvers, and ecocritics. Anthropomorphism needs to be replaced, as I have said, with ecomorphism, the willingness to imagine all things not in relation to human beings but rather in relation to an ecosystem, a natural system that is always also a human system. Each ecosystem includes everything: all of the people, the buildings, the nonhuman creatures, the manmade substances and the natural substances alike. Ecomorphism is easy. It says that everything should be seen, everything should be thought of, as part of this larger urba-natural system.

Humanity also needs to get rid of anthropocentrism, a tendency that has done even more damage than anthropomorphism, although the two are closely related. Anthropocentrism says that human beings are at the center; mankind's activities are seen as central in terms of value judgments, ethical debates, and decision making of all kinds. Anthropocentrism began when the monotheistic God of Judaism and Christianity said that human beings should have "dominion" over all that had been created; that idea is another error that needs to end—right now. Anthropocentrism was also the American pioneers saying, "Let's get rid of these passenger pigeons and buffalos; let's eat them, or put their heads on our walls, or just leave their bodies where we killed them, and—while we are at it—let's get rid of these annoying red men, and oh, yes, let's get rid of their women and their children, too!" Anthropocentrism simply is not true, or it is only true in ways that most often do harm to other people and to other living things.

Once human beings gave up on the idea that nature might control them—that there might be limits to what humans could accomplish—the foundation was laid for the triumph of technology and the completely humanistic tenor of modern life. As Max Oelschlaeger notes, "modern human beings think of themselves as existing without natural limits" (69). In recent years, however, the recognition of nature's power has been reasserted, both by nature and by culture. Numerous diseases seem resistant to our best efforts at defeating them; some like superbacteria (superbugs) are clearly caused by us. The earth bleeding oil from a crack in its surface into the Gulf of Mexico (2010) may reveal localized environmental destruction on a scale that has never been seen. A tsunami in South Asia, Hurricane Katrina, earthquakes in developed and undeveloped nations, volcanoes destroying entire regions of once-urbanized habitation, and perhaps most of all, an increasingly unstable set of climactic conditions: the stage is clearly set for a new world, one in which humans will have to learn to live with nature or die without it.

Timothy Morton has recently suggested that Western culture is in mourning for a concept—"nature"—that never existed in the first place (*Ecology Without Nature* blog). The fantasy that humans once believed in was called "nature," and it is very difficult to give up such a beloved fantasy: "happy, happy nature," "joy, joy, the great outdoors!" Such a fantasy was one version of William Blake's idea of innocence writ large (Fosso, Morton, and Nichols). Like Blakean innocence, post-Enlightenment "nature" had no existence beyond a beautiful aesthetic dream, a fantasy fashioned in each human mind, a mental and linguistic place we might call "Bambi's World." The "Bambification" of the nonhuman world happened to the Western world, and even to the East (consider the cities of Olympic Beijing and Westernized Tokyo in 2010), ever since Rousseau, and Wordsworth, and Goethe (among many other artists and thinkers) created a version of a nature that human beings were supposed to love like their mother, a nature they should long to return to, just like the Garden of Eden. Just as there was no Eden, however, there was never a mother-place called "nature." Humans are set down here on planet earth, not only with Bambi, but also with Bambi's dying mother, placed here by the rules of reproduction and natural selection in a world full of life and also of death. As Darwin taught so clearly, the engine that drives evolution is death, and lots of it. Death or no death, however, it is time to end the mourning, get over the grief, and get on with making a world that all humans can inhabit together and share, a world that can survive for future generations of human beings and the rest of life on earth.

Like ecocentrism, urbanatural roosting will not be so difficult. All it will require is that every one of us should think about, care about, and do something good about every place, every person, every creature, and every thing that each of us can affect on planet earth. The developed world should shape its view of life now with a sense of earth as a nonhuman home, humanity's "spaceship-earth" as the futurists used to say in the 1960s. Many people can make their houses into rural, or urban, ecohomes. I can craft the place I rest into my roost, wherever I may come to rest. Wherever I happen to live on this planet, the rain still falls fast. Wherever I roam, the wind always whistles around me. My habitation is always human—as in *humus*—as in *earth.* There can be no completely urban spot where nature does not remain. There can be no fully wild spot, where the world of humans has been left completely behind. There can now be no place that is not pervaded by human culture: perceived by human eyes and ears, given a name, recorded by cartographers, geologists, and historians. The wildest wilds of the Sahara and the coldest colds of the Poles have been mapped, scanned from the sky, or walked over. The most distant nonhuman spot has been seen, and photographed clearly, from outer space. This is the new world that each human being now inhabits, a world that waits for humanity to begin urbanatural roosting.

Acknowledgments

When my students ask me how long it took John Keats to write the poem "To Autumn," I say, "Well, it took him one afternoon, but it took him 23 years." That is how one feels when finishing a project like this one. There is no appropriate way to perform the courtesy suggested by the term "acknowledgments" except to thank those without whom this book would not have been written. Even that list is too long; so, instead of a comprehensive list, I will thank those who are close at hand, likely to read these words, or indispensable—in some way—for their various and multifarious contributions: Teddy Ako, Nandita Batra, Steve Clark, Jack Cowardin, Peter Hajdu, Steven Hockley and Elizabeth Ashton Nichols Hockley, Liam O'Loughlin, Yoshimitsu Miyakawa, Richard B. Miller, Molly MacKenzie Nichols, Tessa Brooks Nichols, Wang Ning, Emerson John Probst and Gwendolen Smith Probst, Liu Qinghan, Bruce Reid, Michael Reid and Deborah Rizzo Reid, Alan Richardson, Masashi Suzuki, Teku Teku, P. Kingsley Smith and Mary Lee Evans Smith, Roberto Smiraglio and Amy Eliza Nichols Smiraglio, and Thomas Steptoe.

At ASLE, I thank Jim Warren, who had a lengthy conversation with me on a bus-ride to the south ridge of the Grand Canyon that has stayed with me ever since (and whose daughter, Sylvia, wrote a great thesis in my senior English seminar); Kate Rigby, whose friendship and ecocritical thinking have helped to internationalize my own; Kate Singer, who provided me with a most energetic audience of Mount Holyoke questioners; and Scott Slovic, whose comments around a buffet lunch table in Beijing—and subsequent reading and commentary on my chapter on American ecocriticism for a Chinese textbook on environmental writing—saved me from several errors. At Dickinson, Marcus Key, Susan Perabo, Bob Winston, and my colleagues on the sustainability discussion group: the founders—Jeremy Vetter and Meghan Reedy—and Marc Mastrangelo, have offered ongoing collegial friendship and intellectual sustenance. Tom Arnold provided valuable information about the intricacies of Darwinian speciation, the question that literally began this project ("What did Mary Shelley think the word 'species' meant in 1816?").

I also owe a long-ago debt to a remarkable man, my scoutmaster, Carl A. Zapffe. Here is how Dr. Zapffe described himself on his own letterhead: "B. S., M. S., Sc. D., D. Eng. Hon., Professional Engineer, Metallurgy, Physics, Chemistry, Fractology, Geology, Space Science." He was also the spouse of a Dupont and, most important to me, my father's eulogist. Dr. Zapffe loved to camp, and when he camped his motto was—in retrospect—part of the dawning of urbanature in my mind. "Remember, boys!" he would say in his booming voice to a hundred or so of us gathered by the shoreline of Churn Creek on Maryland's Eastern Shore: "whenever you are camping, nothing you can do for yourself in the woods is too good." What this meant practically, to Dr. Zapffe, was air-mattresses, a rustic rocking-chair that accompanied him everywhere, hollandaise sauce for fresh asparagus on the Coleman stove, and the new (1960s) large pop-up tents with screen porches, rain-flies, and light aluminum tent-poles. What it meant abstractly to a bunch of adolescent boys from the suburbs of Baltimore was that the woods were a place to embrace, a locale to inhabit with any conveniences that urban culture might provide.

I am grateful for grants from the Office of Dickinson Provost and Dean of the College Neil Weissman, as well as the Research and Development Committee at the College. The "Great Courses" program of The Teaching Company has provided time and financial assistance that allowed me to deepen my understanding of Emerson, Thoreau, and American Transcendentalism. The CSE (Center for Sustainability Education), a Valley and Ridge Grant, and the Willoughby Fellowship Program—all at Dickinson—offered collegial, financial, and technical assistance at crucial stages in the development of this project. In this regard, I thank especially Neil Leary and Sarah Brylinsky. I am grateful to Kelly Winters-Fazio for a thousand bits of administrative, clerical—and at least as many other forms of thoughtful—assistance and advice over two decades of collegial work. I thank students in a number of my classes, especially "Thoreau, Wilderness and American Nature Writing," "Darwin and Romantic Natural History," "British and American Nature Writing," and "Writing About Nature," as well as the Nanzan University students I have taught at Dickinson and in Japan in the spring of 2010. Among my students, I think especially of Evan Gregoire, Breanna Marr, Brett Shollenberger, and Joanna Sprout, models of undergraduates whose intellectual sophistication and academic maturity belie their years and consistently amaze me with their insights. They will find some of their questions—and provisional answers to those questions—echoing in these pages.

I am grateful to many librarians at the British Library (the original Bloomsbury Reading Room as well as the new facility at St. Pancras), the Library of Congress, and the Museum of Natural History in London, the American Philosophical Society in Philadelphia, and the Waidner-Spahr Library at Dickinson (especially Jim Gerenscer and his colleagues in the May Morris Reading Room and Special Collections for assistance with their outstanding holdings in early natural history). In all of these libraries I did much of the research into original—or early editions—of these poets and natural historians. I have preferred earlier to later editions of poetry in most instances (and record those debts in my citations), since they often capture more of the original energy of experiences in the nonhuman world. On the editorial front, I am supremely grateful to Marilyn Gaull, the editor every author dreams of, one who praises lavishly at the same time that she corrects aggressively; she knows what our friendship means to me. At Palgrave Macmillan, I thank Brigitte Shull, Lee Norton, Joel Breuklander, and Rohini Krishnan (at Newgen Imaging in Chennai, Tamil Nadu).

Parts of this work have been published elsewhere. I am grateful to these original sources for permission to reprint works here, all of which have been revised—some extensively—since earlier appearances: *The Wordsworth Circle* for "The Anxiety of Species: Toward a Romantic Natural History," *The Wordsworth Circle* 28.3 (1997): 130–136, also available web page http://users.dickinson.edu/~nicholsa/ Romnat/anxiety.htm; *Romantic Circles* for "The Loves of Plants and Animals: Romantic Science and the Pleasures of Nature," *Romantic Circles Praxis Series*, available at the website, http://www.rc.umd. edu/praxis/ecology/nichols/nichols.html, University of Maryland (November 2001); The American Philosophical Society for "Roaring Alligators and Burning Tygers: Poetry and Science from William Bartram to Charles Darwin" (from *The Proceedings of the American Philosophical Society* 149:3 (2005): 304–316, also available online at http://www.amphilsoc.org/sites/default/files/490302.pdf; and finally, The Blue Oceans Institute for "Face to Face with Wild Dolphins," *Sea Stories: An International Journal of Art and Writing*, http://seastories.org/2010/04/welcome-to-sea-stories/, Hibernal Issue (2006/7), a publication of the "Blue Oceans Institute," a valuable resource for anyone who is interested in the fate of 70 percent of the earth's surface. Additional discussions of urbanature can be found at the *Romantic Circles* invited Thematic-Thread blog-posts by Timothy Morton (UC-Davis), Kurt Fosso (Lewis and Clark), and me from October to December 2008: *Ecocriticism*, 9–12/2008, http:// www.rc.umd.edu/blog_rc/, and also at my own blog: *Urbanature*, http://ashtonnichols.blogspot.com/. My chapter epigraphs are taken from Whitall N. Perry's magisterial *Treasury of Traditional Wisdom: An Encyclopedia of Humankind's Spiritual Truth*. London: George Allen & Unwin, 1971, a *tour-de-force* volume that should be required reading for those who—like Emerson and Thoreau—find so-called perennial wisdom to be a veritable fount (or is it "font") of knowledge, insight, and awareness. I thank Charles Lloyd Garrettson III for the great cover photograph of an unoccupied Romantic naturalist's seat.

My family sustains me in ways that grow more powerful with the passing of the years. My four daughters—and their partners—continue to be sources of countless conversations, ideas, and intellectual (as well as familial) exchanges that push my own thinking in new, and valuable, directions: film history and theory, Italian language and culture, environmental and other forms of sustainability, nature writing, postcolonial ecocriticism, prison writing, and much, much more. My wife, Kimberley Anne Nichols, as always, has been with me through every page of this volume—literally and figuratively—and, although she has received dedications in two of my earlier works, she receives another one here, but now in multigenerational form. She knows how much this dual dedication means to both of us; I am confident that the rest of the family knows how much it means to all of us.

Works Cited

Age database. "An Age Entry for *Homo sapiens.*" *Human Ageing Genomic Resources.* Web. May 28, 2010.

Altick, Richard D. *The Shows of London: A Panoramic History of Exhibitions, 1699–1862.* Cambridge, MA: Belknap P of Harvard UP, 1978. Print.

"The Ancient Bristlecone Pine." sonic.net & U of Arizona. Web. May 27, 2010.

Arnold, Matthew. *Selected Poetry. Representative Poetry Online.* UTEL Edition. Toronto: U of Toronto P, 2005. Web. June 7, 2010.

Ballantyne, Coco. "Fact or Fiction?: Smog Creates Beautiful Sunsets." *Scientific American.* July 12, 2007. Web. June 22, 2010.

Barber, Lynn. *The Heyday of Natural History: 1820–70.* London: Jonathan Cape, 1980. Print.

Barr, J. S. *Buffon's Natural History, Containing A Theory of the Earth, A General History of Man, of the Brute Creation, and of Vegetables, Minerals, &c.* Trans. J. S. Barr. 10 vols. Covent Garden: Barr, 1792. Print.

Barrett, Andrea. *The Voyage of the Narwhal.* New York: Norton, 1998. Print.

Bartram, John. *The Correspondence of John Bartram, 1734–1777.* Ed. Edmund Berkeley and Dorothy S. Berkeley. Gainesville: U of Florida P, 1992. Print.

Bartram, William. *Travels and Other Writings.* New York: Library of America, 1996. Print.

Bate, Jonathan. *The Song of the Earth.* Cambridge, MA: Harvard UP, 2000. Print.

Batra, Nandita. "Dominion, Empathy, and Symbiosis: Gender and Anthropocentrism in Romanticism." *The ISLE Reader: Ecocriticism, 1993–2003.* Michael P. Branch and Scott Slovic, eds. Athens: U of Georgia P, 2003: 155–72. [*ISLE* 3.2 (Fall 1996): 101–20]. Print.

Beecher, Henry Ward. *Proverbs from Plymouth Pulpit,* New York: Appleton, 1887. Print.

Benford, Gregory. "Leaping the Abyss: Stephen Hawking on Black Holes, Unified Field Theory, and Marilyn Monroe." *reason.com.* April 2002. Web. May 28, 2010.

Bennett, Michael. "Urban Nature: Teaching Tinker Creek by the East River." *ISLE* 5.1 (1998): 49–60. Print.

Bennett, Michael and David W. Teague. *The Nature of Cities: Ecocriticism and Urban Environments.* Tucson: U of Arizona P, 1999. Print.

Berry, Wendell. "Preserving Wildness." *Home Economics: Fourteen Essays.* San Francisco: North Point P, 1987: 137–51. Originally published in *The Landscape of Harmony: Two Essays on Wilderness & Community.* Hereford: Five Seasons P, 1985. Print.

Bewick, Thomas. *A General History of Quadrupeds.* Newcastle: S. Hodgson, R. Beilby, and T. Bewick, 1790. Print.

Blake, William. Ed. David V. Erdman. *The Complete Poetry and Prose of William Blake.* New York: Random House, 1988. Print.

Blanchan, Neltje. *Birds: Selected from the Writings of Neltje Blanchan.* New York: Doubleday and Doran, 1917. Print.

Blunt, Wilfrid. *The Ark in the Park: The Zoo in the Nineteenth Century.* London: Hamish Hamilton, 1976. Print.

Bogdan, Robert. *Freak Show: Presenting Human Oddities for Amusement and Profit.* Chicago: U of Chicago P, 1990. Print.

Bradley, A. C. *A Commentary on Tennyson's* In Memoriam. 3rd ed. London: Macmillan, 1920. Print.

Buell, Lawrence. *The Environmental Imagination: Thoreau, Nature Writing, and the Formation of American Culture.* Cambridge, MA: Belknap P, 1995. Print.

Buffon, George Louis Leclerc, Comte de. *Barr's Buffon: Buffon's* Natural History; *containing a theory of the Earth.* 10 vols. London: J. S. Barr, 1792. Print.

———. *The Natural History of Insects, compiled from Swammerdam, Brookes, & Goldsmith.* 1792. [bound with Buffon, *System*]. Print.

———. *The System of Natural History Written by the Celebrated Buffon.* Perth: R. Morison, 1791. Print.

Byron, George Gordon, Lord. *Byron's Letters and Journals.* Ed. Leslie A. Marchand. 12 vols. Cambridge, MA: Harvard UP, 1973–1983. Print.

Carson, Rachel. *Silent Spring.* Boston: Houghton Mifflin, 1962. Print.

Chagnon, Napoleon. *Yanomamo: The Fierce People.* Boston: Holt McDougal, 1977. Print.

[Chambers, Robert]. *Vestiges of the Natural History of Creation.* London: John Churchill, 1844. Print.

"China Plans Mount Everest Cleanup in 2009." *USA Today.* June 23, 2008. Web. May 27, 2010.

Clare, John. *Poems Descriptive of Rural Life and Scenery.* London: Taylor and Hessey, 1821. Print.

Coleridge, Samuel Taylor. *Anima Poetae: From the Unpublished Note-books of Samuel Taylor Coleridge.* Ed. E. H. Coleridge. Boston: Houghton Mifflin, 1895. Print.

———. *Coleridge's Poetry and Prose.* Ed. Nicholas Halmi, Paul Magnuson, and Raimonda Modiano. New York: Norton, 2004. Print.

———. *Notes and Lectures upon Shakespeare and Some of the Old Poets and Dramatists with Other Literary Remains.* Vol. 1. Ed. Mrs. H. N. Coleridge. London: William Pickering, 1849. Print.

Crèvecoeur, Hector St. John de. *Letters from an American Farmer.* London: Davies & Davis, 1782. Print.

Cronon, William, ed. *Uncommon Ground: Rethinking the Human Place in Nature*. New York: Norton, 1996. Print.

Darwin, Charles. *Charles Darwin's Letters: A Selection*. Ed. Frederick Burkhardt. Cambridge: Cambridge UP, 1996. Print.

———. *Darwin*. Ed. Philip Appleman. 3rd ed. New York: Norton, 2001. Print.

———. *On the Origin of Species by Means of Natural Selection*. London: John Murray, 1859. Print.

Darwin, Erasmus. *The Botanic Garden: A Poem, in Two Parts*. Part I "The Economy of Vegetation." Part II: "The Loves of the Plants." London: Joseph Johnson, 1791. Print.

———. *Phytologia; or the Philosophy of Agriculture and Gardening*. London: Joseph Johnson, 1800. Print.

———. *The Temple of Nature; or, The Origin of Society. A poem, with philosophical notes*. London: Joseph Johnson, 1803. Print.

———. *Zoonomia; or, The laws of organic life*. 2 vols. London: Joseph Johnson, 1794. Vol. 2, 1796. Print.

D'Holbach, Paul Thyry, Baron [M. de Mirabaud, pseud.]. *Nature, and Her Laws: As Applicable to the Happiness of Man, Living in Society, Contrasted with Superstition and Imaginary System*s. 2 vols. London: Henry Bohn, 1834. Print.

Dillard, Annie, *Pilgrim at Tinker Creek*. New York: Harper and Row, 1988 [1974]. Print.

Dixon, Terrell. *City Wilds: Essays and Stories About Urban Nature*. Athens: U of Georgia P, 2002. Print.

Dolan, Brian, ed. *Literature and Science 1660–1834: Chemistry*. Vol. 8. London: Pickering & Chatto, 2004. Print.

"Ecotecture: Designing and Building with the Environment in Mind." *New York Times Magazine*. 20 May 2007.

Elder, John. *Imagining the Earth: Poetry and the Vision of Nature*. Athens: U of Georgia P, 1996. Print.

Emerson, Ralph Waldo. *The Journals and Miscellaneous Notebooks*. Ed. William H. Gilman and William H. Parsons. Vol. 8. Cambridge, MA: Belknap P of Harvard UP, 1970. Print.

———. "Nature" in *Essays and Lectures*. New York: Library of America, 1983. Print.

Estok, Simon. "Theorizing a Space of Ambivalent Openness: Ecocriticism and Ecophobia." *ISLE* 16.2 (Spring 2009): 203–226. Print.

Evelyn, John. *The Diary of John Evelyn*. Ed. E. S. de Beer. 6 vols. Oxford: Clarendon P, 1955. Print.

Evernden, Neil. *The Social Creation of Nature*. Baltimore: Johns Hopkins UP, 1992. Print.

Flint, Richard W. "American Showmen and European Dealers: Commerce in Wild Animals in Nineteenth-Century America," in Hoage and Deiss: 97–108. Print.

Fosso, Kurt, Timothy Morton, and Ashton Nichols. *Romantic Circles, Thematic Blog*: "Ecocriticism." Sept.–Dec. 2008. Web. June 20, 2010.

Fowles, John. *The French Lieutenant's Woman.* Boston: Back Bay Books, 1998. Print.

Fresh-Air Fund. Serving Children Since 1877. 2009. Web. June 20, 2010.

Gilligan, Carol. *In a Different Voice: Psychological Theory and Women's Development.* Cambridge, MA: Harvard UP, 1982. Print.

Giorbran, Gevin. "Stephen Hawking and the Time Has No Boundary Proposal." *Timelessness.* May 16, 2007. Web. June 1, 2010.

Goethe, J. W. von. *Goethe on Science.* Ed. Jeremy Naydler. Edinburgh: Floris Books, 1996. Print.

Goldsmith, Oliver. *A History of the Earth and Animated Nature.* 4 vols. Philadelphia: Mathew Carey, 1795. Print.

Handke, Shawna L. "The Urbanature Way." walkthestreets. Web. Oct. 2, 2009.

Hardy, Thomas. *Tess of the D'Urbervilles.* Ed. Scott Elledge. 3rd ed. New York: Norton, 1991. Print.

Heringman, Noah. *Romantic Rocks: Aesthetic Geology.* Ithaca, NY: Cornell UP, 2004. Print.

Hess, Scott. "Imagining an Everyday Nature." *ISLE* 17.1 (Winter 2010): 85–112. Print.

Highfield, Roger. "Hawking: Man Must Leave Planet Earth." *London Telegraph.* Nov. 30, 2006. Web. June 1, 2010.

Hoage, R. J., Anne Roskell, and Jane Mansour. "Menageries and Zoos to 1900," in Hoage and Deiss: 8–19. Print.

Hoage, R. J. and William A. Deiss. *New Worlds, New Animals: From Menagerie to Zoological Park in the Nineteenth Century.* Baltimore: Johns Hopkins UP, 1996. Print.

Hobbes, Thomas. *Leviathan.* Oxford: Oxford UP, 1996 [1651]. Print.

"How Many Species Are There?" *World Resources Institute,* quoting Thomas, C. D. 1990. "Fewer species." *Nature* 347 (1990): 237. Web. May 10, 2010.

Iliffe, Rob, ed. *Literature and Science 1660–1834: Natural Philosophy.* Vol. 7. London: Pickering & Chatto, 2004. Print.

Irmscher, Christoph. *The Poetics of Natural History: From John Bartram to William James.* New Brunswick: Rutgers UP, 1999. Print.

Kalka, M. B., A. R. Smith, and E. K. V. Kalko. "Bats Limit Arthropods and Herbivory in a Tropical Forest" and K. Williams-Guillen, I. Perfecto, and J. Vandermeer. "Bats Limit Insects in a Neotropical Agroforestry System." *Science* Apr. 4, 2008. Web. May 23, 2010.

Keats, John. *The Complete Poems.* Ed. Miriam Allott. London: Longman, 1975. Print.

———. *Lamia, Isabella, The Eve of St. Agnes, and Other Poems.* London: Taylor and Hessey, 1820. Print.

———. *Selected Poem and Letters.* Ed. Douglas Bush. Boston: Houghton Mifflin, 1959. Print.

Keim, Brandon. "Salamander Discovery Could Lead to Human Limb Regeneration." *Wired Science.* July 1, 2009. Web. May 28, 2010.

Keynes, Randal. *Annie's Box: Charles Darwin, His Daughter, and Human Evolution.* London: Fourth Estate, 2001. Print.

Knickerbocker, Brad. "World First: In 2008, Most People Will Live in Cities." *Christian Science Monitor.* Jan. 12, 2007. Quoting Worldwatch Institute "State of the World." Web. Apr. 13, 2010.

Leopold, Aldo, *A Sand County Almanac.* New York: Oxford UP, 1949. Print.

Lindroth, Sten. "The Two Faces of Linnaeus," in *Linnaeus: The Man and His Work.* Ed. Tore Frangsmyr. Berkeley: U of California P, 1983. Print.

Linnaeus, Carolus. *Systema Natura.* Stockholm: Laurentii Salvii Holmiae, 1735. Print.

Liu, James J. Y. *The Art of Chinese Poetry.* Chicago: U of Chicago P, 1962. Print.

Locke, John. *Two Treatises on Civil Government.* London: Routledge, 1887. Print.

Lopez, Barry. *Crossing Open Ground.* New York: Vintage Random House, 1989. Print.

Louv, Richard. *Last Child in the Woods: Saving Our Children from Nature-Deficit Disorder.* Chapel Hill: Algonquin, 2005. Print.

Lyell, Charles. *Principles of Geology: Being an Attempt to Explain the Former Changes of the Earth's Surface by Reference to Causes Now in Operation.* 3 vols. London: John Murray, 1830–33. Print.

Malamud, Randy. *Reading Zoos: Representations of Animals and Captivity.* New York: New York UP, 1998. Print.

Malthus, Thomas R. *An Essay on the Principle of Population.* London: J. Johnson, 1798. Print.

McCarthy, Michael. "Five-Year Plan Marks Last Attempt to Breed Salmon in Thames." *Independent.* Nov. 24, 2003. Web. May 25, 2010.

McKibben, Bill. *Hope, Human and Wild: True Stories of Living Lightly on the Earth.* Minneapolis: Milkweed, 2007. Print.

———. *The End of Nature.* New York: Random House, 1989. Print.

Merwin, W. S. "Foreword." *Last of the Curlews.* By Fred Bosworth. Washington, DC: Counterpoint, 1995. Print.

Moore, Bryan L. *Ecology and Literature: Ecocentric Personification from Antiquity to the Twenty-First Century.* New York: Palgrave Macmillan, 2008. Print.

Morris, Solene, Louise Wilson, and David Kohn. *Darwin at Down House.* London: English Heritage, 1998. Print.

Morton, Timothy. *Cambridge Companion to Shelley.* Cambridge: Cambridge UP, 2006. Print.

———. *Ecology without Nature.* Cambridge, MA: Harvard UP, 2007. Print.

———. *Ecology without Nature: Ecology, Nature, Culture, Science, Philosophy.* Blogspot. Web. June 22, 2010.

Muir, John. *The Mountains of California.* New York: Century Company, 1894. Print.

Murphy, Patrick. *Farther Afield in the Study of Nature-Oriented Literature.* Charlottesville: U of Virginia P, 2000. Print.

Nabokov, Peter and Lawrence Loendorf. *Restoring a Presence: American Indians and Yellowstone National Park.* Norman: U of Oklahoma P, 2004. Print.

Neuzil, Mark and Bill Kovarik. *Mass Media and Environmental Conflict: America's Green Crusades.* Newbury Park: Sage, 1996. Chapter 3: "The Mother of the Forest: How to Make a Park." Web. Nov. 5, 2009.

Nichols, Ashton. "Roaring Alligators and Burning Tygers: Poetry and Science from William Bartram to Charles Darwin." *Proceedings of the American Philosophical Society.* 149.3 (2004): 304–15. Print.

——— . ed. *Romantic Natural Histories: William Wordsworth, Charles Darwin, and Others.* Boston: Houghton Mifflin, 2004. Print.

——— . *A Romantic Natural History: 1750–1859.* 2000–2006. Web. June 7, 2010.

———. "Thoreau and Urbanature: From *Walden* to Ecocriticism." *Neohelicon* 36.2 (December 2009): 347–54. Print.

Nordhaus, Ted and Michael Shellenberger. *Break Through: From the Death of Environmentalism to the Politics of Possibility.* (Also subtitled *Why We Can't Leave Saving the Planet to Environmentalists* [Mariner, 2009]). Boston: Houghton Mifflin, 2007. Print.

Oelschlaeger, Max. *The Idea of Wilderness: From Prehistory to the Age of Ecology.* New Haven, CT: Yale UP, 1991. Print.

Oerlemans, Onno Dag. *Romanticism and the Materiality of Nature.* Toronto: U of Toronto P, 2002. Print.

Orr, David W. *Earth in Mind: On Education, Environment, and the Human Prospect.* Washington, DC: Island, 2004 [1994]. Print.

——— . *Ecological Literacy: Education and the Transition to a Postmodern World.* Albany: State U of New York P, 1992. Print.

——— . *The Nature of Design: Ecology, Culture, and Human Intention.* Oxford: Oxford UP, 2002. Print.

Orwell, George. *Shooting an Elephant and Other Essays.* New York: Penguin, 2003. Print.

Paley, William. *Natural Theology; or, Evidence of the Existence and Attributes of the Deity, collected from the appearances of nature.* Oxford: Oxford UP, 2006 [1802]. Print.

Pennant, Thomas. *British Zoology.* 4 vols. London: Chester, 1768–70. Print.

Philbrick, Nathaniel. *In the Heart of the Sea: The Tragedy of the Whaleship Essex.* New York: Penguin, 2001. Print.

Phillips, Dana. *The Truth of Ecology: Nature, Culture, and Literature in America.* Oxford: Oxford UP, 2003. Print.

Priestman, Martin. *Romantic Atheism: Poetry and Freethought, 1780–1830.* Cambridge: Cambridge UP, 2006. Print.

Richards, Robert J. *The Romantic Conception of Life: Science and Philosophy in the Age of Goethe.* Chicago: U of Chicago P, 2004. Print.

Richardson, Robert D. *Emerson: The Mind on Fire*. Berkeley: U of California P, 1995. Print.

Rigby, Kate. *Topographies of the Sacred: The Poetics of Place in European Romanticism*. Charlottesville: U of Virginia P, 2004. Print.

Ritvo, Harriet. *The Animal Estate: The English and Other Creatures in the Victorian Age*. Cambridge, MA: Harvard UP, 1987. Print.

———— . "The Order of Nature: Constructing the Collections of Victorian Zoos." In Hoage and Deiss: 43–50. Print.

Robbins, Chandler S., Bertel Brunn, and Herbert S. Zim. *Guide to Field Identification of the Birds of North America*. New York: Golden Press, 1966. Print.

Roosting: Weber's Quotations, Facts and Phrases. San Diego: ICON International, 2008. Print.

Ross, Andrew. *The Chicago Gangster Theory of Life: Nature's Debt to Society*. London: Verso, 1994. Print.

Rousseau, Jean-Jacques. *The Social Contract and the First and Second Discourses*. Ed. and trans. Susan Dunn. New Haven, CT: Yale UP, 2001 [1754]. Print.

Runk, David. "Detroit Wants to Save Itself...by Shrinking." AP. *San Francisco Chronicle*. March 21, 2010. D1. Web. May 25, 2010.

Sachs, Aaron. *The Humboldt Current: Nineteenth-Century Exploration and the Roots of American Environmentalism*. New York: Viking Penguin, 2006. Print.

Secord, James A. *Victorian Sensation: The Extraordinary Publication, Reception and Secret Authorship of "Vestiges of the Natural History of Creation."* Chicago: U of Chicago P, 2001. Print.

Shakespeare, William. *Representative Poetry Online*. U of Toronto English Library. Sonnet LXXIII. Web. June 7, 2010.

Shellenberger, Michael and Ted Nordhaus. "The Death of Environmentalism: Global Warming Politics in a Post-Environmental World." 2004. Web. May 5, 2010.

Shelley, Mary. *The Frankenstein Notebooks*. Ed. Charles E. Robinson. 2 vols. New York: Garland, 1966. Print.

———— (with Percy Shelley). *The Original Frankenstein: Two New Versions*. Ed. Charles E. Robinson. New York: Vintage Random House, 2008 (1816–17). Print.

Shelley, Percy Bysshe. "Essay on a Future State." *Essays, Letters from Abroad, Translations and Fragments*. Ed. Mary Shelley. 2 vols. London: Moxon, 1852. Print.

———— . *Poetical Works*. Ed. Mary Shelley. London: Moxon, 1839. Print.

———— . *Shelley's Poetry and Prose*. Ed. Donald H. Reiman and Neil Fraistat. New York: Norton, 2002. Print.

Simili, Raffaella, ed. *Il Teatro Della Natura di Ulisse Aldrovandi*. Bologna: Editrice Compositori, 2001. Print.

Sinfield, Alan. *Alfred Tennyson*. Oxford: Blackwell, 1986. Print.

Slovic, Scott. "Numbers and Nerves: Seeking a Discourse of Environmental Sensitivity in a World of Data." *Tamkang Review* 32.3/4: 47–70. Print.

Smith, Eric Todd. "Dropping the Subject: Reflections on the Motives for an Ecological Criticism." *Reading the Earth: New Directions in the Study of Literature and the Environment.* Moscow: U of Idaho P, 1998.

Snow, C. P. *The Two Cultures.* (Rede Lecture 1959). Cambridge: Cambridge UP, 1960.

Solnit, Rebecca. "Detroit Arcadia: Exploring the post-American landscape." *Harper's Magazine* (July 2007): 65–73. Print.

Speyrer, John A. Book review of *To Be an Invalid: The Illness of Charles Darwin* and *Darwin's Illness. Primal Psychotherapy Page.* Oct. 3, 1995. Web. June 7, 2010.

Stallings, Tyler. "The Lore of Humankind in Jeremy Kidd's New Work." *Jeremy Kidd: Fictional Realities.* Laguna Beach: Laguna Beach Art Museum, 2006. Web. May 25, 2010.

Stanley, S. M. and X. Yang. "A Double Mass Extinction at the End of the Paleozoic Era" *Science* 266: 5189 (Nov. 25, 1994): 1340–44. Web. May 25, 2010.

Stearn, William T. "Linnaean Classification, Nomenclature, and Method," in *The Compleat Naturalist: A Life of Linnaeus.* By Wilfrid Blunt. New York: Viking, 1971. Appendix. Print.

Stein, Jay M., ed. *Classic Readings in Urban Planning.* Washington, DC: Island Press, 2001. Print.

Tenenbaum, David. "When Did Life on Earth Begin? Ask a Rock." *Astrobiology.* Oct. 14, 2002. Web. May 29, 2010.

Tennyson, Alfred, Lord. *In Memoriam.* London: Moxon, 1850. Print.

Tennyson, Hallam. *Alfred Lord Tennyson: A Memoir by his Son.* 4 vols. Leipzig: Bernhard Tauchnitz, 1899. Print.

Thomas, Dylan. *The Collected Poems of Dylan Thomas.* New York: New Directions, 1957. Print.

Thoreau, Henry David. *A Week on the Concord and Merrimack Rivers, Walden, The Maine Woods, Cape Cod.* New York: Library of America, 1985 [1849, 1854, 1864, 1865]. Print.

———. "Walking." *Walden, Civil Disobedience, and Other Writings.* Ed. William Rossi. Norton Critical, 3rd Edition. New York: Norton, 2008. Print.

Tocqueville, Alexis de. *Democracy in America.* Trans. Henry Reeve. Vol. 2. New York: Appleton, 1904. Print.

Turner, Jack. *The Abstract Wild.* Tucson: U of Arizona P, 1996. Print.

Tyson, Edward. *Orang-Outang, sive Homo sylvestris* ["Man of the Woods"]. London: 1699. Print.

"urbanature.org." Architects in New Zealand and Singapore: 2000–06. Web. June 14, 2010.

"The UrbaNature Signature from Honda." *Jakarta Post.* Feb. 22, 2010. Web. June 7, 2010.

Veltre, Thomas. "Menageries, Metaphors, and Meanings." In Hoage and Deiss: 19–32. Print.

Vidal, John. "UN report: World's biggest cities merging into 'mega-regions.'" *Guardian.* March 22, 2010. Web. May 25, 2010.

Wasserman, Earl. *Shelley: A Critical Reading.* Baltimore: Johns Hopkins UP, 1977. Print.

Water Science. "How much water falls during a rainstorm?" *Rain: A Valuable Resource.* USGS. Web. June 1, 2010.

"What Killed the Dinosaurs?" *DinoBuzz.* U of California (Berkeley). Web. May 24, 2010.

White, Gilbert. *The Natural History of Selborne.* New York: Penguin, 1997 [1789]. Print.

White, Matthew. *Historical Atlas of the Twentieth Century.* March 25, 2003. Web. June 7, 2010.

White, Stephen B., Richard A. Dolbeer, and Theodore A. Bookhout. "Ecology, Bioenergetics, and Agricultural Impacts of a Winter-Roosting Population of Blackbirds and Starlings." *Wildlife Monographs* 93. *Journal of Wildlife Management* 93 (Apr. 1985): 1–42. Print.

Whitman, Walt. "Song of Myself." *Leaves of Grass.* Philadelphia: David McKay, 1891–92. Print.

Williams, Terry Tempest. *Refuge: An Unnatural History of Family and Place.* New York: Pantheon, 1991. Print.

Wilson, Edward O. *Biophilia: The Diversity of Life, Genes, Mind, and Culture.* Cambridge, MA: Harvard UP, 1984. Print.

——— . *Naturalist.* Washington, DC: Island Press, 1994. Print.

Wittgenstein, Ludwig. *Philosophical Investigations.* Ed. G. E. M. Anscombe and R. Rhees. Trans. G. E. M. Anscombe. Oxford: Blackwell, 1953. Print.

Wordsworth, William. *The Oxford Authors.* Ed. Stephen Gill. Oxford: Oxford UP, 1984. Print.

——— . *The Prelude: 1799, 1805, 1850.* Ed. Jonathan Wordsworth, M. H. Abrams, and Stephen Gill. New York: Norton, 1979. Print.

Yeats, William Butler. *The Collected Poems of W. B. Yeats.* Ed. Richard Finneran. New York: Scribner, 1996. Print.

Yolton, D. Bruce. *Urban Hawks and Other Wildlife in Central Park and NYC.* Web. May 25, 2010.

INDEX

Abbey, Edward, 5, 64
Adam and Eve, *see* Garden of Eden
Adirondacks, 80, 170, 199, 200, 201, 204
Aesop, 81
AIDS (virus), 15, 47, 50, 81, 141
Aldrovandi, Ulysses, 130–1
Altick, Richard, 155, 156, 166–7
animal life, 35, 43, 71–5, 78–9, 86, 92, 99, 155–60, 183–4
animated nature, 2, 14, 22, 49, 141
Anning, Mary, 43
anthropocentrism, xv, 30, 80, 88, 184, 206
anthropomorphism, 12, 17, 50, 77–8, 80–1, 87–8, 93, 97, 110, 124, 159, 205–6
Anubis, 196
Aristotle, xvi
Arnold, Matthew, 182
    "Dover Beach," 182
Artemis (of Ephesus), 104
ASLE, 209
atheism, 59, 111

Babbage, Charles, 143
Bambi (Disney), 207
Barr, J. S. (translator), 38
Barrett, Andrea, 152–3
    The Voyage of the Narwhal, 152
Bartmann, Sarah (or Baartman), 166–7
Bartram, John, 92
Bartram, William, 92
Basho, 32
Bate, Jonathan, xvi, 170–1, 193
Batra, Nandita, 80–1

Beckett, Samuel, 148
Beecher, Henry Ward, 135
Bennett, Michael, xxi
Benson, E. F., 159–60
Berry, Wendell, 29
    "Preserving Wilderness," 29
Bewick, Thomas, 50–1
biology, 17, 27, 38, 41, 111, 141, 143
    origins as a science, 27–9
birds, 20, 37, 57, 77, 112–14, 185, 192
    eagle, xvii, 57, 120, 121, 122, 123, 124, 153, 185, 191, 192
    hawks, 121–3, 148, 185, 203
    Kiptopeake hawk-watch, 121–3
    pileated woodpecker, 37
    songbirds, 37
    vulture, 83
    warblers, 20–1, 37
    wood thrush, 36, 83
Blake, William, xvi, xviii, 2, 8, 30, 49, 80–1, 142, 157, 171, 185, 190, 196
    "Auguries of Innocence," xviii, 52, 157
    "The Book of Thel," 117
    "The Fly," 80–1
    "Marriage of Heaven and Hell," 8, 88, 190
    "The Tyger," 2, 49, 142
Blue Ridge Mountains (Virginia, West Virginia), 5, 17–18, 70, 120, 176, 192, 194, 197
bobcat, 71–2, 76
Boston, MA, 3, 205
Buck, Frank, 155

Buddha (Buddhism), 96, 191
Buell, Lawrence, xvi, 170
Buffon, George Louis Leclerc,
    Comte de, 28, 38–9, 50–1, 92,
    97, 141
  anticipates Darwin, 38
  Barr, J. S. (translator), 38
  echoes Tennyson, 39
  Histoire Naturelle, 38, 50, 141
Burns, Robert, 9
Burroughs, John, 64
Byron, George Gordon (Lord), 44,
    58, 128, 131, 158–9, 186
  Journal, 158–9

cannibalism, 144
Carson, Rachel, 64, 80
  Silent Spring, 80
Central Park, xxi, 82, 187, 203
Chagnon, Napolean, 168
Chaillu, Paul du, 43
Chambers, Ephraim, 25
Chambers, Robert, 57–61
  *Vestiges of the Natural History of
    Creation*, 57–61
chimpanzee, 28, 44, 128–9, 132
Chunee (elephant), 157–9
cicada (periodical), 69–71
cicada killer, 105–7
Clare, John, 8, 142
climate change, xvii
cod (fish), 107, 181
Coleridge, Hartley, 142
Coleridge, Samuel Taylor, xix,
    14–15, 21–2, 24, 26, 36, 39,
    58, 88, 96–7, 100, 142, 153,
    162–3, 169, 194
  Anima Poetae, 96–7
  "The Eolian Harp," xix, 14, 21–2
  "Frost at Midnight," 27, 100,
    162–3, 169
  "Kubla Khan," 153
  Notes on Shakespeare, 26
Columbus, Christopher, 33, 41
consciousness, xiv, 30, 35, 44, 76,
    79, 96, 111, 152, 175, 188, 193

Constable, John, 147
Cook, James (Captain), 41
Copernicus, Nicolaus, 9, 15, 59, 142
creation, 15, 16, 28, 40–1, 57–60,
    108, 132, 139, 184, 198
Crèvecoeur, Hector St. John de, 33
Cro-Magnon, 28, 108
Cronon, William, xiv, 29, 64
Curitiba (Brazil), 80, 201, 204

Dante Alighieri, 124
Darwin, Charles, xvi, xviii–xix, 6,
    14, 16, 25, 27, 28, 38–42, 44,
    56, 57, 58, 59, 60, 87, 107,
    128, 132–3, 143, 154, 159,
    176, 181–3, 207
  Annie Darwin, 58, 111
  Beagle, 154
  Down House, 132–3
  Galápagos Islands, 72–5,
    154, 187
  Letters, 14
  Origin of Species, xix, 14, 16, 27,
    57, 107, 143, 154, 159
Darwin, Erasmus, xix, 21, 23–4,
    28, 39–41, 44, 87, 88–92,
    93–4, 97, 98, 100, 128, 141
  The Botanic Garden, 23–4, 91,
    98, 150
  Phytologia, 40
  The Temple of Nature, 40,
    90–1, 104
  Zoonomia, 40, 87, 91, 141
Davy, Humphry, 142
Descartes, Rene, 192
Detroit, 35, 187, 189
D'Holbach (Baron), 3
Dillard, Annie, xvi, 3, 5–6, 30,
    108, 146, 170, 174–5
  Pilgrim at Tinker Creek, xx,
    174–5
dinosaurs, 43, 56, 59, 62, 108
Dixon, Terrell F., xxi, 10, 202
  City Wilds, 202
DNA (deoxyribonucleic acid), 23,
    28, 40, 140

dolphin, 54, 72–5, 160
  Pacific dolphins, 72–5

eagles, xvii, 57, 121, 122, 124, 153,
    185, 192
Earth Works Garden (Detroit), 35
ecoambience, 31, 79
ecocentrism, xv, 17, 30, 45, 77,
    80–1, 156, 184–5, 191,
    204, 207
ecocriticism, xvi, xx, 4, 46, 64, 66,
    145, 156, 161, 168, 172, 184,
    193–4, 198, 200
ecoempathy, 80
ecofeminism, 80
ecohome, 31, 45
ecology (oikos), xv, 17, 28, 29, 31,
    34, 47, 52, 79, 91, 162, 186–7,
    189, 201, 202
ecomorphism, 17, 31, 45, 77–9,
    80–1, 110, 159, 184–5, 206
ecosystem, 26, 133, 184, 185,
    186, 206
ecotecture, 31, 45
Einstein, Albert, 22, 60, 185, 198
élan vital (life-force), 9, 21, 24, 126
Elder, John, 198–9
Eliot, T. S., 194
Emerson, Ralph Waldo, xxi, 5, 11,
    32, 129
Enlightenment, xiv, 8–9, 79
environment, xvii, xx, 10, 17, 30,
    34, 36, 79, 80, 82, 83, 133,
    153, 162, 168, 170, 176, 186,
    189, 193, 200, 201
environmentalist, xv, xx, 10, 17, 29,
    30, 66, 82–3, 183, 200, 202
Estok, Simon, 183
eudaimon (the good life), 180
Evelyn, John, 86–7
Evernden, Neil, xiv, 174
evolution, 16, 40, 41, 44, 56, 58,
    60, 79, 111, 129, 132, 133,
    134, 154, 159, 176, 181–2
extinction, 16, 41, 59, 62, 109,
    111–12, 176, 190

Fleming, Alexander, xxii–xxiii
Fowles, John, 110
  The French Lieutenant's
    Woman, 110
Frankenstein, 28, 38, 39
Frankenstein, Victor, xix, 38,
    90, 131
Franklin, Benjamin, 94
Fresh-Air Fund, 48
Fuseli, Henry, 104, 196

Galápagos Islands, 72–5
Galvani, Luigi, xix, 38, 128
Ganesh, Eoh, xiv
Garden of Eden, xxi–xxii, 168,
    199, 207
  Adam and Eve, xxii, 34, 61, 168
  "dominion" over nature, xxii, 34,
    80, 206
Genesis, 9, 14–15, 16, 191
geology, 41, 47, 90
Gilligan, Carol, 80
God, 14–15, 21, 34, 43, 59,
    75–6, 86, 107, 110, 126, 141,
    182, 206
  deity, 14, 110, 126, 182
  Jaweh (Judeo-Christian), 21, 34,
    80, 182, 196
  primum mobile (first mover), 32
Goethe, Johann Wolfgang von, 15,
    93, 128, 143, 207
Goldsmith, Oliver, 49, 50, 88, 141
Goldsworthy, Andy, 187
Google Earth, xv, 4, 187
gorilla, 43–4
Gould, Stephen Jay, 28, 97, 168
Grant, Ulysses S., xxi
Great Chain of Being, 15–16, 24,
    25, 89, 91, 150
Gulf of Mexico (oil spill), xvii

Hagenbeck, Carl, 155
Hallam, Arthur Henry, 58
Handke, Shawna L., xiv
Hanno of Carthage (the
    Navigator), 43

Hardy, Thomas, xviii, 32, 109–12,
  117, 159
  Tess of the D'Urbervilles,
    109–11, 117
Hawking, Stephen, 28, 60, 190,
  197–8
  no beginning, no end, 135, 197–8
  unified-field theory, 60
hawks, 120–3, 148, 185
  peregrine falcon, xiii, 82, 120,
    121, 122
  red-tailed, 121, 122
  sharp-shinned, 121, 122
hawk-watching, 120–3
  Hawk Mountain, 120–1
  Kiptopeake, 121–3
  Waggoner's Gap, 121
Heisenberg's Uncertainty
  Principle, 22
Hendrix, Jimi, 190–1
Heraclitus, 22
Herschel, John, 99
Hess, Scott, 30
Hobbes, Thomas, 32, 144
Homo sylvestris, 44, 128
  see also orangutan
Hooke, Robert, 141
Hottentot Venus, 166–7
Humboldt, Alexander von, 42, 169
Hume, David, 40
Hunt, Leigh, 156

Iliffe, Rob, 143
imagination, xiv, 35, 49, 50, 75, 99,
  142, 176
Indians (Native Americans), 11,
  17–18, 32–3, 48, 177, 186,
  199–200
Industrial Revolution, 156, 171
insects, 20, 69–71, 90, 92, 97, 101,
  105–7, 137–40, 185
Irmscher, Christoph, 92

Jenyns, Soames, 25
Joyce, James, 148

Kant, Immanuel, 87
Katrina (hurricane), xvii, 47–8,
  189, 206
Kaza Park (South Africa), xxi
Keats, John, xvi, xviii, 6, 11,
  28, 50, 58, 75, 80, 88, 97,
  114–18, 140, 142, 169, 171,
  174, 209
  "To Autumn," 11, 97, 114–18, 209
  Letters, 6, 75–6, 140, 171
  "Negative Capability," 140, 171
  "Ode on a Grecian Urn," 169
  "Ode to a Nightingale," 11,
    27–8, 50, 80, 87, 98–9, 142
Kemble, Fanny, 60
Kerala (India), 80, 201, 204
K.E.S.T.R.E.L., 122
Kirby, William and William Spence
  (entomologists), 97, 117–18
Kublai Khan, 153

Lake District (Cumbria, UK), 12,
  168, 170
Lakoff, George, 100
Lao-Tse, 32
Lawrence, D. H., 32
Leopold, Aldo, 5, 64, 97, 204
  A Sand County Almanac, 204
lightning, 27, 43, 94, 111, 124
Lincoln, Abraham, 57
Linnaeus, Carolus, 27–8, 88–9, 132
  Systema Natura, 27
Liu, James J. Y., 32
Locke, John, 10, 79
London, xviii, 11–14, 43, 61, 98,
  154–6, 192, 198, 203
Longhi, Pietro, 134–5
Lopez, Barry, 77–8, 170
  Crossing Open Ground, 78
Loudoun County (VA), 8, 148
Louv, Richard, 6
  Last Child in the Woods, 6
Lucretius, 59, 60
Lyell, Charles, 43
Lynch, Kevin, xx

Malamud, Randy, 155, 159, 160, 166
Manhattan, *see* New York City
MapQuest, xv, 4, 187
Marco Polo, 153
Matthiessen, Peter, 170
Mauritius, xiii, xv
Maya, 189–90
McKibben, Bill, xvi, xx, 80, 170,
    191, 201, 204
    The End of Nature, xx, 191,
        201, 204
    Hope, Human and Wild, xx,
        80, 201
Mead, Margaret, 168
Melville, Herman, 32, 51
    Moby Dick, 51
Mendel, Gregor, 25
Merwin, W. S., 123–4
metaphor, 8–9, 24, 77, 81, 88,
    93, 100, 142–3, 173, 184–5,
    202, 205
Mimosa pudica, xix, 23, 25, 28, 91,
    93–4
    see also sensitive plant
Montagu, Ashley, 168
Monty Python, 81
Morton, Timothy, xvi, xx, 29, 31,
    79, 207
    Ecology Without Nature, 29, 31,
        79, 207
Muir, John, 64
Murphy, Patrick, 198
museums, *see* natural history
    museums

NASA, 65, 66, 204
Native Americans, 11, 17–18, 48,
    177, 186, 199
    see also Indians
natural history, 2, 9, 14–17, 18,
    23, 27, 38, 42, 51, 93, 97, 99,
    127–34, 141, 142, 153, 186
    Buffon's *Histoire Naturelle*, 38
    Goldsmith's *Animated
        Nature*, 49

natural history museums, 42,
    127–34
    American Museum of Natural
        History (New York), 17
    Bologna, 128, 129–31
    Florence (La Specola), 42, 44,
        127–30
    London, 42, 43, 133–4
    Naples, 42, 128, 129, 131–2
    Rome, 128, 129, 133–4, 186
natural selection, 16, 28, 41, 57, 79,
    183, 207
natural theology, 141–2
natural year, 3, 5, 18, 20, 165, 197
nature, xviii, 29–34, 44, 48, 52,
    93, 99, 144–5, 148, 157, 163,
    173–4, 187, 201, 207
    as an idea, xviii, 29, 93, 99,
        173–5, 207
    and humans, xviii, 29–34, 48–9,
        50–2, 58, 110, 144, 207
    natura, xviii, 17, 27, 172,
        202–3
    and the material world, 50,
        59–60, 153, 175, 182, 188
    as the nonhuman, 29, 30, 110,
        134, 162
    tzu-jan, 32
    -versus-culture, 192, 199
Neanderthal, 28
Newton, Issac, xvi, 15, 27–8,
    60, 198
New York City (Manhattan), xiii,
    xviii, 8, 10, 17, 48, 61, 78,
    123, 192, 200, 201, 203–4

Oelschlaeger, Max, 206
Olmsted, Frederick Law, xxi
orangutan, 44, 128, 129
    see also *Homo sylvestris*
Orr, David, xxi, 47, 77
    Ecological Literacy, 77
    The Nature of Design, 47
Orwell, George, 158
Owen, Richard (Sir), 42–3, 108

owls, xvii, 67, 92
   long-eared, 67, 112–14
   screech, xvii, 114

Paley, William, 141
penicillin, xxii–xxiii
penicillium, xxii
Pennant, Thomas, 141
peregrine falcon, xiii, 82, 120, 121
Peterson, Roger Tory, 188
Phillips, Dana, xiv, 198
Pinker, Steven, 100
plant life, 19–20, 24, 55, 85, 88–9, 91–2, 98
Plato, 179, 188
   Crito, 179
poison tree (*Bohun upas*), xix
Priestley, Joseph, xix, 142

Queen Victoria, 57–8, 59, 157

Raffles, Stamford, 154, 155
rhinoceros, 134–5, 152, 154–5, 156
Richards, Robert J., 143
Rigby, Kate, 171, 209
Ritvo, Harriet, 156, 157, 158
Robbins, Chandler S., 114
Robinson, Charles, 38, 169
Romantic ecocriticism, xvii, xx, xxii, 4, 18, 48, 64–6, 156, 161, 168, 170, 172, 186, 200
Romanticism, xxi–xxii, 14, 17, 29–30, 126, 186, 140–3
Romantic natural history, 9–10, 16, 18, 38, 50, 93, 109–10, 128, 141, 144, 152, 176
Romantic poetry, xiv, xviii, 22–7, 49, 58, 93–101, 114–18, 140–2, 146–8, 192–3
Roost, The (cabin), 3, 5, 9, 19, 36, 45, 47, 56, 61, 65–7, 69–71, 77, 112, 120, 123, 124, 137–40, 162

roosting, xii, xiii, xvii, xxi, 5, 17, 34, 44, 45, 79, 165, 199, 200–2, 207–8
   and birds, xvii–xviii, 34, 77, 82
   and humans, xvii–xviii, 34, 44, 82, 165, 199, 207–8
Ross, Andrew, xx
Rousseau, Jean-Jacques, 10, 15, 32, 79, 168, 174, 207
Rush, Benjamin, 92

salamanders, 17, 55–6, 132, 152, 203
Sappho, 9
Savage, Thomas, 43
sensitive plant, xix, 23, 29, 93–4
   see also *Mimosa pudica*
sexual lives of plants, 24, 39–40, 88–9, 109
Shakespeare, William, 179
   Hamlet, 26, 180
Shelley, Mary, xix, 21, 28, 38, 39, 58, 90, 131, 143, 168, 169
   Frankenstein, 28, 38, 39, 168, 169
Shelley, Percy Bysshe, xviii, xix, 11, 22–7, 29, 58, 80, 87, 88, 93, 124, 131, 142, 146–8, 169, 173, 174
   "The Cloud," 22–3, 80, 94, 146–8
   "Death," 23
   "On Love," 26, 173
   "Mont Blanc," 11, 24, 87
   "Mutability," 22
   "Ode to the West Wind," 25–6, 27, 124–7
   Prometheus Unbound, 87
   Queen Mab, 141
   "The Sensitive Plant," 23, 142
   "To a Sky-Lark," 11, 80, 93, 142
   "Witch of Atlas," 94–5
Shenandoah River, 8, 61, 70, 123, 146
Singer, Kate, 209

Slovic, Scott, 193–4, 209
Smith, Eric, 198
snakes, 6, 42, 55, 71, 86, 109, 129, 152, 153, 159–60, 193, 203, 204
Snow, C. P. (two cultures), 16–17, 143
Snyder, Gary, 32
Socrates, 98, 179–80
soul, 13, 21, 71–6, 86, 87, 90, 92, 95, 100, 109, 180
species, 14–15, 21, 23, 28, 34, 38–44, 47, 58, 65, 81, 93, 105, 107–8, 111–12, 117, 130, 132, 153, 155, 161, 166, 176, 181, 183, 185, 190, 199
    extinction, xvii, 16, 41, 59, 62, 109, 111–12, 176, 190
    varieties, 28, 39, 167
La Specola, 44, 129
    see also natural history museums, Florence
spiders, 6, 42, 52, 61, 86, 179, 100
Spirn, Anne Whiston, 46
Stallings, Tyler, xiii

Teague, David W., xxi
Tennyson, Alfred (Lord), xvi, 39, 58, 107–9, 182
    In Memoriam, 39, 58, 182
Tennyson, Hallam, 182
Teton National Park, 17
Thomas, Dylan, 24
Thomas, Lewis, 97
Thoreau, Henry David, xiii, 3, 5, 6, 7, 11, 31, 44–5, 52, 64, 86, 87, 139–40, 170, 171–2, 174–5, 183–4, 186, 203
    Concord, MA, 5, 31, 32, 64, 175
    Journal, 139–40
    Ktaadn (Mt. Katahdin), 87, 172–4
    The Maine Woods, 64, 87, 171, 173–4
    Walden, 6, 7, 64, 86, 171–2, 183–4, 186

Walden Pond, 3, 11, 64, 87, 170, 183
"Walking," xiii, 3, 44
A Week on the Concord and Merrimack Rivers, 64, 171–2
wildness, 3, 64, 173, 186, 203
tiger, 2, 49–52, 108, 129, 162
    "Tyger, tyger," (Blake), 2, 49
Tocqueville, Alexis de, 33
Turner, J. M. W., 147
Turner, Jack, xx
Turner, Mark, 100
Tyson, Edward, 141

United Nations, 34, 201
urban, xv, xxi, 30, 35, 46–7, 64, 82, 140, 161, 171, 185, 187, 189–90, 192, 200–4, 208
urbanature, xii, xiii–xv, xx–xxiii, 3–5, 11–12, 17–18, 30–1, 35, 47, 64, 66, 77, 80–2, 127, 132, 152, 155, 157, 161–2, 168, 170–1, 173, 175, 188–9, 199–200, 202–8
    as idea, xiii, xv, 30, 35, 47, 152, 155, 161–2, 188
    and roosting, xii, xvii–xviii, xxi–xxii, 4–5, 36, 127, 191, 199–200, 204, 207–8
urbanature.org, xiv
US Park Service, 17–18
Ussher (Bishop), 60

Vedas (Hindu scriptures), 32, 184
vegetarianism, 180, 183–4, 185
Venus flytrap, 91, 133, 150
Vestiges of the Natural History of Creation, 57–61
Victorian, xii, xvi, 57, 58, 59, 60, 61, 63, 107–11, 141, 155, 158–9, 166, 181–2
Volta, Alessandro, 38, 42

Wang Wei, 31
Warren, Jim, 209

Warren, Sylvia, 209
wasps, 7–8, 105–7, 137–9
Wasserman, Earl, 24, 25
White, Gilbert, 31
Whitman, Walt, 32, 85–6
wilderness, xiii, xvi, 10–11, 17, 18,
    29, 30–2, 45, 47, 64–6, 82,
    86, 96, 144, 175, 186, 191–2,
    198, 200, 202–3, 210
wildness, xiii, 3, 29–30, 44–5, 52,
    64, 75, 157, 160, 162, 173,
    186–7, 203, 204, 208
Williams, Terry Tempest, 5, 170
Wilson, E. (Edward) O., 97,
    130, 187
    Naturalist, 187
Wittgenstein, Ludwig, 174, 188
Wordsworth, William, xvi, xviii,
    xix, 3, 11–14, 22, 39, 58, 77,
    87, 96, 97, 168, 170, 174, 193
    "Composed Upon Westminster
    Bridge," 11–14

"Goody Blake and Harry Gill," 39
"I wandered lonely as a cloud,"
    80, 95
"Nutting," xxii, 83
The Prelude, 3–4, 87, 95, 168–9
"Surprised by Joy," 58
"Tintern Abbey," 193
"The World is Too Much with
    Us," 14
Wright, Frank Lloyd, 187, 202

Yanomamo (tribe), 168
Yeats, William Butler (W. B.), 199
    "The Song of the Happy
    Shepherd," 199
Yellowstone National Park, xxi, 10,
    17, 82, 186–7, 199–200

zoos, 42, 44, 50, 152–62
    captivity, xv, 151, 157, 160–1
    and colonization, 155
    humans on display, 42, 153, 166–7